JUSTICE IN SOUTH AFRICA

Perspectives on Southern Africa

Justice
in South Africa

by
ALBIE SACHS

UNIVERSITY OF CALIFORNIA PRESS
BERKELEY AND LOS ANGELES

University of California Press
Berkeley and Los Angeles

Copyright © 1973, by Albie Sachs
ISBN: 0-520-02417-6
Library of Congress Catalog Card Number 72-97749

Printed in the United States of America

264406

CONTENTS

CONTENTS
PART II THE MODERN MACHINE

TABLES

PREFACE

Race discrimination can be found in many parts of the world. South Africa is unique in being the one country in which such discrimination is still openly supported by the Government and expressly written into the laws. Newly painted segregation notices can be found on all public amenities – on post offices, railway stations, beaches, parks, buses, ambulances, taxis, telephone kiosks and urinals. In recent years the surface area of the country has been systematically divided into zones for occupation by different racial groups, and vast numbers of people have been forced to vacate their homes to make way for persons of appropriate pigmentation. In order to sift the population and allocate each individual to his legally defined racial category a special system of race classification has been instituted. Intermarriage and sexual activity across the colour line have been forbidden on pain of imprisonment, and separate systems of education have been established for separate racial and tribal groups. Jobs have been reserved along racial lines, and the controls placed upon the movement and labour of Africans have become so extensive that upwards of a million Africans are prosecuted under various race-statutes each year.

These facts are generally well known, and the term apartheid has become internationally synonymous with segregation. What is less known is the manner in which the system of segregation is enforced. It is here that the courts have played a crucial role, and this book is a study against a background of social history of how the courts have been used over the centuries to regulate race domination in southern Africa.

The story begins with a description of the system of justice in the poorly developed slave-holding settlement established by the Dutch in the middle of the seventeenth century. The dominant legal system in South Africa did not evolve, it was imported, and its adaptations are thus more interesting than its pedigree. Its principal doctrines and technique were shipped with the early judges and law books from Holland and England to the Cape, from where they spread with white settlement and conquest through the rest of southern Africa. Roman-Dutch law survives as the common law of the country.

The slave-holding settlement was not very large in terms of area or population, but it lasted for nearly two centuries and was the base for subsequent penetration and conquest of southern Africa. Slave society created relationships and attitudes which were to endure long after the abolition of the legal forms in which they had first appeared. Liberation of the slaves was carried out with relatively little disruption–not by war, rebellion or local abolitionist pressure, but by British Act of Parliament–and the actual situation of the slaves *vis-à-vis* their masters did not change very much. Legal emancipation was not the same thing as social emancipation, and many features of the master/slave relationship were reproduced in labour legislation and pass laws and sustained by social practice and attitudes. In particular the notion that certain types of work were fit only to be done by black men under white supervision survived into the industrial era.

The introduction to the Cape of English judges and English-style court procedures in 1828 laid the foundation of the modern court system in South Africa. The formal equality of all before the courts was recognised, and the rules of evidence and procedure were modelled on those existing in England. The need to reconcile the theory of juridical equality with the practice of race inequality gave the legal system a contradictory character that has persisted to this day. On the one hand the courts provided a forum where the poor and the dominated could seek redress of grievances in an atmosphere of decorum; on the other they furnished the machinery for the massive suppression and punishment of persons threatening the peace and property of the dominant community. South African courts have been by no means unique in serving these two apparently contradictory ends, but they have done so to a degree probably without modern parallel.

The early British judges were lawyers of vigour and panache. They travelled widely, supervised the activities of local magistrates, acted as informal commissions of enquiry, and generally symbolised governmental authority in the vast areas under their jurisdiction. The extension of their circuit courts coincided with the first large-scale contacts between white colonists and black Bantu-speaking tribesmen, and as more and more tribal lands were conquered and annexed, the courts became increasingly important instruments for binding the different racial, linguistic and class groups to a common political authority. A relatively advanced system of justice in a relatively underdeveloped territory gave to the judges a particular lustre and prestige, and ensured for them and their successors what one historian has called an especially brilliant place in South African history. With the development of other organs of government, the pre-eminence of the Judiciary became less noticeable, but the importance of judges and magistrates as instruments of social control never diminished.

Increasing industrialisation intensified rather than reduced compulsory segregation in South Africa, and gave the courts a greater rather than a lesser role in the enforcement of segregation. It also emphasised the extent to which race differentiation was being artificially maintained. Large-scale evasion of the law and growing participation in crime constituted one expression of African resistance to the dominant legal order; crowd revolts and clashes with the police were another. Eventually direct challenges were issued, both inside and outside the courts, to the whole character of the legal order. As social conflict increased, benevolent judicial paternalism became more difficult to maintain, and the courts lost some of their earlier liberalism and prestige.

The last decade has been described as a period of permanent emergency. During this time a number of former defenders of the Judiciary have become its critics, while former critics have risen to its defence. The debate has been conducted circumspectly, since some of the judges have shown great sensitivity to criticism. Supporters of apartheid have tended to argue that the judges have simply been carrying out the law as laid down by Parliament in their traditionally neutral and fair manner. Opponents of apartheid, on the other hand, have tended to claim that in implementing the laws the judges have leaned unduly in favour of the Executive and abandoned their former impartiality. The question that has to be asked is to what extent the judges can be held responsible for carrying out laws which are clearly intended to be discriminatory and which cause great hardship when enforced. In this connection it is suggested that the main charge which the Judiciary might be called upon to answer is that instead of investing their office with the prestige associated with the pursuit of justice, they have allowed the prestige associated with their office to be used for the pursuit of manifest injustice.

Part One
THE HISTORICAL SETTING

CHAPTER ONE

Law Enforcement and Race Attitudes in a Slave-owning Society: The Dutch Settlement at the Cape 1652-1795

The modern legal system in South Africa today, with its flourishing legal profession, bustling courts, vast prison population and busy gallows, had its humble beginnings in the small refreshment station established by the Dutch East India Company at the Cape in 1652.

The first Court of Justice met in a hall in the centre of the Commander's earthenwork fort. The setting was exotic, the judges untrained and the procedures, especially in criminal matters, barbarous by modern standards. Round the walls hung skins of lions and leopards and the polished horns of slain buck, whilst opposite the entrance stood the figure of a stuffed zebra. The judges consisted of the Commander and his advisory council, none of whom were legally trained. They made no claim to be independent from the Executive, in fact they were the Executive; nor were they separate from the Legislature, for inasmuch as they had power to assist the Commander in framing local decrees they were the Legislature as well. The multi-purpose hall in which they met was also used as a Church on Sundays, the zebra being moved out during divine service. This unity of functions was not inappropriate for a tiny refreshment station, but it caused increasing strain when the settlement expanded and gave birth to a large class of independent farmers with interests separate from those of the Company.

The Dutch settlement was never more than a small enclave in the southern African sub-continent, and even after a century and a half of development it did not impinge directly on the lives of the great majority of inhabitants of the territory now known as South Africa. It was governed primarily as a trading station, a half-way house for ships sailing to and from the East Indies, and few of its institutions survive in immediately recognisable form today. Roman-Dutch law – a late Middle Ages inter-marriage of Germanic custom and Roman law – still exists as the common law of South Africa, but the contribution made to it by the Dutch courts at the Cape was nil. Yet the period of Dutch settlement was of great importance to subsequent South African history, since the little victualling depot became the base for later white penetration and it was through importation of slaves and contact with the indigenous inhabitants that the dominant white attitudes towards colour and labour were first nurtured.

Although at first the Commander's Court operated largely as a court martial with jurisdiction only over Company servants, when the settlement expanded the court broadened its character and began to handle a variety of cases, both criminal and civil, involving a variety of persons–Christian and Moslem, bondsmen and free, men and women.

The society that developed in and around the settlement was a multi-racial one in which Company servants, colonial settlers, slaves, manu-mitted slaves, Khoi Khoi (so-called Hottentots) and their descendants intermingled in a single legal order. The court enforced inequalities of civic status between owners and slaves, masters and servants and white and coloured, but maintained an identity of personal law. Save for limited recognition of Islamic law given to non-slave Moslems with regard to matters of family law and succession, all inhabitants, regard-less of colour or status, came under the Roman-Dutch law and such statutes as were of local operation.

Most legal historians are agreed that the laws at the Cape were in a state of great confusion, and that they were generally administered in an arbitrary fashion by untrained judges. A Commissioner sent to enquire into the government of the Cape during the last years of Dutch rule exclaimed in a much-quoted statement: "Behold the sorry state into which the administration of justice has fallen!", and the most that even a relatively sympathetic modern historian could claim on behalf of the Dutch legal system at the Cape was that it was 'viable' (Visagie).

The Cape settlement was in effect a colony of a colony, being subject to the control of the Company's overseas headquarters in Batavia, which which in turn was subordinate to the Directors in Holland. An endless stream of statutes and instructions flowed from both sources to the Commander, later called the Governor. In addition a vast mass of local decrees were issued, frequently conflicting with each other and with the Batavian ordinances. Since the Cape did not possess any form of printing press until the beginning of the nineteenth century, promul-gation of new laws took the form of public declamation or announce-ment in church; the decrees in manuscript were then filed away in the Governor's office. The court itself lacked precise instructions on how it should conduct its proceedings, directives being cast in such general form as: "The Governor must be gentle, godfearing, friendly and courteous, ready to converse with and aid the good, but severe and terrible to the wicked" (1685). The court judgements were very bare, containing merely the verdict and such authorities as had been quoted in argument, with the result that no body of precedent grew up for the guidance of later judges. If there were too many statutes, there were too few textbooks, and by 1739 the law library attached to the court contained only ten books, though this might have been regarded by the judges as a virtue rather than a deficiency.

There do not appear to have been many lawyers practising at the Cape during the period of Company rule, but court records mention the name of an advocate as early as 1688 followed by that of another one in 1706. By 1715 the question of attorney's fees had already become an issue, preceding in priority by three-quarters of a century the question of what rules should govern the formal admission of attorneys. In 1791 four attorneys were admitted, followed by a fifth the next year and a sixth the year after. Advocates and attorneys performed functions roughly similar to those of barristers and solicitors in England, with advocates having the higher official status and being entitled to wear hats in court.

Probably the most important of all the officers of court was the Fiscal, who from 1688 was called the Fiscal Independent because from then onwards he was appointed by the Directors in Holland and was responsible to them rather than to the local administration. His main duties were to defend the property and revenues of the Company, and to initiate prosecutions of criminal offences. In a general atmosphere of petty extortion the Fiscal was the most oppressive of all officials, and since he personally received a third share of all fines imposed he was well placed to enhance his fortune through overzealous or fraudulent use of his office. One writer described him as combining the acuteness of the lawyer with the greedy watchfulness of the customs officer, and to this day the predatory butcher bird in the Cape is popularly known as the Fiskaal.

The Company's monopoly of trade with passing ships and its exclusive control over the importation of slaves limited the amount of civil litigation, and obliged farmers with claims against the Company to seek their remedies by petition to higher authority rather than by suit in the local court. Law enforcement at the Cape was thus at first largely a matter of maintaining Company discipline, protecting Company property, and guarding Company morals but later it included regulating relationships between masters and slaves and masters and Khoi servants.

The introduction of slaves to the Cape was destined to have a profound effect on master-servant relationships in South Africa, and to

establish the pattern, early recognised in legislation and judicial attitudes, whereby privilege was associated with racial type. Factors of
race and skin colour, however, played little or no part in determining
the social attitudes of the first Company servants and settlers, whose
behaviour towards groups and individuals was conditioned largely by
whether or not such persons were Christians, rather than by whether
they were black, brown or white. The social and legal gap that existed
between Christian and non-Christian could be crossed by means of
baptism, which, particularly in the case of women slaves, opened the
way to marriage and full legal and social integration into the Christian
community. Thus the first Dutch commander arranged a special bridal
feast in his home to celebrate the marriage of his surgeon to a Khoi
woman, and many other marriages were contracted between Dutch
settlers and freed women slaves. The most popular as well as the most
ardently Dutch of all the Governors at the Cape in the eighteenth
century was in fact the son of an inter-racial marriage.

As the number of slaves increased, however, what had started off as a
means of cheap labour became a settled institution, so that the slave was
no longer merely an unpaid servant but a valuable piece of property
who contributed as much to the owner's status as to his patrimony. Most
labour, skilled and unskilled, was done by slaves, and whites became increasingly disinclined to suffer what they considered to be the degradation
of doing work fit for slaves. Gradually it came to be thought by colonists that slavery was the proper condition for all dark-skinned people.

Slaves were imported from all the many regions where the Dutch
East India Company traded, while their number was added to by West
Africans seized as prize cargo from British, French and Portuguese slave
ships. The increase in the proportion of slaves to colonists is given in
the following table:

TABLE I

POPULATION OF COLONISTS AND SLAVES AT THE CAPE
IN THE EIGHTEENTH CENTURY

Year	Colonists	Slaves
1701	1,334	891
1753	5,533	6,045
1795	14,927	16,839
1797	21,746	25,754

The relative smallness of the Cape settlement can be gauged from the following figures estimated for the year 1790 for other slave-holding societies. In the United States of America there were 757,000 blacks, all but eight per cent slaves, and consituting twenty per cent of the total population. In the British West Indies there were 455,000 blacks, who made up eighty-six per cent of the population. In the French colony of Saint Dominique 450,000 blacks, of whom six per cent were free, accounted for more than ninety per cent of the population (Brion Davis).

Most of the Cape slaves were employed on heavy domestic or farm work, but others were used as cooks, musicians or artisans. ("Jason, of Madagascar, appears to be of good character, and told me after I had purchased him that he could cook and knew how to make all kinds of pastries, sweet meats, marchpanes and other sweet things, and could play on the flute, hautboy and French horn.")

Life for household and artisan slaves was much easier than for those who worked in the vineyards and wheatfields. Many of the children of the former went to slave schools where they were taught by slave teachers, while some sat alongside their masters' children at general schools. A small number of artisans and pedlars were even permitted by their masters to trade on their own account, and a few were manumitted by will on the death of their masters. (However, only 893 slaves were manumitted between 1715 and 1792, mostly as a result of purchase by free relatives or friends.) Good conduct, however, often reduced a slave's chances of manumission by raising his economic value.

Those slaves who worked as farm labourers not only had to perform arduous work but were grouped by their owners, who wished to achieve the maximum discipline for the minimum cost, into large and tightly supervised field-gangs. Thus one of the consequences of the introduction of slavery at the Cape was the development of extensive rather than intensive agriculture, since it was uneconomical for the colonists to supervise small groups of slaves. The sons and grandsons of small-holding European peasants therefore became the owners of large semi-autonomous estates, exercising paternalistic control over slaves who were closely bound to them and with whom they were in constant contact. One writer has suggested that it was these slave-worked farms which were to constitute the ideal model of race relations for later generations of white South Africans, and that in its milder form it was slavery that provided the basis for 'Cape liberalism" which he felt could better be described as 'Cape paternalism' with an injection of nineteenth century British humanitarianism (Van den Berghe).

Whereas the social conditions of slaves varied greatly, their legal condition was rigidly defined. The Dutch common law relating to slavery was based entirely on the well-developed principles of the Roman law of slavery, and long after slavery was abolished in Holland, these principles were applied in the courts of the overseas settlements. When the Fiscal was asked by the British early in the nineteenth century to prepare a report on the law relating to slaves at the Cape, his main source of reference was the Digest of Emperor Justinian published fourteen centuries earlier. This provided that slaves were the property of their masters who had bought them or who had owned their mother at the time of their birth. They could be sold or hired out at the will of their master, and on their master's death they passed with his other property to his heir. A purchaser of a slave could sue the seller for rescission of the contract or reduction of the purchase price for any latent defect found in the slave.

The law of slavery has rightly been described as practically an enumeration of the rights of the master, but provided a slave obeyed all lawful commands he was entitled to food, clothing and shelter and protection from bodily injury. By and large the slave was the object rather than the subject of rights. In addition to being liable to punishment by the court for ordinary contraventions of the law he could also be punished directly by the master for what were called domestic offences, such as carelessness, disobedience, drunkenness, impudence, desertion, minor household thefts, and other similar offences. For these misdemeanours the master could by statute impose a whipping with a sjambok of up to thirty-nine lashes, which according to one critical observer, was loosely interpreted by some farmers as a whipping for as long as it took the farmers to smoke a pipeful of tobacco (Barrow). More serious offences had to be reported to the authorities, who alone had the right to imprison a slave or place him in irons, save that as a temporary measure to prevent escape the master was permitted to impose physical restraints.

A slave had no legally recognised dignity which could be injured, but a corporal offence against him was punishable according to the circumstances. Unlawful and intentional killing of a slave was technically murder, though the fact that death was caused by excessive punishment was regarded as an extenuating circumstance. If a slave was injured or abducted it was not he but his master who could maintain an action, which was for damages suffered for financial loss to the master. Discontented slaves could complain to court officials of ill-treatment and if their complaints were verified then their masters were obliged to sell them. If, as was frequently the case, the officials held that the complaints were ill-founded then the slaves were liable to severe punishment from the court in addition to possible retribution from their masters. One slave complainant, for example, was chained to a wheelbarrow and sent to Robben Island for life, and it was not surprising that slaves tended to express their grievances through arson, sabotage and desertion rather than through official channels. In order to control ill-treatment, the Company decreed at one stage that the shackling of slaves be performed only by the Company blacksmith and that no slave be buried without prior official examination. There were also cases in which the court imposed severe sentences on slave-owners who had inflicted lethal thrashings and torture on their slaves, but not even the most heartless killings led to the execution of a master. The evidence of slaves could be received in court even though not given on oath, subject to a judicial discretion as to its credibility.

There were no large-scale slave rebellions, except in the imaginations of the colonists, but there were a number of minor revolts, and many slaves attempted desertion. Some absconders stowed away on passing ships, but most fled to the interior where the more successful ones grew food, fished and ate berries under the protection of the Khoi Khoi, whilst the others led the desperate lives of outlaws. Where the masters were not strong enough on their own to punish insubordination or arson or to recapture escapees they could call upon the services of the garrison at the Fort. The slow-moving, rank-conscious mercenaries were not, however, the most effective men for giving chase, and as time went on the colonists' militia and frontiersmen's commandos did most of this sort of police work. Vengeance on recaptured slaves was severe, the emphasis being on mutilation rather than death, which latter punishment would have deprived the owner of part of his property.

The criminal prosecution of slaves took place in the same courts as were used to try freemen, and generally both classes were liable to the same range of punishments. Some offences such as bigamy and adultery could in fact only be committed by freemen, because marriage amongst slaves was not legally recognised. Criminal process and punishment was harsh for slaves and freemen alike, and it would seem that as a general rule law enforcement was far more severe amongst the Dutch colonists than amongst the indigenous inhabitants of southern

Africa. It would be tempting to regard the tortures inflicted at the Cape as a direct outgrowth of the colonial slave situation, but in fact the practices which now seem so cruel and so inconsistent with the jurisprudence of enlightened seventeenth century Dutch jurists such as Hugo de Groote (Grotius), were part and parcel of the ordinary administration of justice in Holland, just as they were judicially approved in most of western Europe until the French Revolution and the Napoleonic Wars. The effect of slavery was not to invent or to legitimise torture, but to intensify its severity and to delay any humanising reforms. It could even be argued that although the treatment of slaves as chattels facilitated the use of violence against them, it also diminished the use of torture, since torture was the prerogative of the court, and slaves were usually punished directly by their masters without trial or reference to the court. What the rack was to the Fiscal, the whip was to the farm-owner, and like the master of a ship, the farm-owner relied heavily on strokes as a deterrent to mutinous conduct. The slaves had no property out of which to pay fines, and a flogging was both speedy and inexpensive and calculated to cause pain without incapacitating the slaves for work.

The purpose of torture was not primarily to get information or to punish the prisoner, but to get him to confess his crime out of his own mouth. Failure to make a confession even under the most rigorous torture was not usually regarded as a proof of innocence but as a sign of extreme criminality and lack of repentance. The stage at which the torture was applied was when an accused denied guilt after being confronted with substantial incriminating evidence at a preliminary court hearing. (If he pleaded guilty then he would be sentenced at a full hearing of the court without having to undergo torture.) The examining judge would order him to be subjected to 'more stringent examination' and he would then be taken to the torture room (Van Leeuwen–trans. Kotze, vol. 2, p. 588).

As late as 1798, the year in which torture was abolished in Holland, a leading Dutch jurist, van der Linden, wrote that though he disapproved of torture in the wide sense, a little bit of flogging properly used could be most beneficial. If the accused contumaciously denied guilt at the preliminary hearing then he should be proceeded with in a slow and calm manner. First he should be shown the apparatus for flogging. Then if he still remained obdurate, he should be undressed and taken to the flogging post, all the while being exhorted to admit guilt. Then he should be given lashes, but not so severely as to constitute punishment. "It is not the force of the blows that will soften the heart of the captured thief or housebreaker; it is the apparatus and the accompanying exhortations, which by means of the stings of conscience will cause him as it were to lose countenance, to forget his stubborn resolve to persist in denial, and in such a moment to make confession" (Van der Linden, II, p. 235).

At the Cape the flogging post was one of the milder instruments used by the prosecution to induce an accused person to make a confession. From its earliest days the court made use of the rack and the thumbscrew, and as the settlement progressed and the administration of justice became more specialised, these mediaeval relics were supplemented by instruments which could instil terror and inflict pain in a more refined and modern manner. Thus the Criminal Law Rolls of 1732 reveal that elaborate machinery for torture by suspension had been created. After being escorted to the torture room the accused would be hoisted by a rope tied to his hands and suspended by a pulley from the ceiling. Weights would be attached to his toes – the weights varying according to the degree of torture ordered by the judge – with full torture consisting of 50 lb. weights attached to each big toe.

Slaves were by no means the only persons to be subjected to pre-trial torture. White men and women were amongst the victims, and the records tell of a white woman who was castigated with rods for refusing to confess that she had ordered the killing of a cow belonging to a Khoi herder. They also refer to the case of a white man who, after having had weights hung from his toes, only 'confessed a little' to having killed a black man.

Where a recognised distinction between slaves and freemen existed was in the degree of severity of punishment imposed on each after trial and conviction. Thus defamatory and warning punishments were imposed on white colonists, whilst the most extreme forms of death sentence were reserved for slaves. Defamatory punishments presupposed that the accused had a reputation in the community, and were imposed on colonists guilty of infringing public morals. Thus a bigamist was made to bear a placard reading: THE TAKER AND POSSESSOR OF TWO WIVES. Punishment by imitation consisted of exposing the miscreant on the gallows with a noose around his neck or getting him to kneel blindfolded while shots were fired or a sword was waved over his head. In the early years capital punishment was frequently inflicted by drowning, which was used to kill sailors and slaves alike, but later more prolonged and painful methods of execution were adopted, with condemned slaves being the main victims. Similarly mutilation was a punishment reserved mainly for slaves.

Right until the period of British rule sentences of death could be carried out in ways ranging from hanging to strangling (for women), breaking on the wheel or cross with or without a *coup de grâce*, decapitation, quartering and chopping off the limbs, and even burning. This last mode of execution was imposed, though only rarely, for arson, and as late as 1804 a person was sentenced to die by fire.

Freemen sentenced to death were usually hanged, shot or strangled, whereas slaves were subjected to the more lingering forms of death, such as being stretched on the rack or broken by iron clubs while crucified. The severest degrees of death were reserved for runaway slaves who committed murder whilst in flight. Thus a slave convicted of "two frightful murders . . . which make the hair of a rational being stand on end, and his entrails to shudder and freeze" was ordered to be punished ". . . in a land where justice and righteousness (were) maintained as the pillars of the public peace" by the harshest death sentence possible: being tied to the wheel, having his flesh pinched and being broken alive by eight blows of the club without the mercy stroke. Another slave was bound naked to a cross, had ten pieces of flesh nipped from him by red hot pincers at lengthy intervals, his right hand hacked and thrown into his face, his body quartered and dragged in portions through the town, and his head secured to a pole as prey to the birds. That such excruciating forms of execution were common throughout the Dutch trading empire is evidenced by the sentence imposed on the male partner of a woman sent as a convict from Batavia to the Cape, namely that he be "Bound on a cross, when his right hand shall be cut off, his body pinched in six places with red-hot irons, his arms and legs broken to pieces, and after that to be impaled alive before the Town House on the Square, his dead body afterwards to be thrown on a wheel outside the town at the usual place, and to be left as prey to the birds of the air. Prisoner also to pay all costs."

Executions were carried out in public, and far from diminishing in severity and scale as the settlement progressed, were effected by more executioners using better equipment and attended by greater ceremony. Improvement of techniques unaccompanied by any softening of objectives resulted in cruel executions occupying a larger rather than a smaller place in Cape society, and even those visitors most sympathetic to the way of life of the colonists recorded in their journals the horror they felt at witnessing the painful deaths of the condemned men. One of the most extraordinary features remarked upon by these visitors was the stoicism with which many of the victims bore their tortures. On one occasion the keeper of the Company Records was driven to express astonishment at the spirit of a slave who, as the paramour of a white woman and the murderer of her husband, was impaled on an iron prong until death: four hours after the prong had been thrust through his body he was given some arrack to drink, but advised not to have too much otherwise he would become drunk, to which he retorted that it did not matter, as he sat fast enough and there was no danger of his falling. According to the Records he lingered on for two days, joking with spectators and saying scoffingly that he would never put his trust in women again.

The public executioner, like the hangman of today, was paid on a piecework basis. A statute of the mid-seventeenth century fixed his tariff of fees as follows (converted into 1970 sterling prices):

For every person he might kill–6 shillings.
For suicides whom he hanged on the gallows–2 shillings.
For punishment where death did not follow, such as flogging, brand-ing with a red-hot iron, cutting off ears, boring a hole through the tongue, cutting off a hand, pulling out the eyes–2 shillings.
Torturing–1 shilling and 4 pence.

The one area of punishment which at first glance seemed to have softened over the years was mutilation, which was inflicted on runaway slaves. Early court records refer to the cutting out of tongues, and the cutting off of ears and other forms of defacement, whereas later cases more frequently involved branding on the back. The main reason for the change, however, appears to have been that the sight of deformed persons was too much for the gentler-born inhabitants, and it was to protect them rather than the slaves that the back was mutilated rather than the head.

It has been pointed out that slavery is paradoxically a great cultural leveller inasmuch as it rapidly shatters the culture of origin of the slaves and encourages miscegenation. Slaves arriving at the Cape from all over Asia and Africa were given European names by their new masters, who often called them after the months of the year or Biblical or classical personalities: thus Jupiter cleaned the shoes, Hercules rubbed down the horses and Juno lit the fire. In a settlement where there was a general shortage of women, Dutch colonists tended to cohabit with slave women, while slave men tended to have sexual relationships with Khoi women; an early Governor noted that three-quarters of the children born to women slaves had Dutch fathers. For their part, the slaves and Khoi women who looked after the colonists' children had a great influence on the language of their masters, which they helped to simplify so that eventually it was to prove more popular and enduring than High Dutch. Yet the narrowing of the cultural gap between slaves and masters did not lead to any amelioration of the conditions of the slaves, nor did the increase in prosperity and stability of the settlement result in any softening of their masters' attitudes towards them. On the contrary, as time passed the colonists' attitudes towards the slaves became noticeably harder, emancipation was made more difficult, and a series of harsh statutes was passed to control the conduct of slaves. It was not the status of the slaves that improved with the growing sophistication of the settlement but the machinery for their control and punishment. Thus statutes were passed a hundred years after the settlement was established forbidding slaves from being on the sidewalk except in attendance on their masters, prohibiting them from carrying lighted pipes in the street (a security measure against arson), and penalising them for jostling colonists in the street. Provision was made for them to be flogged if they entered the church or even the porch or made any noise outside during divine service, or if they entered a burial ground during the funeral or went into the public gardens unaccompanied by their masters, unless they did so in charge of their masters' children. It was also decreed that any slave whether man or woman, whether with weapons or without, who raised his hand against his master should be punished by death without mercy (1754).

Finally even the adoption of Christianity no longer served to enable a slave to become his own master, for the Church Council in Cape Town declared that neither the laws temporal nor the laws spiritual prohibited the retention of baptised persons in slavery (1792). From this time onwards the great social and legal divide was no longer between Christian and non-Christian, but between white master and black slave or servant. A significant indication of the extent to which colour had superseded religion as the determinant of status was the instruction given in 1780 that Company black servants were no longer to be sent to arrest white offenders.

A similar process of hardening attitudes took place in the relations between colonists and Khoi Khoi. A well-known South African jurist has recently declared that the Cape was *res nullius* (belonging to nobody) which became Dutch territory by occupation; implicit in this

view is the assumption that the indigenous people belonged to the
land, the land did not belong to them. This, however, was not the view
of the indigenes themselves, nor of the first European settlers. The
hunting bands (the San or so-called Bushmen) occupied territories
over which they recognised prior rights amongst themselves, while
the herders (Khoi Khoi–the Men of Men–or so-called Hottentots)
had a system of government that included arbitration procedures and
law enforcement agencies; both groups resisted encroachment by the
Dutch on their land. The first Dutch Commander clearly recognised
the prior title of Khoi Khoi to occupation and pasturage of neighbouring territory, and the famous hedge which he erected and which has
been claimed as the first manifestation of apartheid in South Africa
was designed not only to keep the Khoi Khoi out but to keep his own
men in. In the first years of the settlement it was the Khoi Khoi who
had contempt for the Dutch, who watched enviously as Khoi shepherds
drove vast herds of cattle and sheep past the Fort. A leading Dutch
jurist had referred to a rule laid down in the middle of the seventeenth
century that "the Aborigines shall be undisturbed in their liberty and
never enslaved; they shall be governed politically and civilly as our-
selves, and enjoy the same measure of justice" (Voet 1:5:3), and Company officials at the Cape initially tried to follow a policy of peaceful
trading and non-interference with their neighbours. Gradually, however, the Dutch and the Khoi Khoi came into armed conflict; the Khoi
Khoi suffered some heavy blows, and certain sections became increasingly dependent on the settlement economy for their livelihood.
Military defeat was followed by economic dependence and social
subordination, and the one-time independent pastoralists were absorbed
into the expanding settlement as farm labourers, domestic servants and
herders. Technically they were not slaves and they were not bought
and sold at public auctions, but they were completely dependent on the
farmers, they had no redress for grievances and they were treated as
runaways if they left service. In the opinion of country farmers they
were a docile and cheap form of labour at the disposal of their masters
whose personal authority over them was final. In the first years of
contact, convicted Khoi Khoi were handed over to their own people for
execution, but later they were subjected to the same punishments as
convicted colonists and slaves. Because most of them lived in the frontier regions they tended to have less contact with the settlement courts
than did the slaves, but they were subjected to a considerable amount of
domestic correction by their masters. 'Terribly violent means' were

used to prevent them from lodging complaints against their masters, and when a few managed to get a hearing from officials, redress seldom followed.

Race attitudes of the dominant section of the community, whether on the frontier or in Cape Town, have remained essentially unchanged since the end of the eighteenth century. What has changed is their rationalisation. The emphasis then was on the Christian and his religion, now it is on the white man and his 'civilisation' (Macrone).

Slavery was eventually abolished at the Cape not as a result of insurrection, civil war or pressure from an indigenous abolitionist movement, but by external compulsion in the form of a British Act of Parliament (1834). Yet the legal emancipation of slaves did not lead to their social emancipation. The buying and selling of servants and absolute restraints upon their mobility were outlawed, but many of the features of the master-slave situation were reproduced in labour legislation and pass laws, and sustained by social practice. Farmers continued to pay their workers on a subsistence level, and the close interdependence of farmers and farm workers coupled with strong paternalism and rigid social distance have endured to this day. Other social products of slavery at the Cape which are still much in evidence are the Afrikaans language, the deeply entrenched divisions between brown and white Afrikaners, the racism of the Dutch Reformed Church in South Africa, and the position of dominance exercised by white persons over persons brown and black. Even scholarship is frequently imbued with strong racial assumptions. The author of the one extended work on slavery in the Cape writes that if "the Hottentots had not been so lazy the Dutch would not have had to import slaves. . . . A regular trade in slaves was kept up almost from the beginning of European civilisation . . . but many of the slaves had so little taste for work that they had scarcely arrived at the Cape when they began to desert" (De Kock). A leading criminologist, on the other hand, writes of a period when slaves and Khoi women were virtually defenceless against the sexual attacks of their masters, that it is nothing short of astonishing how few cases the records reveal of rape committed by slave and Khoi men against their white mistresses (Venter).

POSTSCRIPT

When the British occupied the Cape in 1795 to prevent it from being seized by the French under Napoleon, they undertook not to withdraw any of the rights and privileges of the inhabitants. Thus the right to own slaves was upheld for several decades and in fact the first years of the British occupation saw a very steep rise in the number of slaves held at the Cape. However, the privilege of torturing suspects and imposing different degrees of severity in capital punishment was something the new administration would not allow. After witnessing an execution which he found to be most harrowing, the British Commander wrote to the Cape Court of Justice that in England death itself was the supreme penalty and no degrees of severity were permitted in how the condemned man was to be killed. On receiving this letter the judges were most alarmed and forecast a great increase in capital offences. In their reply to the Commander they pointed out that there was nothing discriminatory in the use of the rack, which was applied to suspects, or, rather, to which suspects were applied, irrespective of race, colour, creed or status. They assured the esteemed Commander that even in Holland, where there were no slaves, the very same gradations of severity were recognised as those in force at the Cape, and, moreover, these gradations were equally applicable at the Cape to freemen and slaves. With regard to slaves who committed offences against colonists, especially against their masters, however, there was a distinction in punishments inflicted but this was not peculiar to the Cape . . . "on the contrary it is grounded upon analogy with the criminal law, according to which the distinctions of persons is one of the essential points by which the degree of punishment is measured in most civilised nations. . . ." Death by torture could be abolished without ill effects in the case of free people, they declared, but to abolish it generally would only encourage revolt among the slaves.

Apparently the public executioners were even more alarmed than the judges. According to the secretary to the British Commander, one of them "made an application for a pension in lieu of the emoluments he used to receive for the breaking of arms and legs". The other waited upon the President of the Court to know from him "whether it was the fashion amongst the English to break upon the wheel". A few days later, because, it was thought, of fear of redundancy, the hangman hanged himself.

CHAPTER TWO

Enter the British Legal Machine: Law, Administration and Race Relations at the Cape 1806-1910

INTRODUCTION

When in 1814 pressure from British merchants forced court proceedings in the colonised portion of the Cape to be thrown open for the first time to the public, the existing court-room in Cape Town was found to be too small to accommodate spectators. The site chosen for a new and larger building was the yard of the former Government Slave Lodge, which shortly after the second and final British occupation of the Cape in 1806 had been converted into a centre for administration (the slaves having been selected and removed by respectable people on payment of £30 per head). The new court was duly completed and at the opening ceremony (1815) Chief Justice Truter declared that "it had been erected with great expense and peculiar ingenuity, purposely to give the administration of justice in this Colony, all the external lustre, which can tend to place its dignity and freedom in the most exalted point of view . . ."

The hoped-for lustre did not manifest itself immediately. The Cape judges were at various times in the nineteenth century accused of being impetuous, overbearing, theatrical, licentious, over-lenient, over-strict, lazy, intriguing, stupid, prejudiced, incompetent and deaf, and two of them (including the first Chief Justice of the Supreme Court) were nearly impeached for misconduct. Part of the population adulated them for being representatives of British justice, another part detested them for the same reason, while the majority of the population were simply not asked for their opinion.

Yet for all the criticism and controversy, respect for the judiciary grew amongst all sections of the community, especially during the long period when de Villiers was Chief Justice (1876-1910). Just as the elegant Supreme Court building in Cape Town gave lustre to the judges, so did the judges impart a measure of brilliance to the Cape administration. By the end of the century the Royal Colonial Institute in London was told that the Cape Colony had been particularly fortunate in its judges who in point of integrity, learning and impartiality could bear comparison with any judicial body in the Empire. The *Cape Law Journal* ("the oldest periodical of its type in English in the world") agreed, declaring that the Cape judges were men of unquestioned probity and fearless independence and that the Cape system of criminal law was as nearly perfect as could be desired and worthy of adoption by the British Government itself. Fifty years later the distinguished South African historian de Kiewiet singled out the judges for the only undiluted accolade in a substantial book ("the specially brilliant role played by the judiciary in South African history").

This chapter examines the growth of the legal system at the Cape from its 'sorry state' at the beginning of the century to its allegedly 'near perfect' condition at the end, and discusses its role in the maintenance of what were regarded as proper relations between masters and servants and white and black. This was a time of expansion and conquest, when the small refreshment station at the western Cape grew to be the headquarters of a huge colony that spanned the whole of southern Africa. It was also a period when the discovery of diamonds and the re-discovery of gold to the north opened the way for rapid industrial and commercial development, and led to the final destruction of tribal and Boer independence and the establishment of British hegemony throughout the sub-continent.

In this setting the concept of British justice assumed particularly great importance. On the one hand it was seen as an instrument for extending Imperial control, on the other it was proclaimed as the guardian of the property and liberty of all British subjects, whether white, brown or black, English-speaking or Afrikaans. The courts lay at the heart of government, since they were used not only to extend the area of effective administration in a territorial sense (via magistracies and the Circuit Court), but also to bind diverse peoples to a common political authority. A court-centred administration modelled on British lines and adapted to the Cape social situation became the basic instrument of rule. The alternative of government by a military bureaucracy was considered from time to time, but apart from the special unpopularity it might have incurred amongst people grown accustomed to access to the courts, it would also have involved greater expense for the British taxpayer. Thus once conquest was complete, soldiers and punitive expeditions financed by the British Exchequer gave way to magistrates and police paid for by the Colonial Government. Eventually the British-type legal administrative machine encompassed the whole of South Africa, where it operated subject to the directives of a sovereign white-dominated Parliament and to the scrutiny of an influential white-dominated press.

Today it is Afrikaners rather than Englishmen who are largely in charge of this apparatus of control, but the system they employ and the specific techniques they use remain substantially unaltered. Judges, magistrates, lawyers, policemen and prison officers follow methods of organisation and styles of work derived almost entirely from their predecessors in the Cape Colony. The Dutch settlement and the Boer Republics might have provided much of current racial ideology in South Africa, and Natal the policy of separate development, but it was the Cape that supplied the present-day machinery of rule.

TRANSITION

The short period of rule at the Cape (1803-1806) by the Batavian (Dutch) Republic saw the beginnings of many modernising reforms not the least of which was the reconstitution of the Court of Justice around a core of salaried, legally trained judges enjoying considerable independence and prestige. Yet juridically speaking very little survived from that period; neither law reports, textbooks, opinions nor decrees. Outside the archival papers, the only physical relic of note was the Bench or, as a later judge was to put it, *the* Bench, denoting not a collective of judges but a collective of seats, consisting of five cane-backed chairs joined firmly together "to uphold . . . the pipe-smoking . . . grave and reverend signeurs . . . who upheld the laws" (Cole). Only two of the incumbents stayed on after the second British occupation, and neither achieved any particular fame. Yet a number of other officials, some Cape-born, others out from Holland, elected to work for the British administration even though this entailed an oath of allegiance to the British Crown. These men staffed the lower ranks of government for two decades after the occupation, and filled nearly all posts connected with the administration of justice. J. A. Truter, after having been under a cloud for his part in looting the Treasury as the British troops approached Cape Town, practised as an advocate and prosecutor until August 1812, when he was appointed Chief Justice. Thereafter he became the right hand man of successive governors and chief adviser on reform of land tenure (1813), tax collection (1814) and criminal procedure (1819). More than any of his colleagues he became the prototype of the many Afrikaners who subsequently were to rise to high office by skilful collaboration with the British. Born in Cape Town in 1763 as plain Johannes Andries Truter, he died in 1845 heaped with honours as Sir John Truter, the first South African to receive a British knighthood (1820).

Other leading personalities of the old regime manned the court which toured the countryside on the so-called Black Circuit of 1812 sent by the British Governor to investigate complaints from missionaries that white farmers were maltreating Khoi labourers. It was also Dutch and colonial-born lawyers who tried the leaders of the short-lived Slagter's Nek rebellion, whose resistance to British authority and subsequent execution was to make them martyrs in the eyes of future Afrikaner rebels. Significantly, this revolt was sparked off by the defiance of a white farmer who had fired on and been killed by a group of Khoi troopers sent to compel him to attend court on a charge of ill-treating a coloured servant. Eventually five of the rebels were hanged in a grim public execution – Afrikaners of the countryside condemned by Afrikaners of the town.

The problem of fractious frontiersmen was not something that first arose during British rule. Since the early days of the Dutch settlement attempts had been made to keep under rein the more distant farmers, and in fact one of the first appearances in court by Truter as a young advocate had been in a case where he had sought and gained an order for banishment against a farmer "for cattle bartering from Hottentots and shooting some of the latter" (1789). What was new about the British was their greater determination and efficiency and their greater willingness to incorporate armed Khoi Khoi into the police force. The Governors of that time were in general far less liberal in political outlook than their Batavian Republic predecessors had been. They came from a class of High Tory that tended to apologise for slave-owning and sympathise with the problems of landowners, and they loathed anything that smacked of Jacobinism. Yet being autocratic Conservatives they believed that the job of the Governor was to govern. How better both to govern more effectively and to quieten the philanthropic non-Conformist missionaries than by extending and invigorating the whole court system? Both to those who cried out for and to those who thundered against EQUALITY, the same answer could be given, one that combined the virtues of morality and effectiveness, of modernity and stability – JUSTICE. Justice did not tamper with social differentiation, on the contrary, it regularised it; it gave all inhabitants a forum for the expression of grievances; it established the machinery for the systematic investigation of complaints; and it gave an aura of impartiality to the extension of government control.

It was this very aura of impartiality that caused most affront to the white frontiersmen. The least that they expected of an active government – the only good government being a moribund one – was that it should be partial. Yet here was the law not only refusing to punish insubordinate servants, but actually giving them a chance publicly to defame their masters. From now on it was clear that the law could be used to discipline not only coloured servants, but also their white masters: thus if a slave raised his hand to his master, he would be guilty of an assault, and if a master lashed his slave more than 39 times (reduced in 1823 to 25 times) he too would be guilty of an assault.

This new willingness on the part of the courts to hear complaints from servants and to receive the evidence of Christian slaves (1823) and all non-slaves irrespective of colour or occupation, would have counted for little, however, had there not been people prepared to bring cases of alleged cruelty to court. The men who did this in some areas and to some extent were the Nonconformist missionaries sent out mainly by the London Missionary Society. They were enthusiastic, practical and, above all, safe from reprisals; through their activities they added a new and enduring element to South African political life, the white man who acted as 'champion of the natives' and did so by manipulating the machinery of white power rather than by helping to organise black resistance.

The missionaries received a valuable ally at a crucial stage in the person of a former Attorney-General of New South Wales (Saxe-Bannister) who after living at the Cape from 1827 to 1830, published a book in England criticising aspects of the colonial administration of justice. In some respects he thought that judicial institutions at the Cape were excellent, and he especially admired the public prosecutors in the country areas, whom he regarded as the guardians of the oppressed and a check on magistrates. Unfortunately, however, the courts were not vigorous enough in punishing abuses; in his view they neglected their special responsibility for redressing the inequalities which had been brought about during the long period in which the coloured poor had been stripped of their possessions. Yet one of the local magistrates, understood to be generally well disposed, and of a mild character, very recently remarked in regard to a clear case, in which success was partly gained, that he thought the rest (equally plain) should be waived. The time, said he, was "when Hottentots would have got no justice: now they wanted too much". The writer mentioned a number of other cases he had got to know about at first hand, which prompted him to urge that the outcome of trials be published in the *Colonial Gazette* in order that they might achieve maximum educational and deterrent effect. In one case an elderly Khoi man had been thrashed and kicked by a white farmer who had mistakenly suspected him of theft. The farmer was fined and ordered to pay damages in a civil suit, the writer's complaint being that the amounts were too low. Another matter arose out of a dispute over boundaries, which had led a group of white farmers to flog a Khoi farmer and leave him hanging by his arms all night. Eventually after much delay and some attempts at obstruction by lower court officials, the case came before the Circuit Court which awarded the injured man £20 and costs, a fairly substantial sum for those days. Other cases involved convictions for assault of a white woman for ill-treating a slave, of a white constable for beating a Khoi suspect, and of three white men for illegally punishing a slave—all were ordered to pay fines. A Khoi man who stole a sheep was, on the other hand, sentenced to undergo a whipping. Two other interesting matters which were heard outside the Colonial court's jurisdiction related firstly to the trial and execution by their chief of four Africans on a charge of murdering two Colonial soldiers, and secondly to the trial and execution by his chief of a San hunter on a charge of murdering a missionary. Both these cases were brought on the requisition of the colonial authorities, whose representative attended the trials as observer. Finally he mentioned the case of eleven Khoi Khoi who successfully petitioned the Supreme Court as paupers for relief from a contract of servitude unlawfully imposed upon them for debt.

In those years the influence of men like Saxe-Bannister on the Colonial Office was greater than it was to become later in the century. One example of this influence was the pressure put on the Governor at the Cape to end the practice whereby women slaves, who could not be whipped as were their menfolk, were punished by confinement on Sundays. The Governor complained that many of these women were so depraved that Sunday was not a day of rest for them but a day of debauchery and dissipation, and he also asked why the masters should be punished as well by being deprived of their labour on working days, to which the Colonial Secretary replied that he could not see how bad character could be improved by a day in solitary confinement meant for instruction and repose. Ultimately, however, it was the setting up of a Supreme Court in the Colony that was destined to have a greater effect than missives from the Colonial Office.

After the defeat of Napoleon and the conclusion of the Peace Treaty of 1814, the Cape was regarded by its rulers as a full British colony to be governed in the British interest. Lack of local educational facilities together with a deliberate policy of anglicising the administration made it inevitable that the ageing survivors of the Batavian Republic administration would be replaced by men imported from Britain. Commissioners of Enquiry were sent out from London and they recommended *inter alia* a complete overhaul of the judicial system, the introduction of British judges, the application of British court procedures and the gradual assimilation of the local Roman-Dutch law to that of England. The use of the English law of evidence, they asserted, could "not fail to produce the most beneficial consequences . . . even under the disadvantages to which it is liable from the strong prejudices of the white population and from the imperfect sense of religious and civil obligation by which the uninstructed portion of the Colonial Population is distinguished".

Following on their recommendations a Charter of Justice was enacted for the Cape in 1827 and confirmed by a second Charter in 1832. These Charters together with accompanying ordinances and rules of court completely transformed the local judicial establishment. At the head of affairs were well-paid judges drawn from the English, Irish and Scottish Bars; at the lower end were magistrates invested with wide-ranging judicial and administrative responsibilities. The styles and forms of British legal procedures were introduced: preliminary examinations and trial by jury in serious criminal matters, furnishing of indictments, provision for bail, examination and cross-examination of witnesses, in fact most if not all of the characteristic features of the British trial based on the adversary system.

The proceedings of the new Supreme Court of the Cape of Good Hope were commenced on 1st January 1828, when four judges, nine advocates, four attorneys and eight notaries took the oath of allegiance. The judges had been attracted by a good climate and a good salary (£2,000 p.a. for the Chief Justice and £1,500 p.a. for the Puisne Judges), while each seemed to have had strong personal motives as well for taking up posts in what must have seemed to them to be a near-wilderness. Thus one was alleged to have killed a man in a duel (Menzies), another had already served as legal adviser to the Governor at the Cape (Kekewich), a third was a sailor turned lawyer whose globetrotting career was eventually to take him to five continents (Burton), whilst the fourth was probably trying to get away from his wife (Chief Justice Wylde). As a group they were well-educated–

Menzies was a close friend of Sir Walter Scott—and they possessed a flamboyance, panache and independence of spirit quite new to officials at the Cape. Under their leadership the whole legal system took on a more vigorous character; one immediate consequence of their arrival was that demands for 'freedom of the press' could be met, because newspapers could be made subject to the fixed provisions of the law as interpreted by the courts, rather than to the capricious feelings of the Governor. These British judges may have been following in the wagon-ruts of their Cape predecessors, but they did so with an energy and a style that proved to be both new and lasting.

LIBERTY, EQUALITY, SERVILITY

The Charters of Justice and accompanying legislation made no reference to the colour or status of litigants or witnesses and to that extent may be regarded as having entrenched the technical equality of all before the lawcourts. The criminal courts tried white, black and brown prisoners, and the civil courts heard litigation involving members of all racial groups. Witnesses of all colours and every station could give evidence, and theoretically there was no weighting in favour of or against any class or group of witnesses. In the field of substantive law, too, steps were taken to secure a greater measure of formal or civic equality—in fact this was the only period in South African history when legislation was used to revoke rather than entrench race differentiation. Ordinance 50 of 1828 declared that "Hottentots and other free persons of colour are . . . entitled to all the rights of law to which any other of His Majesty's subjects . . . are entitled". It also expressly abolished the Vagrancy laws of 1809 and 1819 which had prohibited all non-slave coloured persons from moving from one place to another without a written permit from a local official. Soon afterwards (1834) the owning of slaves was abolished throughout the British Empire, and the process of establishing formal equality was complete.

Yet these measures made no provision for the acquisition by Khoi Khoi or ex-slaves of the land, education and political rights necessary for them to achieve any effective social and economic equality. Slave labour was converted into cheap labour; the great majority of coloured people at the Cape, whether ex-slave, Khoi Khoi, or descendants of mixed unions, had no means of subsistence other than to work for white employers on whatever terms were offered to them. Thus the actual situation of baasskap (domination) remained very much the same before and after the legislative reforms. The arming of Khoi Khoi troopers and the establishment of the Kat River Settlement might have counted for more than statutory declarations abolishing servitude, but this line of development was halted after the Kat River Rebellion of 1851.

When representative government arrived three years later, the franchise was deliberately restricted on economic and not on racial lines, but no black or brown person was ever elected to the Cape Parliament. Masters and Servants laws (1841, 1856 and 1873) were made applicable to all masters and all servants, irrespective of race. They required that contracts of service be annually registered and made insubordination or desertion of service criminal offences, but since most masters were white and most brown people were servants, the effect of this apparently race-free law was to consolidate rather than weaken race domination.

The net effect, then, of these legislative measures was not to constitute a revolution, but to remove certain barriers to emancipation; not to eradicate racial domination, but to sanction its class rather than its colour or cultural aspect; and not to destroy privilege, but to regularise its operation and restrain its arbitrary exercise. With regard to the use of force and the infliction of punishment, the area of permissible self-help open to farmers and other employers was reduced and the effective jurisdiction of the State increased. At the same time the State with its extensive resources could now be called upon to exercise systematically, publicly and on a large scale the sort of control over labour which the farmers had formerly exercised haphazardly, in private and on an individual basis.

For many of the white frontiersmen the bargain appeared inequitable, and they voted against it with their wagons. To them the right to punish servants was a matter of discipline and not of law, and warranted interference just as little as did the right to punish children (or, for those who had contact with schools, the right to chastise pupils). A farmer thought he knew far better than any magistrate how to handle his workers. A thrashing swiftly delivered seemed far more appropriate than punishment after a time-consuming trial at a distant courthouse, especially since fines could not be met and imprisonment deprived the farmer of his labour. At a time when the magistracy had not been firmly established and police and penal establishments were almost non-existent outside of Cape Town (with killing, whipping and banishment being the main forms of punishment open to the court) the advantages of a court-centred system of controlling labour and maintaining 'proper relations' between white and brown were not as obvious as they were to become later. To aggravate the feeling of injury, these apparently foreign ideas about the regulation of master/ servant relationships were conveyed in a foreign tongue and, with the arrival of the new judges, by foreign men.

ROBES AND OXWAGONS

These early British judges had a complicated task to perform, one not made easier by the wrangles, intrigue and scandal in which they were constantly involved. Today South African legal scholars tend to view their contribution purely in terms of the dispute as to whether English law has polluted or enriched the stream of Roman-Dutch law, and looked at in this narrow way all that need be said is that the Scottish Menzies was a 'staunch upholder' of Roman-Dutch principles, whereas the other judges were more eclectic and inclined to fall back on English legal precepts. Their real contribution, however, lay not so much in what they did to the principles of the law, as in what they did for the activities of the court. They invested judicial office, if not always with a dignity, then with a sense of importance, and they drastically renovated procedures and methods of administration, bringing them into line with British practice.

Their job was not merely to interpret the law but to create it: thus they introduced new Rules of Court and drafted an ordinance which made English rules of evidence applicable to the Cape Courts; they also drafted ordinances dealing with the handling of insolvent and deceased estates, the setting up of a Land Register, the qualifications for jurors, and the establishment of the office of Master of the Supreme Court with responsibility for looking after the estates of minors and lunatics. As general legal advisers to the Governor, they concerned themselves with all proposed legislation, and not only with measures directly related to the administration of justice. It was Judge Burton, for example, who drafted the famous Ordinance 50 of 1828, for which activity the white colonists forgave him only when he later awarded damages against the leading missionary and philanthropist, John Philip, on the grounds that Philip had wrongly accused a magistrate of oppressive behaviour.

The opinions of the judges were sought and given weight to by members of the Governor's Advisory Council and later by members of the Legislature. The first Chief Justice was for a time in fact a member of the council of advice, but he proved to be so disputatious that he was diplomatically relieved of this office and told he was needed more urgently on Circuit. When, however, representative government was inaugurated in 1854 he became *ex officio* President of the Legislative Council (like the Lord Chancellor in Britain who presided over the House of Lords), a position which his successors in office continued to hold until Union in 1910.

The judges "in those days were more jealous than they have always been since of the executive's use of emergency powers", and exercised considerable influence over the drawing up of treaties with African leaders (where this was done) and defining the modes of government in the frontier territories. They saw themselves not as mere executants of the law but as watchdogs of constitutionality and representatives of the Crown. The military might conquer, but the judges were needed for good government. On one occasion Judge Menzies while on circuit was so anxious to keep Emigrant (Trekker) families under British jurisdiction, that he actually purported to annex in the name of the Crown large portions of territory north of the Colonial border.

The Colony was poor but litigious and the judges worked hard for their good salaries. Travel on Circuit was particularly arduous, since by 1850 the court's jurisdiction extended to an area of 130,000 square miles, and distant towns were 800 to 900 miles apart. Thus twice a year every year for three months at a time the judges, who until 1860 travelled in oxwagons over roads 'in a state of nature', covered more ground than did the Voortrekkers, and they had to be on time. The towns were filled with prisoners waiting to be tried and with dignitaries waiting to be entertained (Nagmaal-the Dutch Reformed Church's Communion Feast-was usually made to coincide with the Circuit). Each town accordingly represented a non-stop whirl of judicial and gastronomic activity. The Circuit judge was regarded as second in importance only to the Governor, and his arrival "in this Colony (where but few distinguished occasions occur) an event of peculiar import". Thus the first judge to travel through the Transkei was greeted with triumphal arches, fireworks and addresses (though compulsory jury service dampened the enthusiasm). Escorted into town by a cavalcade of police, the judges generally drove in open carriages with two horses, while the local people stood in the street and removed their hats. Whether or not justice was seen to be done, the judges were certainly seen, and so effective were they as recruiting agents that nearly all their successors on the Bench in the late nineteenth and early twentieth centuries came from small country towns.

To those who criticised the expense of the Circuit, it was pointed out that the judge abroad was the best schoolmaster in the country, exercising a profound moral influence wherever he went. Even if the costs of a Circuit in fact exceeded the value of property stolen in the Circuit area, this was said to be to the credit of the judges, since just as "the Celestial Emperor pays his physicians when he is well and stops their fees when he is sick . . . so one . . . should not begrudge the expenses of the circuit court because the state of crime is what it is, but rather the reverse" (Porter). Nevertheless, savings were made in the costs of travel and entertainment, and by the end of the century judges were complaining of being forced to proceed *in forma pauperis*.

In order to ease the load of the Cape judges a separate Eastern Cape Division of the Supreme Court was created with its headquarters in Grahamstown. The successive annexations, however, of the Transkei, East Griqualand and Pondoland resulted in the judges being responsible for covering two giant Circuit areas instead of one. The introduction of landau carts drawn by teams of horses opened up a new era of speed but did little to overcome what was by now the greatest hazard of Circuit travel–swollen rivers. Complaining of the absence of bridges, the *Cape Law Journal* pointed out that "the judge who perhaps but yesterday was seated in Court bewigged and scarlet gown'd . . . may a day or so later be seen crouched in a small wooden box, suspended from a wire rope, being hauled by jerks across a rushing, flooded river". For counsel the indignities could be even worse. "On one occasion a smasher hat and an eyeglass constituted the only articles of apparel upon the form of the prosecuting Barrister, as he waded, holding his clothes aloft, through a river which was more than ordinarily full." It was not reasonable, concluded the *Journal*, that every six months a Judge and Circuit Bar should be expected to face odds in arriving on time.

To get through all their work on Circuit the judges frequently held court at night. One energetic judge managed to handle cases in eleven Circuit towns in only a month by means of sitting from 6 a.m. to near midnight and then leaving for the next town at daybreak. As late as 1891 the *Law Journal* referred to the practice of lighting the court with candlesticks placed on the Bench, the jury-box and tables, with the result that "the effect at a recent sitting for the conclusion of a notorious murder case was quite ghastly".

In Cape Town itself the activity of the judges was far less heroic. For some time there was so little work for them to do that three judges would sit together to hear the most trifling matters (1878). This was so despite the fact that in 1856 the procedure of automatic review–a unique South African contribution to criminal procedure–had been introduced, whereby all magistrates' court cases in which the sentences imposed exceeded one month's imprisonment, or £5 fine, or twelve lashes, were automatically sent on review to the Supreme Court.

By the 1850s judges were no longer being appointed solely from Britain. The elevation to the Bench of such persons as Ebden, Cloete and Watermeyer, perhaps lowered the level of judicial rhetoric but raised the standard of Roman-Dutch law scholarship (assisted by the publication of law reports dating back to 1828). Until 1868 the Colonial Office kept a balance between British-born and Colonial-born judges, with the Chief Justice always being an Englishman or Scotsman, but from 1868 onwards all Cape judges were appointed from members of the Cape Bar, and after the coming of responsible government in 1872, the Cape Government itself made all appointments.

The quality of judges during the mid-century varied considerably. Thus Chief Justice Hodges (1858-1868), who was said to have no prejudices except against the letter 'H', was strong on improving jail conditions but weak on points of law, whereas his predecessor and successor, Bell (1855-1858, 1868-1874), was strong on points of law but weak on tact. Newspapers were unafraid to attack tyrannical or unjust judges, and used the most scathing language to do so. Judge Dwyer (1868-1886) was openly referred to as a 'hedgehog' and a 'ginger-pop' judge, and one paper ascribed his wearing of gown and wig to "the custom of covering those parts of the body which are in any way deficient".

It was only when Paarl-born J. H. de Villiers was elevated to the Bench as Chief Justice in 1874 that the court received a leader who combined dignity, tact and legal acumen with a concern for improving the standards of justice. Merely 30 years old when he took office, it was expected that the passed-over judges would refuse to administer the oath to him, so "he rose from his seat and administered the oath to himself and said 'Call the first case, Mr Registrar' ". For the next thirty-six years he presided with forbidding gravity over the court, achieving for it an international regard during a period when rapid economic and political development brought South Africa to the attention of the world. As a jurist his greatest achievement lay in the way he moulded Roman-Dutch law to meet the needs of a modern, developing economy, which earned for him from his most eminent successor, Sir

James Rose-Innes, the title of 'master-builder of South African law'.
His demeanour was as distinguished as his scholarship, and so great
was his eventual fame that to appeal from a judgement of his to the
Privy Council was regarded almost as an impertinence. What he brought
to the Bench was a sense of authority. He was learned, grave, courteous
and prepared to stand up to the Government; being unconcerned about
unpopularity (or perhaps taking his popularity for granted) he became
popular. A friend and protégé of such liberal statesmen as William
Porter and Saul Solomon ('champion of the natives'), he took his
stand on "the fundamental principle that no man's fundamental rights
should depend on the colour of his skin" (Innes). More than most of
his contemporaries in the upper reaches of Cape society he saw what a
valuable role the Supreme Court could play in integrating conquerors
and conquered into a common society sharing common values and
standards of conduct. Unlike most of his colleagues who belonged to
Volunteer Regiments, he was not a military man, but a strong believer
in civil authority. He publicly condemned moves to make flogging
compulsory for stock-thieves, and on at least two occasions severely
embarrassed the Executive by ordering the release on habeas corpus
(and its Roman-Dutch equivalent) of brown and black political leaders
(Willem Kok and Pondo chief Sigcau). To arguments that the detention of such 'troublemakers' was necessary for the security of the
Colony, he replied that "actual justice done with an equal hand does
more to keep the peace than anything else". His fame as a judge spread
to Britain, and he became the first Colonial judge to be appointed
member of the Judicial Committee of the Privy Council.

Contrary to the current notion that South African judges have traditionally given politics as wide a berth as possible, de Villiers never left
politics alone. The only time the *Law Journal* ventured to criticise
him was when he offered to form a Government in the Cape on a
'broad South Africa' policy: the *Journal* observed that just as a mathe-
matical line was length without breadth, so his platform was breadth
without length, and advised him to stay on the Bench. When the
National Convention met after the Anglo-Boer War to consider union
of the four colonies, he was the natural choice for President. For
twenty years he had worked actively to create an Appeal Court for all
states in southern Africa, seeing in it the forerunner of political union;
and when eventually such Union and such Court were simultaneously
established in 1910, he was selected as first Chief Justice of South
Africa.

Barristers and Gentlemen

By accident or design the first case on the roll of the new Supreme Court in 1828 involved the appointment of an advocate to look after the interests of a child of a slave who was claiming that he had been manumitted. At that stage the Bar consisted of only nine advocates, all of whom had been either judges or advocates in the previous court, and additions thereafter came very slowly. When de Villiers commenced practice the number had dropped to four (1866), and this included the Attorney-General. There were accordingly at this stage as many judges as full-time barristers.

By the time James Rose-Innes joined the Bar (1878) the number in practice had risen to twelve, and by 1901 the *Law Journal* was able to report that "Themis smiles in the forum on more than thirty ardent admirers".

Of the first thirty advocates admitted after 1828 approximately half had English and half Afrikaans names. All except two had qualified by virtue of having been called to the Bar either in London, Edinburgh or Dublin; although examination courses were set in the Cape from 1854 onwards, it was customary until well into the twentieth century for the great majority of aspiring advocates to proceed to Britain (and often to Holland) for their legal education, which usually included taking degrees at Cambridge or Oxford. Out of the dozens of well-known judges who sat on the Bench during this period only three (Buchanan, Innes and Curlewis) had received all their legal training in South Africa.

Most of the early advocates with British names appear to have been servants of the Crown or else immigrants, who like the early judges came to the Cape not so much to advance their careers, as for personal reasons, such as ill-health (Thomas Upington, Robert King) and ship-wreck (Alfred Cole). The Irish Bar contributed a particularly large number of advocates and judges (Porter, Griffiths and Upington–all Attorney-Generals–Fitzpatrick, Dwyer and Connor–all judges–and King QC), prompting the *Law Journal* to carry an article by an American lawyer who protested that Ireland was the only country in the world where English was spoken and the Irish did not rule.

The Cape Bar accordingly was small, elitist and strongly influenced by British styles and traditions. The division between barrister and solicitors was maintained, as was the practice of appointing judges purely from the ranks of practising barristers. In the latter part of the century the title Queen's Counsel was awarded to certain leading advocates, and although all advocates and many judges discarded the wearing of wigs, presumably because of the heat, they continued to wear British-style gowns and bibs. The British honours system further bound lawyers and judges at the Cape to Britain, since they were prominent amongst the recipients of royal knighthoods. After the letters patent of the first Queen's Counsel sank en route to the Cape, appointments were made locally by the Governor without an oath of loyalty being taken. Knighthoods, however, were awarded with great ceremony by members of the Royal Family on occasional visits to the Cape, and were much applauded by the *Law Journal*, which urged that the supposedly inexhaustible Fountain of Honour should not dwindle in the process of distribution over Territories south of the Equator. A limited right of appeal to the Privy Council in London also cemented ties between British and Cape lawyers, and enabled the *Law Journal* to point out with pride that more than one quarter of humanity had such an appeal as a birthright (in fact only about two dozen persons a year actually availed themselves of this birthright).

The advocate's oath of admission involved not only a declaration of fealty to Victoria but a solemn undertaking that "... I do from my heart abhor, detest and abjure as impious and heretical that damnable doctrine and position that Princes excommunicated ... by the Pope ... may be deposed or murdered by their subjects ..." Catholics not planning to kill Victoria were, however, admitted, as was at least one Unitarian (Porter) and one Jew (Jacobs). Most of the advocates were members of the Anglican or Dutch Reformed Churches, with a fair sprinkling of Nonconformists and Presbyterians. Many of the leading South African lawyers–both English and Afrikaans–were Freemasons. There were not many schools at the Cape, but nearly all the Colonial-born advocates who subsequently achieved fame seem to have attended only two, the South African College School in Cape Town and, more remarkably, a Reverend Templeton's school at the village of Bedford in the eastern Cape. This latter had within its walls at one time a future Prime Minister (Schreiner), two future Chief Justices (Innes and Solomon) and a number of future eminent lawyers and civil servants.

Friendships at the Bar tended to be strong and lasting, partly because the number of advocates was so small and partly because the hazards of the Circuit were so great. The association which produced the most enduring results was the one between the ageing Attorney-General Porter and the youthful advocate de Villiers. Porter was the most distinguished lawyer and gifted orator at the Cape during the middle portion of the nineteenth century; a Unitarian of strongly liberal views, he used all the authority of his office to encourage a low and non-racial qualification for the franchise for the first representative government (he drafted the Constitution). He was a vigorous opponent of the death penalty, and his failure to persuade the Cape Parliament to abolish it was one of the factors which persuaded him to refuse the Chief Justiceship in favour of de Villiers. He turned down all the many honours offered to him, refusing even to allow his portrait to be painted, but possessed such authority that he could silence the most querulous of judges (doing so once with the famous statement that a witness had in error "addressed me, my Lord, as 'My Lord,' my Lord, instead of my Lord, my Lord, as 'My Lord', my Lord"). Porter took de Villiers under his wing, sponsored him for Parliament and encouraged his candidature for the Chief Justiceship; he also transmitted to him a calm, eloquent style and a deep respect for justice through law. Porter and de Villiers may be regarded as the individuals who did the most to establish the traditions and ethics which South African barristers like to feel characterise their profession, while Innes and Schreiner were their most influential successors.

In those days admission to the Bar led almost invariably to a successful political and judicial career. Young barristers on circuit were quickly snapped up as Parliamentary candidates, and once elected could aim to become Attorney-General–a sort of Minister of Justice practising at the Bar–and then, possibly, even Prime Minister (Upington, Schreiner). Progress was often extremely rapid. Thus Thomas Upington the 'Afrikander from Cork', arrived in Cape Town in 1874 aged 30 and broken in health; within four years he was Attorney-General and within six Prime Minister. Of the twelve advocates at the Bar when Innes commenced practice in 1878, ten became judges, the eleventh a Secretary for Justice in the Transvaal, while the twelfth was the man who Gandhi described as that "famous barrister of South Africa, Mr Leonard".

By the end of the century the development of the diamond and gold fields in the north had drawn many Cape Town and Grahamstown lawyers to Kimberley, Pretoria and Johannesburg, where the volume of work was greater and the scale of fees higher. They took with them the styles and traditions of the Cape, and practised before judges many of whom had themselves come from the Cape. Thus in 1903 a writer in the *Law Journal* claimed that the "Cape Colony, like Africa of old, may well be called the *nutricula causidicorum*—the nurse of lawyers—and every South African colony, except Natal, owes the majority of its Bench, Bar and Side-Bar to the parent colony".

ATTORNEYS AND LAW AGENTS

For a few years after 1806 attorneys were admitted to practice by the favour of the Governor without having to pass examinations or serve indentureships, and the complaint was made that any bankrupt shopkeeper or reduced officer could set up as an attorney. The Charters of Justice and accompanying Rules of Court entrenched the existing division between advocates and attorneys and made it correspond to the English division between barristers and solicitors. They also provided that prospective attorneys should serve five years apprenticeship as articled clerks as a prerequisite for practice, but that persons qualified for practice as solicitors in England, Ireland and Scotland were automatically entitled to practise at the Cape.

Originally there were even fewer attorneys than advocates at the Cape, with only four being admitted at the opening of the new Supreme Court in 1828. For many years they all had their offices in Cape Town, and visited the outlying centres only when the circuit court went round. Nearly all court work was done by law agents, who had no legal qualification but were entitled on payment of a fee to appear in the magistrates court. Examinations for attorneys were introduced only in the last quarter of the century, but they were gradually made more stringent, while a heavy burden of fees and premiums was used further to restrict their numbers. In the 1880s law societies with more than fifty members each were established in the western and eastern sections of the Colony, and gradually the law agents were squeezed out of practice. At the turn of the century almost every town, village and hamlet had as many and often more attorneys than it could support: in Oudtshoorn alone during the ostrich-feather boom there were more than twenty practitioners, and complaints were loud and frequent about the overcrowding of the profession. Unlike the local advocates, the Cape attorneys were for the most part 'home-grown and home-trained', and consequently the Cape Side-Bar was far less affected by English methods and traditions than was the Bar.

By and large attorneys in the Cape never achieved the eminence of their colleagues at the Bar. The only distinguished jurist to emerge from their ranks was C. H. van Zyl, father of a future Governor-General, who collected the first large law library at the Cape, wrote important textbooks on procedure and practice as well as many articles for the *Law Journal*, and pioneered legal education at the Cape. The *Cape Law Journal* was launched by a young and enterprising attorney (W. H. S. Bell) in 1884, and a few Cape attorneys went on to achieve prominent positions in political life. As a profession, attorneys handled a wide variety of legal matters for clients and did much work preparing for trials, but their main contribution to public life in the Cape lay in the economic rather than the purely legal field, where they negotiated sales, drafted agreements and acted as auctioneers and estate agents.

MAGISTRATES, JUSTICES OF THE PEACE AND THE LAW DEPARTMENT

The administration of justice at the local level was transformed in 1827 when resident magistrates were appointed to replace the local officials (*landdrosts* and *heemraden*) left over from the Dutch era. The magistrates were full-time employees of the Colonial Government who combined the administrative tasks of receiving taxes, issuing licences, collecting information, publishing government notices and solemnising marriages with the judicial tasks of hearing all but the more serious criminal and civil cases. Though their jurisdiction was limited in civil cases to relatively small awards and in criminal cases to the imposition of short terms of imprisonment, heavy lashes and low fines, it was in their courts that most trials took place and it was they who represented the administration of justice to the man in the veld.

For many years the absence of sufficient magistrates was regarded as "one of the chiefest wants" of the Colony. The training of those who were appointed was minimal, and they often lacked the finesse required to handle the frequently conflicting demands of the review judges, their departmental heads and the local public (usually meaning the local white public). Although some magistrates were highly qualified and competent, "many such appointments also went to retired sea-captains and other gentlemen whose ignorance of law and procedure was abysmal". At a later stage senior officers of the Cape Mounted Rifles were often made magistrates, presumably on the premise that their fierce demeanour would compensate for their lack of legal knowledge.

Pressure from local white employers was strongest in cases of desertion or refusal to work, and theft of stock or produce. In such cases magistrates were expected to ensure that the accused were punished as severely as they would have been by the employers themselves in the days of self-help. Throughout the century the question of punishment of farm labourers continued to be fiercely argued. In 1892 there was a Cabinet crisis over whether a magistrate should be removed from the Bench after he had been criticised by the Prisons Commission for "extreme harshness to Native offenders and refractory Native servants". Strong support for the magistrate came from farmers throughout the Colony, and in 1894 the notorious 'Strop Bill' (Flogging Bill, or, as Olive Schreiner called it: Every man beat his own kaffir bill) was placed before Parliament, which if passed would have once more legalised the thrashing of servants. As members of the local white community, country magistrates were kept well aware of farmers' feelings. Even in the towns magistrates were subjected to pressure by white employers; in one case a lady of standing is said to have called out loudly to a magistrate trying an employee of hers for desertion: "Punish her Percy!"

In the early years when communications were very poor and the administration even poorer, a large number of justices of the peace were appointed to exercise judicial-cum-police functions in the country districts (1827). As the magistracy advanced so did the justices of the peace retire, until eventually they became little more than commissioners of oath. By 1894 they held court only in the most far-flung districts, trying a total of 1,400 cases (compared with nearly 50,000 criminal cases attended to in the magistrates' courts). The majority of cases which they heard related to the Masters and Servants Acts, with the balance being made up mainly of charges of assault, vagrancy, drunkenness and theft.

The country magistrate's duties were as multifarious as his procedures were informal. A policeman turned magistrate later wrote in his memoirs of the time when he was appointed to the Northern Border magistracy (1873) (Hook). His jurisdiction covered an area of 89,000 square miles, and he had power to impose thirty-six lashes with a cat; amongst his first tasks was that of chasing African and San 'squatters' off certain pieces of land. He carried his records in a wagon and held court anywhere. In one case a Boer charged with assaulting an African rode up to the wagon at breakfast-time with the witnesses, who had all come to eat. "The table cleared, the accused stood up for trial just where he'd sat, I sitting in my chair the same. A £5 note protruding from his pocket was the penalty imposed. Afterwards he shod my horse gratis . . ."

Although procedures in the larger centres were never as casual as this, lawyers constantly complained of the magistrates' lack of legal knowledge (as well as of their tendency to act as judge and prosecutor at the same time). The judges were often extremely severe on the magistrates, on occasions not only upsetting their verdicts, but also ordering them personally to pay the costs of successful appeals. One of these orders for costs was in turn successfully taken on appeal to the Privy Council; a newspaper caustically suggested that the judges should now be ordered to pay the costs of the further appeal).

The procedure of automatic review mentioned earlier helped to raise standards in magistrates courts, even though (1894) only a tenth of convictions were so reviewed, and only one in a hundred of the reviews actually led to a conviction being quashed. Those cases in which magistrates were overruled frequently got into the press and the law reports, and also could have affected promotion prospects. Magistrates had no security of office as had the judges; as employees of the Government they were selected, promoted and transferred by the Law Department.

The Law Department came to be regarded as 'the crack Department' of the Colonial Government, an indication perhaps of the important part played by the law in the general field of administration. Of all the Government departments it demanded the highest educational standards and offered the highest pay. The political head of the department was the Attorney-General, who was responsible for courts, police, prisons, the legal profession, the preparation of indictments and the drafting of legislation. Eminent lawyers and statesmen such as Porter, Upington, Innes and Schreiner gave the office a special distinction, while at the end of the century the permanent head of the department Sir John Graham, became a legend amongst civil servants for his industry and high standards. After the conquest of the Republics in the Anglo-Boer War (1899-1902) many Cape officials in the Law Department were sent to the Transvaal to establish a new judicial system there. The statutes which they prepared were based largely on Cape models, and in turn these statutes became the basis for the organisation of courts and rules of evidence and procedure adopted by the whole of South Africa after Union.

THE LAND REGISTER

The development of efficient methods of regulating land ownership and transfer was one of the preconditions for economic growth in the Colony. In the early years of the century, circular farms were still being appropriated with a radius of a half-hour's walk, but the British soon attempted to stabilise land ownership, and later made the Registrar of Slaves responsible for compiling a proper land register, so that he became known as the Registrar of Slaves and Deeds. By the middle of the century only a little over half the Colony's surface area had been granted in legal title–the creation of an efficient and reliable service did not mean that it was used–but the number of deeds passed each year was to rise from only 200 at the commencement of the century to over 10,000 at the end. The Cape Land Register was eventually copied in a number of other colonies, and became the basis for land registration in the whole of South Africa. The *Law Journal*, which regarded it as perhaps the most simple and complete system of its kind in the world, expressed amazement that it had not been adopted in England.

LAW ENFORCERS: ARMY AND POLICE

Punitive raids, wars of conquest, the suppression of crime and the maintenance of 'proper relations' between masters and servants were so closely interrelated in the Colony that police and military functions were often inseparable.

The military consisted primarily of Imperial troops who started by garrisoning the Cape but then increasingly became involved in frontier warfare. The Dutch had originally colonised a portion of southern Africa populated only by Khoi and then by San people, the so-called Hottentots and Bushmen. Shortly before the British occupation of the Cape, however, white farmers moving up the east coast had begun to penetrate areas populated by black, Bantu-speaking farmers, who will be referred to here as Africans. It was the British Imperial troops who finally accomplished what the colonial forces had been unable to do, namely the conquest of African tribal groups along the Colony's eastern frontier. By and large British troops were not drawn into police work, but they provided the shield of force behind which para-military forces and ordinary police units could operate.

At no stage did the white Colonials have any permanent military force of their own; in the first half of the century they set up mainly Afrikaans-speaking commando units, in the second half mainly English-speaking Volunteers, but both the Commandos and the Volunteers operated on a part-time basis only.

Until the 1850s the Commandos were frequently called up to fight on the frontier. They were mounted infantry drawn largely from the countryside, who wore rough clothes, elected their own officers and were prepared to leave their farms for only a few months at a time. Although their numbers in battle increased from 800 in the Frontier War of 1811 to 5,000 + 3,000 reserves in 1846, they combined badly with regular troops and their military effectiveness declined, probably because their African opponents were increasingly able to match them in guns and horses. Their activities were always controversial, and Attorney-General Porter likened them to wolves who attacked the African tribes.

From the 1850s onwards the Commandos were largely replaced on the frontier by the Volunteers, who were based mainly in the towns and organised along the lines of British models. Many judges and lawyers joined the Volunteers—'exchanged the gown for the sword'— and even the normally pacific Porter was praised for his military ardour. In peacetime the Volunteers indulged in uniformed parades while "the possession of a rifle and the opportunity of buying ammunition was much sought after in a country where everybody was scared of a native uprising, everyone wanted to shoot game, and many were keen on target shooting". In wartime the Volunteers usually served as support troops for the Imperial forces, but occasionally they took part in 'small native wars' as members of purely Colonial expeditions; by 1894 their numbers were just short of 6,000.

Because of their part-time nature, Commandos and Volunteers could not be integrated into any permanent machinery for law enforcement, so that a special force had to be created to fill the large gap that existed between the military and the constabulary. This special force of 'soldier-policemen' was the well-known Cape Mounted Rifles (CMR), whose name had first belonged to a cavalry regiment of Khoi Khoi troopers maintained by the Imperial authorities. Their task was to pacify the border areas and to create a court-centred administration in the Transkei, but they also "helped to realise the Government policy towards the Griquas and Basutos", and their activities became increasingly military in character. Eventually their paramilitary character was given statutory recognition and Inspectors and Sub-Inspectors were re-named as Captains and Lieutenants in the "Permanent Colonial Forces both for police and defence". Their numbers fluctuated at around the 700 mark.

Because the CMR was so heavily involved in military work on the frontier, a second force had to be created to do police work in the interior. In the early 1880s the Cape Police force was established with this end in view. Because they had so many duties—listed under twenty-one heads which included patrolling, tracing criminals, inspecting native locations and visiting pounds – the *Law Journal* considered it "amusing to remember that the Cape Police are under the control of the Law Department and not that of the Colonial Defence. . . . [They] really constitute a valuable military and not a civilian corps". While generally praising the police and complaining that they were over-worked, the *Journal* pointed out that they tended to be too influenced by pressure from local inhabitants and sometimes strained evidence to get a conviction; "a man of weak character might sometimes find it difficult to refrain from making an accused or suspected person talk . . .". The Cape Police force was slightly larger than the Mounted Rifles, with an establishment of about 1,000 officers and men.

In addition to these two para-military police forces, whose functions were clearly related to the conquest, integration and subordination within the Colonial legal order of Africans, Griquas and San in the east and north of the Colony, there were a number of police forces who had 'ordinary' police duties similar to those carried out by police-men in England. These were municipal police forces in the main centres, and small local forces in the country areas under the control of resident magistrates. Finally a special Native Affairs Police force con-sisting largely of Africans under white command was established in the Transkei. For many years these ordinary police forces remained smaller than the para-military ones, but towards the end of the century their total numbers increased rapidly and by 1910 they numbered nearly 2,500 men in all, of whom 700 were in the Native Affairs Police.

The racial composition of the various forces was such that whites were in strong control, both with regard to rank and numbers. In the Transkei, the largely white Mounted Rifles were equalled in number by the largely African Native Affairs Police, but elsewhere white police out-numbered their dark-skinned colleagues by approximately five to one.

PRISONS AND PUNISHMENT

The abolition by the British in the Cape in 1796 of extraordinarily barbarous punishments such as breaking on the wheel and mutilation left the judges and magistrates power to impose only ordinarily bar-barous punishments such as hanging, flogging and imprisonment. Banishment and transportation were unsuited to conditions at the Cape, but imprisonment was gradually introduced to supplement fines and whipping. At first prisons were used solely for persons awaiting trial,

condemned persons awaiting execution and civil debtors, and the warders were paid by the masters, relatives or creditors of the prisoners.
Later, however, prisons and convict stations were established to receive
convicts, and they were put on a more organised and regimented
footing. The aimless and unprofitable work done by prisoners in the
early part of the century gave way to labour on public works, and the
whole road system through the mountains of the south-western Cape
was constructed by prison labour, as was the breakwater at the Cape
Town docks. By the end of the century prisoners were being hired out
in large numbers to farmers and mineowners, and at one stage the De
Beers diamond mines in Kimberley were employing more than 10,000
prisoners a day.

As civil government was extended into the interior via the expanding
system of magistracies, a series of small prisons were built throughout
the country. Overcrowding of prisons was chronic, and complaints
of bad treatment became more and more insistent, until the Colonial
Government was compelled to appoint a special Inspector of Prisons.
Then as now the aim of reforming prisoners was accepted in principle
while the officially prescribed diet of those days compared very favourably with that provided today. The main picture is one of prisoners
suffering from neglect as much as from institutionalised harshness, and
of great unevenness in the quality of prison life from one centre to the
next. Criticism of prisons seemed to mount towards the latter part of
the century, but it is not clear whether this was because conditions got
worse or sections of the public became more concerned. An early
target for criticism was the practice of chaining prisoners to the wall in
insecure prisons to prevent them from escaping; later, when prison
buildings were more substantial, the excessive imposition of spare diet
and solitary confinement was condemned.

On one occasion Chief Justice Hodges refused to convict a prisoner
charged with jail-breaking, on the grounds that the prison was so
tumbledown and overcrowded that he would not punish anyone for
attempting to get away "from such a wretched hole". Some years later
bad hygiene led to outbreaks of smallpox and measles in two prisons
and the spread of a disease in a third which necessitated the prisoners
being assisted, some even carried, into court. Criticism was also levelled
at the rule that 'life' prisoners not only had to do hard labour but also
had to spend all their years in chains.

Figures given in the Cape Statistical Register indicate that by the end
of the century there had already been established at the Cape the basic

characteristic of present-day prison populations in South Africa, namely a very large annual intake of short-term prisoners. Thus sentences of ten years' penal servitude, so common in Europe, were said to be almost unknown at the Cape, where even five years hard labour was regarded as an exceptional punishment. Of about 61,000 persons charged with criminal offences in the magistrates' courts in 1894, approximately 55,000 were found guilty and 42,000 admitted to prison. (In the Supreme Court 800 indictments led to a further 600 convictions.) Yet at the end of the year there were only 3,000 persons in custody, which suggests that the overwhelming majority of prisoners received very short sentences. Allowing for the increase in population, the present-day annual number of persons received into prison in the whole of South Africa is proportionately about the same while the average daily prison population is approximately twice as big. Also making allowances for population differences, the annual intake of prisoners at the Cape in 1894 was roughly five times as great as that in England and Wales at the time and the daily average prison population roughly three times as great.

In the sphere of capital punishment the attitudes of those in authority at the Cape appear to have been much more lenient than those in South Africa today. In the early part of the century capital punishment was imposed for a wide variety of crimes, and as late as 1831 a man was hanged for sodomy. A survey published in 1897 suggests that in the 1830s the Supreme Court judges imposed death sentences for serious cases of housebreaking, arson, cattle-killing, theft, incest and rape, and attempted murder, but that thereafter the death sentence was reserved almost exclusively for murder. Death sentences passed in 1841 and 1862 on persons found guilty of rape seem to have been matters of note, and in 1888 a book reviewer in the *Law Journal* doubted whether persons found guilty of rape would ever again be sentenced to death. "It is highly questionable", he observed, "whether the morbid sympathy created by the severity of the punishment for the doomed man might not weaken the results expected from that penalty, and add another wrong to the injury already sustained by the woman." Ten years later, however, the Chief Justice condemned to death a prisoner who had pleaded guilty to rape and attempted murder.

It has already been mentioned that Attorney-General William Porter attempted to get Parliament to abolish the death sentence. The question of abolition was debated by members of the newly created Forensic Society (1893), while the *Law Journal* contained a number of articles which favoured abolition (the first strongly retentionist article appeared only in 1909). Although death sentences were always imposed for murder, once even by de Villiers on an undefended man, there are indications that it was sparingly carried out. Thus the Cape Statistical Register for 1894 records that only one inquest was held consequent on a judicial hanging, and seems to record no other figure for death by execution.

If lynching is as American as cherry-pie, then flogging is as South African as biltong. The authorities at the Cape never seem to have been in doubt about the necessity for using the cat and the cane as major instruments of punishment. What was in issue was whether farmers and local officials should be legally allowed to thrash servants and whether the law should prescribe compulsory whipping for stock theft. Neither of these demands was in fact acceded to, thanks partly to the energetic opposition of de Villiers who saw it as his duty to mention during the course of an address to a jury (1884) that the 30,000 lashes administered in one year in the Eastern Province alone, where stock-theft was on the increase, were proof that lashes were not the infallible preventive they had been represented to be. Far better, he declared, to concentrate on an efficient police force, properly regulated canteens and control of smuggling.

On the whole magistrates were more prone to be influenced by the demands of white farmers than were the judges. "In some districts," wrote the *Law Journal*, "a 'flogging magistrate' is popular though he may not be humane." In 1894 magistrates imposed whipping in slightly over 1,000 cases, while a further 118 prisoners were whipped for disciplinary offences in prison.

Prison was also used to hold civil debtors, insane persons and witnesses who the authorities feared might abscond. Civil debtors could spend years in prison. The judgement creditor had to pay maintenance for an incarcerated debtor, and one Cape merchant is reported to have set aside £3,000 in his will to ensure that a debtor of his was maintained in perpetuity–only a sermon by a well-known bishop on the 'Unforgiving Spirit' caused him to relent.

A feature of the system which by then was widely known as 'British justice' was that agents of the law were themselves subject to the law. Thus special regulations penalised cruelty or corruption on the part of policemen and warders, and although it was difficult to enforce such regulations, in 1894 over 300 Cape Policemen, guards and constables were convicted under them (compared with nearly 500 prisoners so convicted).

Black and white prisoners were locked up in the same prisons, a fact which judges regarded as constituting a special degradation for the whites and hence a reason for imposing lighter sentences on them. Criticising this approach, the *Law Journal* suggested an opposite course so that the treatment of whites "while in durance vile should be at least in proportion to the height from which they have fallen, a level upon which Europeans are credited almost with an incapacity for crime." The *Journal* was also critical of the fact that whites in a convict establishment and certainly in a jail constituted an upper class of prisoners. By 1894 just over 1,000 prisoners (i.e. a third of the end-of-year total) were accommodated in single cells, from which it might be inferred that association between black and white prisoners took place more at work than in the cells.

There were nearly 450 jailers in charge of prisoners that year, when separate figures for the racial composition of the prison staff were not given. There did not seem to have been any rule forbidding brown or black warders from being in charge of white prisoners; on the contrary, later evidence suggests that such a situation was not uncommon.

Some judges made a point of visiting prisons with a view to exposing abuses, and in an address to a jury in Cape Town which was widely reported a judge went out of his way to criticise the fact that prisoners were not classified. Administrative tradition and economic advantage rather than any purported scientific policy governed penal practice, which might have been as well for the prisoners considering the level of penological thought in those days. In 1892 the *Law Journal* carried an article by a relatively enlightened Transvaal judge under the heading 'The Scientific Study of the Criminal' in which the judge set out the distinguishing features of the criminal as established by science: sugar-loaf form of head; large lower jaw; projecting ears; pale complexion; early wrinkles; abundant hair (baldness rare); rarely good-looking. An extraordinary and ape-like agility enabling him to effect escapes in a wonderful manner. Insensitive to pain (an argument against flogging). The judge pointed out, however, "that an individual was found with all the features of the criminal, but who had notwithstanding led a most respectable life".

WHITE JUSTICE

Though the British Government insisted on the technical equality of all before the law, it did not insist on equality of all behind the law, that is, of all those at the dispensing rather than receiving end of justice. The administration of justice in the Cape in fact remained almost exclusively in the hands of white men – Colonial Office appointees, retired Imperial officers, immigrants from Britain or their descendants, and anglicised Afrikaners. Not only judges and magistrates, but all advocates and attorneys seem to have been white, though there were a few law agents who were not. In the court-room the only dark-skinned person to occupy any official position of importance was the interpreter, who was frequently brown or black.

The law relating to juries contained no colour bar, and was used as a precedent to justify a non-racial franchise, but in practice juries tended to be dominated by whites. A number of blatant miscarriages of justice resulted, and a visiting British writer observed that trial by jury in South Africa sometimes was an arrangement whereby a white man who had forgotten himself in dealing with a black man could be relieved from the consequences. Chief Justice de Villiers conceded that there was much truth in this, but that it was wrong to allege as a general rule that offences of white against black were not regarded as of the same quality as black against white. The courts were open to all, the press was free, and it was not true that juries consisted of white men only; de Villiers said he remembered the intense excitement caused in a few outlying districts by the report that some coloured men were to sit on the jury, but he had since that time presided at trials in remote country districts where white farmers were called out without a word of remonstrance with coloured men, while in Cape Town it was the most ordinary occurrence at the Criminal Sessions to have mixed juries of both races.

The jury system was frequently described as the bulwark of freedom for British subjects, yet one of the freedoms it upheld in the Cape was what was regarded as the time-honoured right of white farmers to thrash recalcitrant brown or black servants. With wry pride Judge Cole in his reminiscences recalled two occasions from his early days as an advocate when clients of his had benefited from this situation. In the first he had defended an Englishman charged with the unmerciful flogging of an African servant. The jury were all English-born, and he asked them: "Do you think it more likely that a Kafir should come here and lie or that an Englishman, your own countryman, should commit atrocities?" The judge's summing up was strongly against the accused, but without even retiring the jury acquitted. In the second case, a wealthy Afrikaner farmer had been charged with murder as a result of his having thrashed to death an African servant with a sjambok. After spurious medical evidence had been given, the accused was acquitted, and the cheering spectators wished to carry Cole on their shoulders out of court. In 1892 the *Law Journal* referred in strong terms to what had become known as the 'East London Case', in which a jury had acquitted a man called Hart and his accomplices on a charge of causing the death of an African by inhuman flogging, torture and exposure. "The presiding Judge, Mr Justice Jones," it wrote, "pronounced the verdict to be a disgrace to the community and declined to thank the jurors . . . for their services."

The strengths and the weaknesses of justice at the Cape were well brought out in two matters which stirred enormous controversy at the time. The first was the 'Koegas Atrocities' case (1879), which arose out of the shooting in cold-blood of captured San prisoners, including women, by white farmers in the north-west Cape. The farmers were charged with murder, and despite a strong summing up against them by the judge, they were, amidst great applause, found not guilty. The furious judge wrote to Saul Solomon asking him to take up and publicise the matter, which Solomon did through the medium of the *Cape Argus*. The paper attacked the jury but more particularly the Attorney-General (Upington) for his failure to have the trial and a second similar one transferred to an area where a less partial jury might have been selected. The Attorney-General sued Solomon and the editor of the paper for libel, and the case was heard before two judges in Cape Town, one of whom was de Villiers. De Villiers held that the most gruesome atrocities had been committed against defenceless prisoners, and that the Attorney-General had behaved reprehensibly, but that nevertheless criticism of him had gone too far and he should be awarded nominal damages.

The other case (1885) flowed from the shooting in the eastern Cape of an African by a farmer named Pelser. Despite many contradictions and improbabilities in Pelser's story, the Solicitor-General of the eastern Cape accepted that Pelser had acted in self-defence, and declined to prosecute him. A Reverend Don thereupon wrote sharply to the press about the Solicitor-General's dereliction of duty, and mentioned in terms that Pelser was "a wretched murderer". The Solicitor-General retaliated by indicting Don for criminal libel, and the case came before a judge and jury in Grahamstown. Neighbours of Pelser's had previously threatened to take the law into their own hands if Pelser was charged, and now Pelser supporters nearly swayed the jury at a bar to which they retired each evening. In the end, however, the jury found in favour of Reverend Don, who was praised by the judge and then by the

Law Journal for "lending himself . . . to the cause of free discussion and impartial justice".

These two cases illustrated that though the courts might not always have been effective in protecting blacks from atrocities by whites, they would give a fair measure of protection to whites who exposed such atrocities.

The one place where an exception was made to the use of all-white or white-dominated juries was the Transkei where for a time all-African juries were empanelled in cases in which Africans only were charged. Despite the fact that "the native juries acquitted themselves most satisfactorily", they were discontinued. In at least one case, however, an African appears to have sat on a jury with whites. Africans were not legally disbarred from being jurors; their names were simply left off the jury lists. Tribal chiefs in the Transkei were permitted in practice to exercise limited jurisdiction over matters involving tribal law and custom, but otherwise the active and extensive judiciary in the Colony remained almost exclusively in white hands.

With regard to recognition of tribal law and custom Cape policy was not marked by its consistency. As more and more Africans were incorporated by annexation into the Cape legal order (at the end of the century Africans constituted well over half of the total population) greater tolerance was shown towards their traditional law in the newly annexed territories. Even in the Colony 'proper', magistrates informally decided cases by tribal custom. A Cape legislator explained to the Royal Colonial Institute in London that the African in the Cape had a department in the government all to himself. A host of officials were

> charged to administer justice and maintain order among native communities, according to an unwritten law in which native precedent and customs are regarded as far as they are right in principle. There are schools for the natives. There are missionaries to the natives. There are native taxes. There are lands reserved for the natives. There is a method for converting natives into citizens. . . . The object of all is to make the African as much like the European as possible (1874).

This dualism of policy was based not so much on principle as on expediency; the primary objective was to cause as little disturbance and expense as possible. It was reflected in a legal dualism whereby a pragmatic interrelationship between Roman-Dutch law and tribal law was maintained, with Roman-Dutch predominating in the Colony 'proper' and tribal law in the Transkei.

If the first half of the century saw the progressive abolition of restrictive laws imposing disabilities on brown men in the western Cape, the second half witnessed the progressive extension of such laws to black men in the eastern Cape. *Pass laws* were revived, this time to deal with so-called 'native foreigners'. As the borders of the Colony were pushed further and further up the coast, such 'native foreigners' became British subjects, remaining 'natives' as far as duties were concerned and 'foreigners' as far as rights were concerned. A similar development took place in relation to *locations*. At first these were tracts of land on the border set aside for African occupation, but gradually they came to be any area defined and set aside for African residential purposes, "the cramped and neglected fragments, like flotsam and jetsam in a flood tide of white settlement, that have become the normal portion of the Bantu population all over South Africa". The combination of locations and pass laws is referred to in a law report late in the century, which speaks of a large pass raid by police on the Queenstown location, after which arrested Africans were brought in batches of twenty before the court. Special legislation was also passed to restrict access by Africans to the so-called white man's *liquor*; though the Innes Act, as the legislation was called, was intended to be a temperance measure and to protect Africans, it in fact led to increasing harassment by the police and a strong sense of grievance. Racial disabilities could also be imposed by administrative action taken in terms of avowedly non-racial statutes. Thus Africans were deliberately lured to the mines and railways by the promise of *guns*, and then later disarmed by boards set up in terms of the Peace Preservation Act (1878) which did more to destroy the peace than any other contemporary piece of legislation. There was no dissimulation about *hut and labour taxes*, which were differentially imposed with the open purpose of paying for administration and forcing Africans to work for white employers. As Innes later put it: "Labour meant labour for other people. No toil, however strenuous, upon a Native's own land was dignified enough to satisfy the tax collector." On the diamond fields at Kimberley another feature of South African life made its first appearance: the housing of African contract labour in *compounds*. Introduced first as a security measure to prevent diamond smuggling, compounds soon proved to be a cheap and convenient measure for controlling migrant workers. Nightly *curfews* on Africans in urban areas were also imposed.

More and more the legal machine which affected the whole population was hitched to the administrative machine which affected Africans only. The established police, court and prison system was used to penalise Africans who broke the special laws aimed at their control. The law thus became involved not only with the maintenance of 'proper relations' between masters and servants, but also with the perpetuation of quasi-colonial relationships between whites and Africans. The process was uneven, and thousands of African Parliamentary voters were exempted from most disabilities. Compared with what was to come the number of Africans prosecuted in terms of differential legislation remained relatively small. Yet a legal-administrative machine for the control of Africans was created which was to be imported in more rigid form into the Transvaal after conquest, and which was then to return to the Cape in harsh all-Union legislation.

It should not be inferred from the above remarks that all the time of the courts was taken up directly with maintaining master/servant and white/black relationships. Out of 47,000 prosecutions brought in the magistrates' courts in 1894, only about 7,700 were brought in terms of special legislation of the kind mentioned: Masters and Servants Act (4,000), Pass Laws (1,500), Vagrancy (1,200) and Trespass (1,000). Of the other offences, Drunkenness alone accounted for over 11,000 prosecutions, Theft for 5,000, Assault for 5,000, Municipal Regulations for 3,500, the Scab Laws for 1,500 and Swearing for 1,000. Many of these latter prosecutions involved protecting the property, persons and peace of the white community, but at the same time 10,000 out of 61,000 persons charged in all these cases were white. [Whites represented 25 per cent of the total population of 1,500,000 and were responsible for 16 per cent of all charges.] It should be remembered too that the magistrates' courts also heard 20,000 civil matters involving claims totalling £200,000, in respect of which most debtors were probably white.

The law reports reflect a wide range of civil disputes, covering such matters as inheritance, insolvency, divorce, water rights and mining claims, while towards the end of the century litigation was indulged in over barbed wire, bicycles and telegraph poles. There were a surprisingly large number of cases involving internal wrangles, mainly over property and partly over doctrine, in the Dutch Reformed and Anglican churches and in the Moslem community; there were also, by contemporary standards, an extraordinary number of actions for defamation.

Judging from the names of parties as revealed in the law reports and in the digest of cases in the *Law Journal*, most civil cases involved white litigants only, whereas most criminal prosecutions involved brown and black accused. Yet there were also cases of coloured men and Africans suing whites over land and cattle or for wrongful arrest, of whites suing coloured men and Africans for breach of contract or eviction, and of dark-skinned persons suing other dark-skinned persons for a variety of causes. As has been shown above, many thousands of whites were prosecuted for criminal offences.

Lawyers fought hard for their clients in criminal as well as civil matters, and even in undefended matters it was not unusual for an accused person of any race to be acquitted because of lack of evidence. Thus in the Supreme Court in 1894 25 per cent of accused persons were acquitted, and in the magistrates' courts 10 per cent. The law reports also contain a large number of judgements of the Supreme Court in which convictions and sentences of the magistrates' courts were set aside on appeal or review. Sometimes the convictions and sentences were altered on procedural grounds, sometimes on points of statutory interpretation and sometimes purely on the evidence. In one case, for example, the judges overruled a decision that a servant who went to the police to lay a complaint about his employer was unlawfully refusing to work. In another they quashed the conviction of a (coloured) man for obstructing a (white) policeman, holding that as the police had been effecting an unlawful arrest the accused had been entitled to offer violent resistance to them. In a further two cases they treated an African's hut as his home and awarded damages against officials who unlawfully interfered with his privacy.

The Supreme Court judges had no testing right in relation to legislation similar to that enjoyed by their namesakes in the United States of America. The sovereignty of the Cape Parliament was subject only to the overriding authority of the British Government, whose veto could not be invoked by the courts but only by an appeal made directly to the Executive authorities in Whitehall. The fluctuating concern of the Colonial Office in London for the welfare of dark-skinned British subjects may be regarded as the Imperial equivalent of a Bill of Rights, and like the American Bill of Rights, this Imperial responsibility was open to a variety of interpretations. Coloured and African leaders might look to the courts for a favourable interpretation of, or so-called loophole in, a Cape Act, but if they wished to have the Act as a whole set aside they had to proceed to London where they could normally expect a polite but fruitless hearing.

The position was different with regard to subordinate legislation, such as municipal by-laws, and the actions of administrative or police bodies. Here the Supreme Court had limited powers of intervention based on its inherent jurisdiction to declare such by-laws *ultra vires* or such actions unlawful. If a by-law or regulation was uncertain, impossible to enforce or in any way contrary to the provisions of the enabling Act of the Cape Parliament, then the Court could declare it *ultra vires*. In this connection it was presumed, on the British model, that Parliament did not intend to permit subordinate authorities such as municipalities to impose special disabilities on any class or section of the community. The Court could accordingly declare that discriminatory by-laws were *ultra vires*, provided, however, that Parliament had not expressly or by necessary implication authorised such discrimination. One case in which this principle was upheld arose out of the claim by an African for return of a stick taken from him by municipal authorities pursuant to a by-law which prohibited 'any native from carrying sticks'. Similarly there were a number of rules of construction which enabled the Court to review the actions of boards, officials or policemen and to declare such actions unlawful if improperly exercised.

The effective constitutional role of the Supreme Court was accordingly limited to a review of subordinate legislation and of administrative and police actions. Schooled in British procedures and applying British canons of construction the judges supervised large areas of administration and local government. They did so on an *ad hoc* basis and only in relation to concrete disputes, either civil or criminal, which came before them. Nevertheless they frequently handed down rulings which embarrassed the administration or the police, and by so doing earned for themselves a reputation for independence and impartiality.

The court system at the Cape, then, fulfilled a variety of complex and interrelated functions. It was central to the spread of government, both geographically and in terms of population groups. It integrated black, white and brown into a common polity in which different rights, duties and disabilities attached to different sections of the community. The lower courts helped to keep the peace, collect debts and maintain relations of domination between master and servant, and white and black. The higher courts supervised the lower courts, regulated proprietary transactions of merchants and landowners, protected the reputations of leading citizens, scrutinised the actions of the administration, and both maintained and restrained the power of the dominant section of the community. As a whole the court system emphasised on a day-to-day basis the subordination of all inhabitants of the Cape to a common law-making authority. Together with the expansion of a single-market economy, the promotion of a single language (English), and the propagation of the belief in a single deity (God), the extension of a single court-centred administration may be regarded as one of the main integrative forces in South African social history. Yet while it bound the diverse peoples of South Africa together in submission to a common authority, it was also destined on an increasingly large scale to enforce separation; the greater the integration, the more rigid the segregation. Much of the remainder of this book will be devoted to a discussion of this apparent paradox.

CHAPTER THREE

In the Interior: The Administration of Justice and Race Relations in the Boer Republics and the Colony of Natal

In order to get away from British government, British taxes and British notions of justice, thousands of white Afrikaner farmers in the eastern Cape in the 1830s packed their belongings into wagons and trekked into the interior of southern Africa. Experience had taught them that it was easier to emigrate *en masse* than to rebel, and what had already been a slow, unco-ordinated movement of the land-hungry became the accelerated and organised exodus of the discontented. Probably the greatest of all their grievances stemmed from the British doctrine of equality before the law, which enabled missionaries to bring servants and ex-slaves to court to lay charges against their masters. Thus the wife of one of the main Voortrekker leaders was herself hauled before court to face a charge of ill-treatment, while the sister of another prominent leader wrote that one of the main causes of the Great Trek was the

> shameful and unjust proceedings with reference to the freedom of our slaves. . . . It is not their freedom that drove us to such lengths, as their being placed on an equal footing with Christians, contrary to the laws of God and the natural distinctions of race and religion, so that it was intolerable for any decent Christian to bow down beneath such a yoke; wherefore we rather withdrew in order to preserve our doctrines in purity.

This was not the departure of outlaws, but the migration of a community determined to maintain what it considered to be proper relations between masters and servants. The advance of the trekker wagons up the east coast was blocked by the military power of the African tribes living there, but the lands to the north were easily penetrable because a decade earlier they had been largely depopulated by the catastrophic *difaqane* (forced migration), the chain-reaction of devastation which followed the growth of the Zulu military kingdom. The Voortrekkers were united by language, religion, attitudes to colour and fear of the British and the Africans, but they were nevertheless jealous of their personal independence and reluctant to entrust their destinies to leaders or governments of any kind. After many vicissitudes, including conflict with and the infliction of heavy military blows against the two most powerful African states in southern Africa (the Ndebele and the Zulu), they settled in the areas between the Orange and Vaal rivers and beyond the Vaal, where they founded the two Boer Republics eventually known as the Orange Free State and the South African Republic, more commonly referred to as the Transvaal. An early attempt to establish a Voortrekker Republic in Natal was frustrated by the intervention of British troops.

The Boers prided themselves on their independence and rural democracy, which were based on the possession by each farmer of his own gun, his own farm and his own entourage of servants. Yet they were far from self-sufficient, being totally dependent on Cape colonists for trade and ministers of religion, and on dark-skinned servants for labour. They forbade the holding of slaves, which, moral objections apart, would have attracted particular odium and given the British further excuse for interfering in their affairs; in any event they had no access to slave traders, and had developed a method cheaper than purchase of obtaining a dependent labour force. All of them had taken coloured servants with them from the Cape, and when they later wished to add to their labour supply they looked to the remnants of the African tribes around them. Some of their new servants they captured during commando raids (these were called 'apprentices') but most of their additional labourers consisted of Africans whose tribal organisations had been shattered by the *difaqane* and who now returned to their ancestral homes where they took up residence again, as 'squatters', labour-tenants and servants of the Boers. The dispossession initiated by the armies of the Zulu king Shaka was completed and made permanent by the Boers, who continually extended their farm-holdings and took further land from the regrouping tribes. A new multiracial community was thus created on the highveld in which the Boer minority exercised political, economic and judicial mastery over a dark-skinned majority. While economic interdependence and cultural assimilation of black and white proceeded, civic inequality and social distance remained as rigid as they had ever been during the late slave-holding period in the Cape.

In the early years of the Republics only the most rudimentary systems of law enforcement existed, and the administration of justice consisted of little more than the maintenance of local discipline by untrained and largely illiterate officials. So little legal knowledge did many of these men possess that the Transvaal government at one stage even felt compelled to make it a criminal offence for magistrates not to acquaint themselves with the law. In the absence of a permanent police force or standing army, commandos of mounted burghers were called out from time to time to quell any major African resistance, and the military officials whose duty it was to call the farmers out for the punitive expeditions also acted as directors of labour, demarcators of land and keepers of the peace. Chronic shortages of funds limited the growth of governmental agencies, but by the end of the century modern institutions had begun to develop, and despite the fact that citizenship was restricted to white-skinned burghers only, the two Republics were cited by a noted American constitutional expert as model democracies (Bryce).

The Boers were firm in their Calvinism, firm in their attachment to their language, and firm in their view that only persons with white skins should qualify for rights of citizenship. The Orange Free State constitution declared that all should be equal before the law, but it was clearly understood that as far as substantive law was concerned, the word 'all' meant 'all burghers' and that only white men could become burghers. The Transvaal constitution was more direct and stated expressly that "the People will countenance no equality between Black and White in Church or State".

Besides being deprived of all civic rights, Africans were forbidden to possess firearms, ammunition or horses or to be abroad without a pass signed by an employer or State official.

In the 1870s, High Courts headed by trained judges were established in both Republics, and they succeeded in attracting some outstanding jurists from the Cape who gave a measure of order and decorum to the administration of justice. Yet although their influence on public life was considerable, their jurisdiction did not effectively extend to supervising white farmers in their relations with black servants. Generally the farms continued to be run as semi-autonomous estates, with ordinary disciplinary offences being dealt with summarily by the masters, and only the more serious offences coming before the courts. In theory, servants had the right to complain to local officials about illtreatment, but they did so at the peril of being punished for laying frivolous complaints.

One further general point which should be made about the administration of justice and race relations in the Boer Republics, is that despite the violence attendant on their birth as states and despite the strong feelings of group identity which characterised their populations, lynching was very rarely resorted to by members of the dominant white communities. Superficially looked at, all the apparent ingredients of lynch-situations would seem to have been present: weak law enforcement agencies, a ruling group with a monopoly of power and a strong sense of racial solidarity, a frontier tradition of lawlessness and commando raids, and a mythology of smiting the forces of darkness. Private violence against African servants, including lethal thrashings, were not uncommon; nor were punitive raids by self-appointed commandos. What was almost non-existent, however, was the banding together of groups of whites in small towns and villages to engage in frenzied attacks, involving violent and obscene rituals, upon defenceless Africans. Neither mob nor vigilante lynchings have been characteristic of the South African scene. It has been claimed that there has been only one recorded case of lynching in the Transvaal, the 'Steynsdorp lynching case' in the middle of the 1890s which led to the trial and acquittal of seven white men. Gandhi was nearly lynched when he returned to Natal from India in 1896, but otherwise in a country where almost every other kind of atrocity has been documented or alleged, there seem to have been no other recorded cases of lynching.

Perhaps the proper approach to the question is to ask why it was present elsewhere rather than why it was absent in South Africa. In the Southern States of the U.S.A. lynching was first used primarily against white men and expressed something in the character of early nineteenth century American society; only during Reconstruction, when white supremacy was under serious threat, was it converted into a weapon of terror and discipline against black Americans. In Europe lynching was from time to time practised against Jews, who, like the black people of North America, constituted a minority group in the population and could more easily fill the role of scapegoats than could members of a majority group such as Africans in South Africa.

THE COURTS AND RACE IN THE ORANGE FREE STATE

Being close to the markets of the Cape, the Boers of the Orange Free State developed a far more prosperous and well-organised community than did their neighbours in the Transvaal. Summing up the requirements of a rural folk who, though sturdy enough, were immune neither to illness, sin nor covetousness, a leading Free State jurist wrote in verse that the greatest needs of the country were for doctors, clergymen and advocates. As far as the supply of advocates was concerned, some of the farmers sent their sons to the Cape or abroad for legal education, whilst the few professional men in the country almost invariably did the same, but the greatest source of recruitment was importation from the Cape Bar. Not many countries have taken the chance of entrusting their destinies to law professors, but the Free State did so, and with signal success, when it invited a law professor from Cape Town to become its President (J. H. Brand, 1863-1888). Under his influence a High Court consisting of three judges drawn from the Cape Bar was instituted in the following decade, from which time onwards Cape legal men dominated political and judicial life in the Republic. The first Chief Justice later became President, and then when he retired from the Presidency he was succeeded by another High Court judge (F. W. Reitz, followed by judge M. Steyn). The Republic's best-known lawyer and last Chief Justice was Melius de Villiers, brother of the Chief Justice of the Cape, and sitting with him on the Bench was the future Prime Minister of South Africa, J. B. M. Hertzog.

So great was the prestige of the judges that when one of them ventured outside of Bloemfontein on the court's first circuit, he was received with immense enthusiasm, and returned home suffering from nervous strain and exhaustion. Just as in an earlier period imported British judges had lent panache to Cape society, so imported Cape advocates gave distinction to Free State life; and if the Cape Bench was invigorated by the addition of anglicised Afrikaners, the Free State Bench came to be strengthened by afrikanerised Scotsmen (Buchanan, McGregor and Stuart). One of this latter group founded a Society for Winter Evening Entertainments in Bloemfontein to whose members he read passages from Dickens; when opening the town's first gymnasium, which he named St Andrew's College, he made an appropriate speech and then, it is said, proceeded in full dress to amaze the audience with some difficult turns on the parallel bars (Buchanan).

This latter judge was in fact the only member of the Free State judiciary who had not received his legal training abroad. All the other judges and a number of other lawyers had spent some years in England and Holland, usually attending universities in both countries, the most popular being Cambridge, Oxford, Leiden and Amsterdam. In their judgements they quoted freely from Latin and old Dutch texts, as well as from the Cape law reports which had great persuasive power but were not binding on them. Although Dutch was the main medium of the courts, the judges and magistrates were normally fluent in English and followed British styles and procedures and applied the English law of evidence. Roman-Dutch law was maintained as the common law of the country, despite the complaints of many burghers that it was inaccessible, and the objections of a few staunch Calvinists that it was apparently connected with Rome.

In civil matters the judges sat alone, but in criminal cases they were assisted by a jury consisting of white Dutch-speaking burghers. Most criminal trials involved the prosecution of Africans, and whenever Africans appeared as accused persons or as witnesses, interpreters were made available to them. It seems that Chief Justice de Villiers spoke a particularly pure form of Dutch, because once when he tried to address an African in Afrikaans, the African replied in Afrikaans that he was sorry but he did not understand English. (Afrikaans was the colloquial form of Dutch, and is now the main language of Government in S.A.) Although the criminal law was directed mainly against Africans there is evidence that the pious and death-fearing burghers took their jury service very seriously and were reluctant to sentence men to death or help with executions. The lack of proper facilities for carrying out hangings, suggests that capital punishment was not a frequent occurrence in the Free State. A Bloemfontein newspaper spoke out strongly against the death sentence, and at least one leading judge is known to have disliked it intensely. In one case the death sentence was imposed on a white man for murdering a coloured man – which he did for gain – but since he was an Englishman and not a burgher, his life was saved as a result of diplomatic pressure. Judging from his name Hofman, an accused in another matter who was actually executed for the murder of two coloured men, might well have been white. There was no rule against the imposition of whipping on white men, but in practice corporal punishment seems to have been used almost exclusively against Africans. The prisons were few and small, and at one stage a special directive was sent to judicial officers requesting them not to fill the jails up unnecessarily with convicts. A provision which might have helped to empty the prisons was one to the effect that convicts might be ordered to work for farmers, with or without pay.

The only comprehensive and accessible records of the judgements of the High Court are contained in the brief quarterly digests produced by the *Cape Law Journal*. They carry sufficient detail, however, to demonstrate that the Free State judges were learned in the law and were not afraid to assert themselves against the Executive or the Legislature. Thus in one matter Judge Hertzog, foreshadowing his later political views on the sovereignty of the people (*volk*), directed that a man who had defamed members of the Legislature could not be found guilty of *lese majestatis*, because only the people and not the Legislature were possessed of *majestas*. In another matter the Chief Justice provoked a constitutional crisis by declaring *ultra vires* a statute which purported to penalise persons who libelled the Legislature. The matter aroused considerable controversy, meetings were held in various parts of the country, and in the end the Legislature was compelled to back down.

Yet the judges were less willing to interpret the constitution against the Legislature when it came to racial matters. Two Indian traders sought to have a law declared *ultra vires* which barred all Indians from dwelling in the country save under permit from the President. They claimed that the law was discriminatory and in conflict with a section of the constitution which stated that "all shall be equal before the law". The High Court held that this provision did not bear the meaning which the applicants claimed for it, and ruled that the statute was valid. As a result of this ruling, the Orange Free State became an almost entirely 'Indian-free' territory, and has remained so to this day.

In another case, however, the judges declared a municipal regulation *ultra vires* which sought to oblige African women to buy weekly passes. The basis of their decision was that the enabling law did not authorise such a regulation; the court held further that approval by the Executive of the regulation and publication in the *Gazette* could not give it a legal validity which it had never possessed. (Interestingly, African women in the Free State were in later years to be pioneers in African anti-pass struggles.) The pass laws were, however, strictly enforced against African men; that officials took advantage of these laws corruptly to extort money appears from at least two matters referred to in the *Law Journal*.

There is today a widely held belief that the race-conscious Boers followed a policy of separate development or apartheid with regard to African tribesmen, whereas the liberal Englishmen pursued a policy of integration; in fact the position was nearer the reverse. The Free State was probably the most racially integrated territory in southern Africa, in the sense that the African population there was more absorbed into the white rural economy and had less opportunity to maintain its tribal identity than anywhere else. (Even today the Orange Free State province has a larger proportion of Africans who are Christian and who speak Afrikaans or English, and a smaller proportion living under tribal conditions, than any other province.) It has been suggested that had the Free State commandos succeeded in defeating the Basuto people, the kingdom of Lesotho might in fact have been granted some autonomy, but the way captured territory was in fact divided up amongst the Boers does not support this contention. For a while there was a small area in the Free State–"this island in the ocean", as the Chief Justice called it–where African tribesmen were permitted total independence. During a succession dispute, a chief who had been sheltering in Basutoland crossed Free State territory to get to this independent enclave, and then proceeded to murder its ruler, but he was acquitted by the High Court on a charge of treason, on the grounds that he was an alien who had committed his offence outside the jurisdiction of the Free State. Despite, or perhaps because of, this verdict, the Free State President thereupon annexed the small tribal homeland.

There was no judicial segregation in the Free State as there was elsewhere in South Africa, and the High Court entertained proceedings in which Africans appeared as litigants, such as disputes over deceased estates. Tribal law was never recognised as a system and no recognition was given to marriages contracted according to tribal custom. Whether the intending spouses were black, brown or white, the only valid marriage in the eyes of the law was one performed according to Roman-Dutch law. This led to a conflict in the minds of the legislators between their Calvinist desire to promote Christian union and their white Afrikaner dislike of having too many Africans using Church and State facilities. As one commentator recently put it, the burgher ideal with regard to African marriages was a simple, monogamous union solemnised by a separate minister in a separate church, out of sight of the white congregation and without uproarious celebrations which kept people away from their labours and gave them a large appetite for meat (Simons).

Thus the court system in the Free State allowed no autonomy to tribal law, and operated as a single, white-dominated judiciary which tried all civil and criminal disputes recognised by Roman-Dutch law or statute, whatever the race or status of the litigants. Only in some very small areas did tribal law receive recognition. It may be said, then, that the administration of justice in the Free State furthered both racial domination and racial integration at one and the same time, domination in the form of white supremacy, and integration in the form of involvement in a common economy and culture.

Law and Race in the Transvaal

The Transvaal High Court was instituted in the 1870s not to satisfy a need expressed by Transvaal burghers, but as a desperate attempt to stave off annexation by the British. The objective was to prove that the Transvaal was capable of supporting a modern administration without outside direction; the judges, however, had to be attracted from the Cape, which was no easy task in view of the Republic's bankrupt treasury. The man who volunteered for the hazards of establishing and presiding over the court was a young Cape advocate named J. G. Kotze. He had studied in Holland and England, where, as he was to say later, he had been greatly influenced by English judges and their even-handed justice. While at the Cape Bar he had travelled the Cape Circuit with Chief Justice de Villiers.

The 'boy judge', as Kotze was called by the visiting novelist Anthony Trollope, was pleased that at his swearing in ceremony he wore a wig, since it hid his youth, yet guided by the motto 'onward, upward and true to the line', he developed into a strong and erudite judge who dominated the court for twenty years, writing 90 per cent of its judgements, and preparing its first law reports. From his early years on the Bench, however, his relationship with the Government was uneasy, and eventually he came into conflict with President Kruger and was sacked for daring to invoke a testing right against statutes passed by the Legislature.

Kruger was a barely literate farmer who believed that the only source of worthwhile knowledge was the Bible. The contrast between him and the urbane lawyers who occupied the Presidency in the Free State was most striking, and was well illustrated when a former Chief Justice and President of the Free State went to the Transvaal to become Kruger's State Secretary (Reitz). This man's son, who had travelled to Europe and been introduced to Kings and Presidents, later wrote that he was amazed to find that Kruger's wife kept dairy cows and sold milk to the neighbours (Denys Reitz). When a statute of her husband in a top hat was unveiled, she suggested that the hat be hollowed out and filled with water to serve as a drinking fountain for the birds. "My father and I laughed heartily at her simplicity," the young man wrote, "but we agreed that it was decent of her to have thought of such a thing." Yet Kruger was a strong, shrewd politician, close to his people in the way of an African chief. He gathered round himself expert and ardent lawyers from Holland and Afrikaner jurists from the Cape, notably J. C. Smuts, and in the last decade of the century stood up with tenacious dignity to Cecil Rhodes and the forces of British Imperialism.

The Transvaal was always less stable than the Orange Free State, both in its boundaries and its institutions; the extension of overlordship over the African people took longer, and the patterns of land ownership were more diverse. In theory the Transvaal Government tried to establish good-neighbourly relations with African tribal groups in the frontier regions, but the avidity of the burghers for land and labour proved more powerful than the restraining decrees issued in Pretoria. Thus the destruction of tribal independence, the appropriation of tribal lands and the conversion of tribesmen into servants, labour tenants and 'squatters' proceeded as strongly in the Transvaal as anywhere else in southern Africa. As in the Orange Free State, a multi-racial society of inter-dependent black and white communities developed, with the minority of white, Dutch-speaking burghers exercising political domination over the black majority. The constitution not only restricted voting rights to burghers, it explicitly laid down that there should be no equality between black and white in Church or State. The original version of the constitution provided that "half-castes to the tenth degree" were prohibited from being members of the Legislature, while a later version stated merely that coloured persons or bastards were excluded, along with persons with an openly vicious character, unrehabilitated bankrupts, and persons who were not Protestant. Englishmen were welcome to work in the country, but not to vote.

The rediscovery of gold in the Transvaal in the 1880s (it had previously been mined by Africans) added a new element of instability to political life, which complicated the functioning of both the courts and the governments, and indirectly brought them into conflict. A large influx of English-speaking persons from all over the world led to the creation of towns on the Rand which soon exceeded Pretoria in wealth and size. Hard on the heels of the prospectors and speculators came dozens of English-speaking lawyers, who began to press the claims of immigrants for the vote and to demand on behalf of their clients that English be allowed as an alternative to Dutch in court proceedings. They also argued that Johannesburg, which boasted of some of the greatest financiers and criminals in the world, should be given greater judicial status than that of a mere Circuit town, and complained of the inconvenience of having to travel to Pretoria for most civil work.

The Transvaal rapidly became economically the most advanced portion of South Africa, but its administrative structures, which had barely coped with the needs of a scattered farming community, were unable to deal effectively with the problems created by the sudden emergence of vast mining towns populated by tough financiers and ruthless adventurers. To hand over power to the new immigrant community would have been to destroy the Boer character of the State, and this Kruger was not prepared to do. On this issue Kruger and Kotze were in substantial agreement. Thus Kotze backed Kruger during the period of the Jameson Raid, when financiers and lawyers in Johannesburg planned an armed insurrection to coincide with the entry into the Transvaal of a batch of soldiers under the leadership of Rhodes' friend, Dr Jameson. He was also firm on the need to maintain Dutch as the language of the courts. Thus in the well known 'Cyanide Patent Case' the costs of which reached the then record total for South Africa of £80,000, counsel suggested to the court that in view of the mass of scientific evidence and the fact that everyone concerned in the case spoke English, the formality of interpretation into Dutch be dispensed with. "However," wrote the *Cape Law Journal*, "the application was met by the enquiry from the Chief Justice: 'What is the interpreter for?' And that," added the pro-English *Journal*, "was precisely what counsel and everyone else engaged in the case could not understand."

Another point on which the two men saw eye to eye was that Africans should have the right to approach the highest judicial and executive bodies in the country. Kotze made this clear in a matter in which an African chief who was being held by the authorities without charge, applied to the High Court for a writ *de homine libero exhibendo*, the Roman-Dutch law equivalent of habeas corpus. Counsel for the state argued that the discriminatory provisions of the constitution deprived Africans of the right to approach the court for relief, but Kotze rejected this argument and declared that the court was "bound to do equal justice to every individual within its jurisdiction, without regard to colour or degree, except where in the particular instance the law expressly provides to the contrary". (When the chief was actually brought before court, however, Kotze ruled that he could be held on a warrant without trial until a rebellion in which he was allegedly involved was crushed.) A few years later Kruger stated in the Legislature that he believed in distinction in the social sphere–the greater the better–but as far as law and justice were concerned the highest body in the country should always be open to receive and consider requests and complaints, no matter from whom, even from the lowest.

In 1897 the Legislature promised to pass a law which would prevent Africans from suing burghers in the High Court, but by the time the Anglo-Boer War broke out two years later, it had not acted on this promise. The right of Africans to seek relief in the High Court may be regarded as more nominal than real, however, since the domination of white over black in the social field was so severe as to make it almost unthinkable that an African or person of mixed descent would dare to litigate against a white person. One of the effects of the opening up of the goldfields was to intensify the rigidity of laws aimed at controlling the movements and activities of Africans. Thus Africans were lashed for walking on the pavements of Johannesburg, and sent to prison for being off their masters' property without displaying their passes, which took the form of badges (hence the phrase 'badge of slavery'). So hostile were members of the Legislature to the idea of dark-skinned people making use of public facilities, that objection was even raised to coloured persons putting money in the Post Office Savings Bank, on the ground that it would be a flagrant violation of the constitution for the State to pay interest to coloured people. Dark-skinned people could not even claim familiarity with whites on a verbal level; a cab-driver who saw Kruger opening a bank and shouted "There goes Oom Paul" (Uncle Paul) was arrested by a member of the Legislature and fined £5 or 20 days by the Chief Magistrate of Pretoria for referring to the Head of State in such familiar terms. The barriers to approaching the High Court, then, were not technical but social. It might be said that even if the High Court was like the Ritz Hotel in that its doors were equally open to rich and poor, it would nevertheless have been prudent for a wealthy African to go round to the kitchen.

Discrimination against Africans was so explicit and all-pervasive, and reflected a subordination so rigid, that it was not Africans who used the courts to challenge discriminatory actions, but members of the small Indian community. Most of these Indians were traders who had entered the Transvaal from Natal, and whose status as British subjects theoretically entitled them to the protection of the British Resident in Pretoria. When under the guise of a sanitation law, they were ordered by the Transvaal Government to remove from their shops to a location where they would have to trade amongst themselves, some of them applied to the High Court for relief. One of the grounds of the application was that although the law under which action had been taken against them was supposedly designed to promote the health of the people, they had in fact been instructed to remove to what was an unhealthy spot. Kotze rejected the application, holding that the Government's duty was an administrative one, and if it were not properly carried out then administrative rather than judicial channels should be used to provide a remedy.

Some years later the same point came up for consideration again in the High Court, which by a majority of two judges to one upheld Kotze's decision. The dissenting judge, who was a Hollander, said that the provision in the constitution prohibiting equality between coloured persons and white could have referred only to such coloured persons as already were in the Transvaal at the time the constitution was adopted, and could not be extended to give the Government power to do what it wanted with 'coolies' who came in afterwards. One of the judges in the majority, a Transvaal Afrikaner, held that the court was bound to accept the principle that every right possessed by the white man could only be exercised to a limited extent or not at all by persons of colour. Since the Government had to indicate by a clear definition what rights a coloured man could possess, in a case of ambiguity a law such as the one in question ought to be interpreted against the person of colour for whose benefit it had been enacted. The third judge, a Scotsman who had settled in the Transvaal, reluctantly decided that he was bound by the earlier decision of Kotze, which, although unconvincing to him, was not so clearly wrong that it should be reversed. He found it most singular that privileges should be granted by means of a law which consisted mainly of prohibition–if the Legislature had meant to bless, the language used by it sounded to him very much like a curse. Kotze's judgement had implied that Indians belonged to a lower level of civilisation, in which a place of trading could not be separated from a place of living, and in his view this was not a wholly indefensible proposition. He hoped, however, that the government would treat the plaintiffs, whom he described as 'Indian merchants', with fairness.

The ambiguity of the status of Indians in the Transvaal was well brought out by the visit there in 1894 of M. K. Gandhi, who went to Pretoria to handle his first major piece of litigation as a barrister. Gandhi found that he was received in friendly fashion by members of the Bar and by leading State prosecutors, and was even able to get a room in an hotel, but he was also rudely pushed into the gutter by a policeman when he walked on the pavement past Kruger's house.

As far as Africans were concerned, the law was seen not primarily as a means of alleviating grievances or securing rights, but as an instrument of control relying mainly on whipping and imprisonment to achieve its objectives. The High Court had jurisdiction to impose as many as 100 lashes per offence, but generally on black people only, since for many years the law stated expressly that whipping should not be imposed on white men. In the early years of the Republic a white man was hanged for the murder of his nephew, but after the High Court was established it appears that execution, like whipping, was carried out on dark-skinned persons only.

For a long time the Republic possessed hardly any prisons, and it was not unusual for white prisoners to be handed over to the magistrate for safe-keeping in his home, while Africans were normally dealt with by summary whippings. The emergence in the 1880s of mining towns on the Rand, however, drastically changed the penal scene, and the number of persons received into prison in a year rose from less than 800 in 1878 to more than 28,000 in 1891. The simultaneous growth of an urban population and of the funds needed for its control was responsible for this extraordinary increase, which may be adduced as a striking piece of evidence in support of the proposition that in a stratified society more industrialisation and modernisation gives rise to more laws, more policemen, more warders and more prisoners. The great bulk of prisoners were Africans–in 1891 three-quarters were black and a quarter white–and those whites who were sentenced to terms of imprisonment seemed to have served only very short periods. Thus although 7,500 whites were received into prison during the year, only 185 were actually in prison on a day when a count was made. Seven years later, however, a count showed that the number of whites in prison on a particular day had risen to more than 2,000.

Not all the white prisoners, it should be mentioned, were criminals in the ordinary meaning of the term. In 1896 the members of the Reform Committee who planned an insurrection to coincide with the abortive Jameson Raid, were jailed for treason, and spent an average of about five months in prison. Prominent amongst the millionaires and lawyers so confined was the editor of the *Cape Law Journal*, who had recently moved to Johannesburg (Bell). The *Law Journal*, which was still being produced in the Cape, loyally campaigned on his behalf, and bitterly attacked the holding of prominent lawyers in "an establishment, which to say the least must be utterly unadapted to the detention of European prisoners, to say nothing of gentlemen accustomed to all the refinements of a civilised life". In later years, however, the editor himself wrote that conditions had not been too bad in prison. Life for dark-skinned prisoners had been very hard, and on a number of occasions he had witnessed or got to know of coloured and African prisoners being flogged, placed in stocks or simply beaten for no reason at all. One sweeper told him that "if Baas (Master) knew how bad prison was he would never have come here", an observation which earned for its maker a cigarend. The Reformers, on the other hand, were regarded as political prisoners and allowed to wear their own clothes; they had none of the comforts of a modern jail, but a great deal more freedom. After being compelled to eat bad prison food for three days, they were allowed to receive a meal a day from their wives, who could visit them each morning. They slept on the floor, got water from a tap in the yard and bathed in a dammed up furrow. Their main complaint was inactivity, and to pass the time they played marbles and poker, drank whiskey and smoked cigars. The warders were at first very strict, but after one of the more disturbed prisoners had committed suicide, their attitude changed and the prisoners could get almost whatever they wanted. Thus a prisoner was told to push a whiskey flask deeper into his pocket where it could not be seen, and another one succeeded in getting transferred to a pleasant nearby hospital simply by complaining that he had got sunstroke playing marbles.

Unlike the Orange Free State, the Transvaal established separate machinery for the hearing of disputes between Africans, but the white-dominated, segregated structures set up for this purpose were never well-developed. At a time when the British exercised direct influence over the Transvaal, the Natal practice of combining judicial segregation with recognition of such aspects of tribal law as were not inconsistent with 'the general principles of civilisations', was adopted. At no stage, however, did the Transvaal recognise the legal validity of marriages contracted according to African custom. In fact the Transvaal was for many years the only South African state which actually had legislation to forbid tribal marriages, on the supposition that they were heathenish and polygamous. It has been pointed out that absorption into a money economy and the development of a migrant labour system proved to be far more injurious to traditional African marriages than any such law, which could not be effectively enforced, but the existence of such a prohibition does suggest that whatever the avowed aim of Boer policy towards Africans, it was not basically designed to preserve tribal institutions. The Transvaal Legislature not only illegalised tribal marriages, it refused to permit 'coloured people' to be married according to Roman-Dutch law, so that for many years there was no system at all whereby Africans in the Transvaal could legally be married. Only in 1897 did the Legislature relent and permit Africans to marry by civil law, and then by the smallest majority after Kruger had assured members that the people wanted neither equality nor polygamy, and that the proposed measure would discourage both evils. Kotze, it should be noted, showed himself to be relatively tolerant towards African customary law, when he held that the second wife of an African accused should be protected by a spouse's privilege from giving evidence in a criminal trial against her husband.

It can be seen that neither Kotze nor Kruger was amongst the extreme repressionists with regard to Africans in the Republic. Kotze was influenced to some extent by British legal ideology, while Kruger belonged to a class of conservative farmers less aggressive in their race attitudes than the younger and more urbanised burghers, who sought to perpetuate in an urban setting rural inequality without the softening features of rural paternalism. Where the two men did disagree, and with increasing asperity, was not over relations between black and white but over relations between the judiciary and the executive. Kotze wished to see the judiciary become a powerful modernising institution, respected in the Transvaal as it was in the Free State and the Cape. Kruger did not object to the judges attending to ordinary civil and criminal cases, but he strongly opposed their taking a stand on questions which he thought belonged to the Legislature and the Executive, and he did not hesitate to reverse by executive action decisions of the judges which he felt to be injurious to the State. Unfortunately for Kotze, he received relatively little support from his colleagues, most of whom were very young and restless, and many of whom were Hollanders not well attuned to South African legal traditions. Judges were appointed and resigned with such rapidity that the *Cape Law Journal* observed that they were not altogether wedded to judicial office. The *Journal* also reported that the style of living adopted by some of the judges shocked a number of burghers; a zealous Republican mentioned that "His Lordship had appeared in spangles and danced upon a public stage 'Ta . . . R . . . .'. The Transvaal Legislature also noted whisperings about debts of the judiciary and other alleged Judicial pecadilloes." Kotze himself was not involved in these scandals, but he invited public criticism of himself and his office by standing for the Presidency in 1893, presumably in the hope of emulating the success of his colleagues in the Free State. He obtained a derisory 85 votes, however, as against more than 7,000 each polled by his two opponents (Kruger and Joubert), and his position became weaker than ever.

Eventually in a series of judgements Kotze took up the position that the Legislature was enacting laws in an unconstitutional fashion, and claimed that the High Court had a testing right to declare such laws invalid. The immediate consequences of his decisions would have been to overthrow the law relating to the pegging of mining claims, while the long-term result would have been to invalidate nearly twenty years of legislation, including that which had sanctioned his own appointment as a judge. Kruger threatened to dismiss Kotze, and lawyers throughout the country divided on the issue, with Smuts supporting the executive and Hertzog the judiciary. The Chief Justice of the Cape intervened in an attempt to reconcile Kotze and Kruger, but his compromise arrangements broke down, and eventually Kotze was dismissed from office. Kruger scathingly told the Volksraad that he thought so highly of the dismissed Chief Justice that "were I to know this would help, I would have him placed in a lunatic asylum and wait until he is restored to health, in order to use his services again. His capacity was high, but he fell into error, in that he accepted the testing right, that principle of the Devil's." Kotze retired to the Cape and was only reappointed to the Bench after the Anglo-Boer War, when once more he became a distinguished judge, now free from controversy. Eventually he spent a total of nearly fifty years in all on the Bench, ending up as a member of the South African Appeal Court, where, in a belated gesture to the Indian community in South Africa, he was to adopt a liberal line of reasoning in direct contrast to his approach in the Transvaal of forty years before.

LAW AND RACE IN NATAL

When the British took over Natal from the Voortrekkers in 1842, one of the conditions which they declared would govern their assumption of power was that there would not be in the eye of the law any distinction of colour, origin, race or creed, but that the protection of the law in letter and in substance would be extended impartially to all alike. This condition was never formally revoked, but by the end of the century Natal had developed a society in which race domination of whites over Africans and Indians was exercised as rigidly and perhaps with more violence than anywhere else in southern Africa. Far from softening race relations and bringing about a greater degree of equality, the law and the courts became major instruments for the maintenance of stratification and privilege.

The first judge to be sent to Natal did lay claim to be administering justice equally to all classes, and it was his boast that within a year his just approach transformed the nature of crime in the Colony in a manner unsurpassed in the world (Cloete, 1848). In support of this claim he quoted figures for the two years in which he had sat on the Bench. In the first year thirty-four people appeared before him, of whom ten were Englishmen and Boers charged with assault upon Africans, while three of the accused were charged with murder and most of the remainder with canteen and housebreaking. In the second year, however, only four persons altogether appeared before him, one of whom was indicted for housebreaking and theft and the other three for fraud, theft and perjury, "offences belonging to and resulting from a more advanced state of society, and committed by persons of comparative respectability. . . . Now everyone may sit in peace under his vine and fig tree . . . enjoying the full confidence that every act of violence or oppression would immediately be punished by the Court."

This judge had been seconded to Natal from the Cape, where he had practised at the Bar after having studied abroad in Holland and England and having been influenced by English traditions of judicial independence and 'evenhandedness'. One example of his interpretation of evenhandedness, however, was to give to the Boers and English settlers only half of the immense tracts of land which they claimed for themselves and to allow Africans (who outnumbered the settlers by perhaps fifty to one) to live in locations on the other half. Many of the white settlers felt this award to be grossly unfair to them, and accordingly they were not displeased when he was dismissed from the Bench by the Governor, who accused him of disloyalty in refusing to strike out an affidavit which contained criticisms of the Governor. The Privy Council subsequently held this dismissal to be frivolous and void, but in the end it was the Governor, who happened to be strongly pro-settler, who stayed on in office and the judge who returned to the Cape. The second judge to arrive in the Colony was a personal friend of the Governor, and although he was to become a noted expert on Roman-Dutch law, he was not conspicuous for his defence of African rights.

This was a time when the judges could have exercised a lasting liberal influence on the administration of justice in the Colony; an index of their authority was that more was spent on the Judicial Establishment than on the magistrates, police, prisons and interpreters combined.

Like the early judges at the Cape, they could have put their stamp on the Colony rather than have allowed the Colony to put its stamp on them, but it was not to be, and most of them were destined to echo rather than counteract the dominant attitudes of the white colonists, and to see themselves as the instruments of the administration rather than its watchdogs. Natal judges tended to be Colonial Office appointees with an authoritarian bent, or else colonists with relatively little legal training who had made their mark in politics rather than in law. There was no division between advocates and attorneys in Natal, and admission to practise could be obtained merely by sitting in court for a stipulated number of days in a year. Natal therefore never developed until after the First World War an elitist group of barristers on the English or Cape pattern, who regarded law as something standing apart from society in the same way as they stood aloof from the public. Until fairly recently the Natal Bench, with a few individual exceptions, was in fact regarded as the weakest in the country, and the editors of the *South African Law Journal* observed that "the light of learning shone dimly from the poorly printed pages of the Natal Law Reports". It was only after the First World War that a separate Bar was established under G. McKeurtan, whom many considered the outstanding South African advocate of this century, and it was only after the Second World War that the Natal Bench began to achieve as much prestige as any other in the country. Weakness in terms of style, erudition, and independence, however, was not necessarily conjoined with weakness in distributing punishments or upholding the authority of the Government.

It has already been mentioned that the Boer Republics were more integrationist than the British Colonies in the sense that they gave less recognition to tribal institutions and allowed fewer Africans to live in partially independent communities on tribally-owned land. Though white appropriation of land in Natal and Zululand was extensive and continuous, it was never as complete there as it was in the Boer Republics, and hundreds of thousands of Africans falling under the white administration continued to live under tribal conditions. For purposes of administrative convenience, a separate structure of rule was established for them in which the chiefs were incorporated as subordinate functionaries retaining some of their traditional powers subject to white supervision. Many decades before the Colonial Office propounded the theory of indirect rule, the Natal authorities adopted the expedient of investing the Governor with the powers of Supreme Chief, which placed him at the apex of an authoritarian bureaucracy that proceeded down-wards through white magistrates to African chiefs and headmen to African subjects. What began as a question of convenience hardened into a policy of segregation and colonial absolutism, that was to find favour throughout South Africa and emerge in modern times as the doctrine of apartheid or separate development. On the purely legal side, this policy in Natal led to the enactment of a code, frequently amended, which gave recognition to various aspects of tribal law, and made it applicable by magistrates to most civil matters in which Afri-cans were litigants. A Native Court was subsequently established to hear appeals in matters litigated upon by Africans, and later converted into a court of first instance for all major civil and criminal matters involving Africans. On the political side the adoption of this policy marked a shift away from an earlier approach of attacking tribal cus-toms as heathenish and barbarian. As the challenge to white supremacy passed from the hands of chief and diviners into the hands of urbanised workers, mission-trained teachers, ministers and clerks, a decaying tribalism acquired merit in the eyes of the settlers. Tribal law obtained more statutory recognition as its social basis crumbled. The Natal Native Affairs Commission set up to enquire into the Zulu (Bambata) rebellion of 1906 specifically suggested that polygamy might be re-garded as a substitute for the vote; it maintained that the civil rights of the African compared very favourably with those of the European, since, "if for his own good he is restricted in the use of liquor, firearms and the franchise, he enjoys a much wider connubial experience than the European".

Provision was made for 'civilised' Africans to be exempted from the operation of customary law, but exemptions became increasingly diffi-cult to obtain, especially when they were made the stepping-stones for attaining the franchise (by 1910 there were believed to be only six Africans on the voters roll in Natal). Interracial actions in which one of the parties was an African continued to be heard in the ordinary courts, and some important questions of succession involving African litigants only were eventually heard on appeal in the Supreme Court. Thus a Natal lawyer wrote incredulously to the *Law Journal* of the scene in the Supreme Court where a large crowd of Africans packed the chamber for three days of a hearing of an appeal, listening intently even though all the proceedings were conducted in English. The judgement of the Court of Appeal was interpreted to the Africans, he said, and the same roar of 'Bayete' (Hail!) resounded through the building as had been heard when the judgement had been given in the court below (1891).

In addition to falling under a separate court system applying a separate system of law, Africans were also governed by a large number of statutes passed by the white Legislature at the behest of the white electorate. As the economy of the Colony developed, these laws, which dealt with matters such as taxation and master/servant relationships, were applied with more rather than less rigidity.

The Natal Supreme Court remained the country's leading judicial body, and although it handled relatively few cases compared to the magistrates' courts and the Native High Court, it had the prestige and the authority to moderate the more severe rulings of the other courts. Yet if some of the judges supported a policy of restraint towards Africans, and if Africans facing political charges sought desperately to be tried in the Supreme Court rather than in special military or Native Affairs courts, none of the judges campaigned as actively as did, say, Chief Justice de Villiers in the Cape, for a less punitive style of law enforcement in respect of Africans. Thus it happened that, in the face of stiff competition, Natal earned for itself the title of the 'lashing Colony'. In 1907 the comparative figures for flogging per annum in the different parts of South Africa were 1 in 400 males in Natal, 1 in 680 in the Transvaal and 1 in 1,100 (approximately) in the Cape.

Leading white Natalians spoke enthusiastically of the whip as a solution to a variety of problems, ranging from cattle-theft to sex crimes to insubordination. Thus after two Africans were sentenced to terms of imprisonment plus 150 lashes each, to be received in three annual instalments, the *Natal Witness* wrote: "By Jumbo, if only we could publish such like punishments all over Kafirdom, we should soon, I guess, see an end of cattle-stealing" (1866). A member of the Legislature referring to alleged attacks by African men on white women declared that "if a rascal who has attempted to do this violence were branded as he ought to be, with a hot iron, given 100 lashes, and then hanged in public, and the Kafirs were made to know why . . . we would stamp this thing out." It was asserted that any attempt to deal with Africans according to the white man's conception of law and justice would only be interpreted as weakness, and accordingly the whip should be used because it was a form of punishment which the Africans respected. "Nothing but the lash will make them understand that we are in control of them."

By way of explanation of these severe opinions, the South African criminologist quoted in the earlier chapter on slavery remarks: "The presence of primitive savages in the small towns of Natal as domestic servants, purchasers of goods or simply as layabouts, created special kinds of criminal problem." To begin with, he writes, there was the danger of sexual assaults on white women and then there was the problem of stock theft; he presents no evidence, however, that assaults on white women were prevalent, and concedes that the severe floggings imposed did little to keep the number of stock thefts down.

The amount of flogging inflicted appeared to decline for a period after 1875, only to rise again after 1890. This temporary decline might have been related to the construction in the last quarter of the century of a number of prisons in the Colony, so that imprisonment could more freely be imposed as an alternative to whipping. Yet many white colonists complained that Africans enjoyed being sent to prison, where they got free board and lodging and from which they emerged as heroes. Notwithstanding these alleged advantages, many Africans did all they could to escape from prison, and for some years all Africans were bound by chains to prevent any of them from escaping. When the prison population soared, however, chaining was no longer practicable, and only special risk prisoners working on outside labour were shackled. By 1894 nearly 30,000 prosecutions were brought in the Natal courts, all but approximately 500 in the magistrates' courts. The prison population on one day in that year was nearly 1,200, of whom 77 were whites.

By the turn of the century more than 20,000 persons were being received into prison each year, of whom approximately one-fifth were white. The daily average prison population a short while later was 2,700. The total population of Natal at the time was approximately 900,000 Africans, 100,000 Indians and 100,000 whites, and the relatively high proportion of whites going to prison—10 per cent of the population contributing 20 per cent of the prison intake—could partly be accounted for by the reluctance of magistrates to sentence whites to corporal punishment.

The prison regulations classified prisoners into three groups, Africans, Indians and Europeans, but the definition of Europeans was unusual in that it included "all persons of European descent, Eurasians . . . , American Negroes, French Creoles and West Indians", and seems originally to have been dictated by dietary rather than racial considerations. In practice it was used to segregate whites from Africans and Africans from Indians. Such segregation was not rigid, however, and black, brown and white prisoners were frequently sent on outside working parties together. In one prison the status of prisoners was clearly reflected in their bathing order; white prisoners were permitted to bath twice a week, dark-skinned prisoners only once, in the same water and after the whites had finished their second bath.

Ironically it was Africans themselves who financed the machinery which was used for their control. In the process of Natal's modernisation, huts were taxed so that prisons might be built. If Africans defaulted on their tax for a year, then they were sent to prisons erected out of the taxes they had paid in previous years. By 1905 the number of Africans prosecuted exceeded 45,000, most of whom were charged in the magistrates' courts for statutory offences. More than 4,000 were charged with desertion and insubordination under the Masters and Servants laws, and a further 1,000 were prosecuted under borough regulations for such crimes as being on the streets at night after curfew hour.

The magistrates were appointed by the Department of Justice, but in their dealings with Africans they acted under the Department of Native Affairs. Many of them were totally untrained, and all were subject to the pressures of white colonists whose interests, with a few exceptions, they tended to put above those of the Africans who appeared before them. For a number of years the police in country districts fell directly under the magistrates' control, who first worked up the evidence against the accused and then sat in judgement upon them. Some of the magistrates made no secret of their hostility towards Africans, and one behaved so roughly towards suspects that he helped precipitate a minor rebellion and was reprimanded by the Colonial Secretary. Defending himself against charges of improper conduct he said, "One of the natives was most insolent, and would not even answer any of the questions put to him, upon which I told (my head constable) to strike him, which he did, giving him about six strokes with a riding sjambok". When the African still refused to answer, the magistrate, satisfied that he "was dealing with men who had no inclinations to keep the law", used a plan "often practised during the Zulu War to gain information from prisoners", which was to take one prisoner aside and fire a revolver over his head and then to threaten the other prisoner that he too would be shot if he refused to co-operate. In the early years of the twentieth century, when twelve Africans who had attacked the police were executed in public by firing squad, the magistrate wrote that he regretted the passing of the good old days when he had seen six Africans publicly hanged before breakfast. Eventually he ended his career as a member of a special Commission established to bring about better relations between Africans and whites (Addison).

Next to the magistrate, the local police sergeant was for the majority of Africans the most important representative of white authority. The Natal Police acted as a military force as much as a constabulary, and were referred to as the country's first line of defence against an African rising. They did to some extent investigate crime, but this was a relatively minor aspect of their duties, which have been described as having been to protect white property and to ensure an adequate supply of labour. Various police forces in Natal were eventually consolidated into one organisation, which proved to be so successful that the Natal scheme was subsequently adopted throughout South Africa; as proof of its success, a police-historian pointed out that in the first year of its existence the number of arrests in the Colony rose from 2,500 to 16,500 (1895).

The white colonists in Natal were never satisfied with their supply of African labour, which was either too small because Africans refused to leave tribal lands, or too great because 'surplus natives' refused to leave white-owned lands. The main complaint was that Africans migrated too frequently and were too undisciplined to undertake heavy farm work, and to remedy this deficiency thousands of labourers from India were imported into the Colony. The occasion for their introduction was the opening up of sugar plantations in the coastal regions in 1860, which led to the second major introduction in South African history of manual labourers to perform heavy farm work under close supervision. Unlike the Cape slaves, however, the indentured Indian workers were entitled to their freedom after serving a five-year contract period, and many of them plus a few non-indentured fellow countrymen eventually settled in Natal as permanent residents. By the end of the century their numbers equalled that of the whites, but they were almost entirely excluded from civic rights and subject to all the rigours of colour discrimination. As far as the criminal law was concerned, the chief offence for which the police watched was refusal of Indians to work for the employer to whom they were bound by contract, while in the civil field the small class of Indian merchants soon began to support a relatively large amount of litigation. Like Africans, Indians were totally excluded from the ordinary Judiciary at all levels, but no segregated court system was created to hear matters in which they were litigants. An Indian barrister did manage, however, to become enrolled at the Natal Bar, and so to break down the *de facto* colour bar which had operated to keep the legal profession throughout South Africa in white hands. This pioneer was M. K. Gandhi, who was embarking upon his first large case since being called to the Bar in London. He had intended to stay in South Africa only for as long as it took for a dispute between two Indian merchants in Durban and Pretoria to be disposed of–characteristically he arranged for it to be settled and for the parties to be reconciled–but he ended up by spending twenty years in the country, during which time he developed the technique of passive resistance and worked out the major elements of his personal philosophy. He wrote later that it was his experience as a non-European lawyer in South Africa that taught him what life must be like for an untouchable in India. Despite the fact the he was more highly qualified than many lawyers practising in Natal, the Natal Law Society tried to prevent him from being admitted to the Natal Bar; the judge brushed their objections aside, but then humiliated Gandhi by ordering him to remove his turban forthwith. Gandhi's status in Natal society was not determined by his profession but by his race. Neither the fact of his having taken elocution, French and dancing lessons in London nor his foppish dress or excellent manners gave him access to the homes of his white colleagues in Natal, though a small number of them, including one man who later became Attorney-General, were quite friendly towards him. He was exposed to so many indignities, such as being thrown off a train, made to travel on the outside of a carriage and refused admission to hotels and barber shops that it came as a relief to him to find that he was not being singled out because of any personal inadequacy. It seems strange that life for Gandhi as a British Indian seemed less beset by obstacles in the Boer Republic of the Transvaal than in the British Colony of Natal, but possibly the rather chaotic social situation on the Rand and in Pretoria favoured him at the time. It was the very determination of the white colonists in Natal to impose restrictions on Indians there, and their greater capacity for doing so, that converted Gandhi from being an ordinary lawyer bent on a career of self-advancement into a public leader dedicated to the progress of his people. At the turn of the century Gandhi was joined at the Bar in Natal by a second Indian, R. K. K. Khan, who appears to have had a successful practice, because he died a wealthy man having made substantial charitable bequests.

Gandhi gradually gave up private practice, and there was far more work from Indian clients than Kahn could handle, so many white attorneys prospered on the basis of their Indian clientele. For their part, the Indians regarded the white attorneys as their eyes and ears. The position was different with regard to Africans, especially in the countryside, where many of the magistrates looked askance at attorneys who appeared on their behalf. The objection was raised that the authority of the magistrates and of the law would be weakened if it was seen to be questioned by lawyers during argument or on appeal. Here again there was a contrast with the Cape, where Chief Justice de Villiers had stressed that justice evenly done was the best means of assuring African submission to the law.

The historical experience of Natal provides a useful corrective to the notion that all harsh laws and attitudes proceeding from white to black in South Africa had their origin in slave society, the Boer Republics and the Afrikaner people. As far as the administration of justice was concerned, the relative efficiency of police and magistrates in Natal meant that racially differential laws there bore more severely on Africans than they did in either of the Boer Republics. It is true that the small body of whites in the Colony who were sympathetic to Zulu interests, prominent amongst whom were Bishop Colenso and his daughters, did on a number of occasions try to use the Supreme Court to protect African leaders from arbitrary actions on the part of the military or the civil authorities, but the amount of success they achieved was slight. On the whole their experience was that writing letters to friends in the House of Commons in London was more efficacious than submitting applications to the Supreme Court in Natal. In its daily administration of the law, the court system was an important agency for maintaining the domination and protecting the property of the white settler community.

It is significant that in the one major case in which the judiciary could be said to have stood up in any noticeable way to the pressures of the majority of white farmers and officials, both the presiding judge (Smith) and the leader of the defence team (Schreiner – head of the Cape Bar) came from outside the Colony; it may be claimed that in this particular matter, international support for the accused counteracted the prejudiced atmosphere in Natal itself. The case was the prosecution of the Zulu king Dinizulu on a charge of treason, shortly after 3,000 Africans had been killed by Colonial forces, for taking part in what has been described as a reluctant rebellion against the poll tax. Acquitting the king of twenty out of twenty-three counts, the judge sentenced him to what was in effect three years' imprisonment, heavy enough to cost him his throne, but still a relatively light punishment against the background of massacres, executions and floggings which had preceded the trial. The *South African Law Journal*, commenting on what was really an exotic judicial experience for Natal, observed that "throughout South Africa the trial and sentence of Dinizulu were looked upon as a vindication of the justice and fairness of the white man in his dealings with the natives" (1911). It might have added that in the eyes of most white Natalians there had been too much justice and fairness, for one of the local lawyers in the defence team was to complain that his appearance on behalf of the chief completely ruined his practice and led to his being socially and professionally ostracised by the white community.

A Natal judge had recently declared that lawyers were a great curse to the natives, and the Chief Magistrate of Zululand had reiterated the view that lawyers undermined the authority of magistrates and the Government, adding that he knew of an extraordinary case of a coolie practising in the High Court—he was sure this man touted, but could not prove it. Finally, the Acting Chief Justice had spoken with regret of the vanishing simplicity of Africans. He felt that an educated African was generally a less useful member of society than an uneducated one, and supported the use of direct taxation to compel Africans to work more. In his experience, Africans of forty or fifty years earlier "were all civil and content with low wages and were more satisfactory in every way as servants. . . . The change from barbarous severity to civilised leniency has upset their equilibrium."

CHAPTER FOUR

The Incorporation of Africans into the Legal Order

THE ADMINISTRATION OF JUSTICE IN TRIBAL SOCIETY–
PRE-CONQUEST

Settled communities of Bantu-speaking people existed in the Transkei in the sixteenth century and probably much earlier, according to oral tradition and the journals of shipwrecked Portuguese sailors. Recent archaeological research has disclosed that vigorous and well-organised communities, almost certainly Bantu-speaking, occupied the Transvaal and the Orange Free State in the eleventh century, leaving behind them a complex abundance of ruins and extensive evidence of mining and metalworking. According to this evidence the claim that black and white entered South Africa at the same time in the middle of the seventeenth century is incorrect. The precise relationship of the early peoples to the present major tribal groups in South Africa has still to be worked out, and only now are South African historians beginning to write up the pre-conquest history of the African peoples. A considerable amount is known, however, through oral tradition and the records of travellers and missionaries, of the principal characteristics of African government and law from the late eighteenth century onwards, and although regional variations existed and changes took place in the course of time, the basic patterns are fairly well established. The following observations are based on some of the better known secondary sources.

As far as the administration of justice was concerned, in traditional African society every man was his own lawyer, and his neighbour's too, in the sense that litigation involved whole communities, and all the local men could and did take part in forensic debate. Women did not ordinarily participate in court cases other than as witnesses, but amongst the men there was little division of functions. The concept of professional judges acting according to formalised rules as part of a specialised and aloof administration was quite foreign to African jurisprudence, as was the notion of men hiring themselves out on the basis of their talent to plead. When pre-judicial attempts to resolve disputes failed, the arguments could be pressed to judgement before the chief, whose word was law; but the chief invariably acted as spokesman for his councillors, who in turn sought to uphold and reinforce the established norms of the tribe. In this context the good chief was reckoned not by the terror he could inspire or the magnanimity he could display, but by his skill in articulating the sense of justice (just-ness) of a relatively homogeneous community, which involved his applying universally accepted rules and precedents to particular disputes in a manifestly appropriate way. His authority derived not from his control of armed force or from his place in a learned bureaucracy, but from his position as leader and representative of the community. His coercive power was dependent not on any praetorian guard or professional police force but on the general body of tribesmen who made up his army. A chief who was corrupt, tyrannical or incompetent risked being deposed or assassinated; alternatively, dissatisfied sections of his tribe could move away from his jurisdiction and establish a new unit elsewhere.

In times of stress and upheaval, such as during the *difaqane* (forced migration) which decimated populations and revolutionised tribal structures in the early part of the nineteenth century, militarist emperor-chiefs like Shaka and Dingane developed structures of rule that were far more authoritarian than those described above, though even amongst the Zulus it was the 'just and generous' king who ruled for a long time rather than the aggressive soldier-kings who forged the kingdom. Generally, too, the procedures were neither benign nor rationally based when sorcery was being investigated, partly because the life of the victim was held to depend on the extraction of a confession. Yet what were innovatory or else peripheral features of tribal adjudication have become widely accepted in white mythology as characteristic and central. Recalling his history lessons at school, Bloke Modisane wrote in his autobiography that "the ancestral heroes of our fathers, the great chiefs our parents had told stories about, were in a class described as bloodthirsty animal brutes. . . . 'Which adjectives did you use?' I asked classmates after writing the examinations. 'I described Dingane as malicious, venomous, ferociously inhuman, beastly, godless; I should get a good mark.' " It is assumed by most whites that all chiefs at all times were ruthless despots and that the cruel procedures used for the 'smelling out' and punishment of witches were characteristic of ordinary litigation.

The ease with which Africans in the Cape adapted themselves to British-type courts came as a surprise to many persons unacquainted with African traditional legal procedures. In 1889 the *Cape Law Journal* commented that the manner in which "the ordinary native parries the most dexterous cross-examination, the skill with which he extricates himself from the consequences of an unfortunate answer, and above all, the ready and staggering plausibility of his explanations have often struck those who come into contact with him in the law courts. He is far superior, as a rule, to the ordinary European in the witness box" (1889). As the *Law Journal* pointed out this forensic skill derived from popular participation in the traditional African lawsuits, which differed from British-style court cases primarily in that they did not involve a class of professional lawyers and judges operating according to a formalised and esoteric set of rules and conventions.

Such difficulties as did arise for Africans in Colonial courts stemmed from these differences in conventions rather than from differences of objectives, as other articles in the *Law Journal* indicated. One story, purporting to be the narrative of 'an uncivilised native', though in fact written by a magistrate, described the tribulations of an African who gave evidence against a long-standing enemy in the Circuit court (1891). First it described the discomfort of having to wear European dress ("my feet, which have known freedom to this day . . . seemed as if they were being quietly roasted"). Then it told of how the narrator agreed to every proposition put to him by the white man who spoke for his enemy, believing that this was the polite thing to do, and that after the white man had finished speaking he would have the opportunity "to thunder forth in (his) best style what (he) knew, convincing everyone that he was an orator and councillor of the chief". Having lost the case as a result of his good manners, he lamented that he wa an old man and knew of only one way of conducting a case, of the nev way he was ignorant. A similar story is told in a pamphlet "Is gratitud to be found among the natives?", where an African witness for th prosecution, after being confounded by the rules of evidence, conclud< by saying that he has never before seen a thief brought up for trial wit a view to acquittal.

On the other hand, it was sometimes the lawyer and not the witne who was discomfited, as when an African witness responded literally t questions:

> *Prosecuting counsel:* Your name is Klaas?
> No Answer.
> *Prosecuting counsel:* Mr Interpreter, please make him answer.

Here a dialogue takes place between the interpreter and the witness.

Interpreter: Yes, I know my name is Klaas.
Prosecuting counsel: Why couldn't you say that before?
Witness: That is my name. You knew that. (1893).

These misunderstandings should not obscure the great similarities of approach and procedure which existed between the traditional and the Colonial courts. If classification is based on the essential nature rather than the detailed forms of the enquiry, then the similarities are more evident than the differences. Both methods of adjudication dealt with much the same range of injuries to person, property, reputation or public order, and both proceeded on the assumption that the truth or otherwise of an allegation could be determined by the orderly presentation of evidence and its rational evaluation. Both systems of jurisprudence investigated problems of veracity in a context of probability, and in both the element of the supernatural existed only on the fringes (the oath and witchcraft). Torture and trial by ordeal were untypical of either, and the major difference lay not so much in the nature of the enquiry as in the selection of people who conducted it. Thus the *Law Journal* was able to describe with great enthusiasm the refinement and skill displayed by tribal litigants and their supporters in settling legal disputes. "The Socratic method of debate appears in all its perfection, both parties being equally versed in it. The rival advocates warm as they proceed, sharpening each other's ardour, till from the passions that seem enlisted in the contest, a stranger might suppose the interests of the nation at stake. . . ." (1889). The article was well received and was soon followed by a fuller account of traditional African government and law, which stressed that the typical form of tribal rule was far from being despotic. Customary law, it pointed out, distinguished roughly between criminal and civil suits on the basis that a man's goods were his own property, but his person belonged to the chief. In cases of treason, murder, assault and witchcraft the injured party was considered to be the chief, and not the victim; in other cases, such as defamation, theft or assault on a man's wife, the man sued in his own name. Possible punishments or forms of compensation included confiscation of cattle or death. Summary executions were usually inflicted for assault on the wives of chiefs or aggravated cases of witchcraft, but otherwise the death sentence "seldom followed even murder, when committed without the supposed aid of supernatural powers; and as banishment, imprisonment and corporal punishment are all unknown in (African) jurisprudence, the property of the people constitutes the great fund out of which debts of justice are paid". Records of cases were kept in the heads of old councillors, and rules were derived from an accumulation of precedent rather than any generalised and systematic collection of laws.

It should be added that execution of judgement, which usually took the form of attachment of stock, was carried out by a special officer. The death penalty was practically confined to cases of suspected witchcraft, and was normally spontaneously carried out after accusation by the diviners, and then reported to the chief. Some of the great chiefs of the nineteenth century were in fact strongly opposed to capital punishment in all circumstances, not excluding witchcraft, although they did occasionally impose banishment for life (Hintsa, Moshweshwe, Montshiwa). Corporal punishment, where it existed at all, played a far smaller role in law enforcement in African states and chiefdoms than it did in the British colonies or the Boer Republics.

DISPOSSESSION NINE POINTS OF THE LAW: COLONIAL RELATIONSHIPS AND COLONIAL ATTITUDES

As the line of white sovereignty thrust up the east coast of South Africa and into the interior, Africans were incorporated in their hundreds of thousands into the new legal order, until eventually in every South African state there were more African subjects than white. The judicial problems that arose did not stem in their essence from any fundamental conflict of cultures between black and white since the two systems of jurisprudence were basically similar in character, inasmuch as both based the determination of liability on essentially rational procedures, in particular the testing of evidence by questions founded on what would have been reasonable in the circumstances. Nor did they flow from any specific legal doctrine, because by that time the common law of both Holland and England asserted the theoretical equality of all before the courts. The main difficulties arose from the context in which justice was administered, since the courts fulfilled a crucial role in the maintenance of colonial-type relationships between black and white. When Africans appeared in court they did so as members of a conquered race, put at a disadvantage by their poverty, their lack of educational opportunities, their menial occupations, and their inferior status in the eyes of most judicial officers and jurors. In the words of one magistrate, they were tried not by their peers but by their superiors.

A marked feature of nineteenth century social life was that greater dispossession of the African tribesmen led to harsher white attitudes towards them and more severe use of the courts as instruments for their control. As long as the indigenous peoples of southern Africa possessed their own armies, they were accorded a certain measure of respect by the white colonists. Treaties were entered into with them, alliances created, and spies sent to their camps to learn about dynastic disputes and other possible sources of division. Africans were not regarded simply as a homogenous mass of persons stamped with the same characteristics, but were divided into friendly and hostile groups, each with their acknowledged leaders and systems of government. Africans responsible for killing white soldiers or missionaries outside the colonial borders were handed over to their chiefs for justice, and it was not unusual for early officials and travellers to describe such chiefs in admiring terms. Thus the private secretary to one of the first British Governors wrote after meeting a young African chief that the chief was "of an elegant form and a graceful and manly deportment; . . . his countenance (was) open, but marked with the habit of reflection, and he possessed in a superior degree a solid understanding and a clear head. . . . He seemed, indeed, to be adored by his subjects . . . and had one wife only". In a later passage he wrote of Africans generally as being a bold, brave and resolute people, a formidable enemy and a fine race of men (Barrow).

A century of frontier wars between white and black for land, cattle, water and security, changed relationships and led to a deterioration of white attitudes, with the result that it became increasingly rare for any white official to speak of African leaders in such a sympathetic way. It was the very similarity of interests and occupations of white and black farmers on either side of the fluctuating boundaries that brought them into conflict, not their differences. White trekker communities, British settlers, and African tribal groups might have spoken different languages and had different concepts of the supernatural, but all derived their incomes from and patterned their daily living around herding cattle and planting cereals on a shifting basis. Decades of contact and interaction reduced such cultural differences as existed: skills in hunting, herding, gathering and preserving food, and travelling were interchanged; white and black learnt each other's languages; and Africans sold their labour or exchanged skins, ivory and copper in return for guns, horses, blankets and trousers (Bibles and brandy were usually given free to selected notables). Yet as the culture gap diminished, the whites sought out differences, not in order to eliminate them, but to emphasise them, since they legitimised violence and confiscation, and

sanctioned permanent subjection. A liberal South African historian has
noted that to European self-esteem, concepts of native debasement, of
inferiority and savagery became convenient modes of thought and
useful bases of action (De Kiewiet).

> The history of the nineteenth and twentieth centuries [he wrote] is
> full of unconscious propaganda of the white race against the black
> race. Although the rifle and the burning torch secured the military
> submission of the tribes, their work was carried on by concepts and
> attitudes, sanctions and sentiments which imputed indignity to the
> natives and increased their submission, till they came sometimes to
> be regarded as a passive commodity, part almost of the raw material
> of the country.

There were some Cape officials, especially in the early years, who tried
to resist this type of thinking. Thus Attorney-General Porter favoured
treaties with African tribes, and condemned commando raids against
them as wolfish and irresponsible.

> When I hear of losses of cattle – of native foreigners in arms [he
> declared] and of the impossibility of preserving anything from the
> audacity of these incorrigible thieves – I do not shut my ears to the
> remonstrances of the sufferers; but when I hear also . . . that the
> purchase price of farms lying in the midst of all the mischief is
> steadily advancing, I cannot feel the evil is of that absolutely ruinous
> description which some persons . . . are in the habit of representing.

Yet as more land was annexed and more Africans were incorporated
as labourers into the white rural economy, voices such as Porter's
became fewer rather than greater. The frontier wars themselves produced waves of anti-African sentiment, but they were not the sole
causes of hostility. The annexation of tribal land, the confiscation of
tribal cattle and the destruction of tribal independence tended to feed
rather than appease the tendency on the part of white colonists to
regard Africans in a generalised way as unreliable but pliable elements
needing to be treated with a firm hand. Now the great fear was of
rebellion rather than of invasion, and of a concerted rising of the tribes
that would lead to a general servants' revolt. In order to forestall the
contemplated barbarities of the rebels, the forces of civilisation were
deemed entitled, both in law and morality, to commit almost any
atrocity themselves. Thus the punishment of rebels went far beyond
military or legal exigencies. When the last major military conflict
between black and white in the Cape broke out, Porter's successor as
Attorney-General advised the Governor that rebels captured in arms

might be shot without mercy, and that there should be no preliminary trial, only an investigation to distinguish between rebels and other enemies. There might have been precedent elsewhere in the Empire for such a course, yet in the Cape the court system was well developed and could well have handled cases of treason and sedition. The Governor was in fact shocked by the harsh advice given him, and declared that the bloodshed in action provided sufficient example for the rebels and that punishment should not be inflicted indiscriminately on rebels whether captured in battle or surrendering. The next year, however, a new Attorney-General made remarks in Parliament which indicated that he condoned the shooting of defenceless men and women prisoners in the north-west Cape (the so-called Koegas atrocities); he was sternly rebuked by a Cape Town newspaper and later by the Chief Justice when giving judgement in a famous libel case, but he undoubtedly represented the opinion of the bulk of white farmers and administrators in the Cape (Upington).

Even relatively liberal whites were ready to point out the advantages of delivering to Africans occasional lessons in blood. A Cape judge who later became a leading administrator declared that when unfortunately it became "necessary to impress upon the savage mind by striking illustrations the duty of submission to civilised superiors", the process should be as short, sharp and decisive as possible; when "once that lesson (had) been thoroughly taught and learnt by heart", the basis would have been laid for an enduring obedience by men of all races to fair laws justly administered (Shippard). The more openly repressionist whites favoured more frequent reminders of the duty of obedience, and to the extent that they succeeded in persuading the authorities to deploy troops in shows of strength, these persons often provoked the very outbreaks which they claimed they wished to prevent. A number of white farmers welcomed punitive expeditions against African tribesmen because they saw them as agencies for increasing their supply of farm labourers and cattle. Like many a crusader before them, white irregulars who accompanied the army and police on campaigns of suppression found no incompatibility in being at one and the same time saviours of Christian civilisation and appropriators of captured booty (though it should be remembered that the 'loyal' African levies were not far behind in zeal when it came to the seizure of cattle). It may even be argued that in the nineteenth century it was the laws of warfare rather than the enactments of Parliament that sanctioned the spoliation by whites of black property. These irregulars were able to take advantage of the benefits of military law without being held back by its restraints; whereas individual private stealth was frowned upon and potentially punishable in the courts, collective public dispossession was legitimised and even acclaimed.

The courts played little or no role in the punishment of rebellion or the distribution of rebels' property. On two occasions, the Cape Chief Justice ordered the release on habeas corpus of alleged rebel leaders who had been detained otherwise than in terms of the law, but normally the courts were too remote for effective access by Africans at the time when such access was required. In general, if the judges intervened at all during the period of rebellion it was not to adjudicate on disputes but to raise volunteers. Thus during the 1877 rebellion, an eastern Cape judge campaigned actively to raise men and equipment, and himself contributed a horse, saddle and bridle. Many of his colleagues belonged to Volunteer Regiments, and, as the *Cape Law Journal* proudly pointed out, saw public service in the arms of the Cape (1898).

While Africans were armed and organised into independent tribal communities–whether legally subject to the sovereignty of white governments or not–they could not be regarded as a passive commodity to be utilised in the same way as water or timber. The wars of disarmament of the late 1870s, however, decisively broke the military power of the tribes, and paved the way for their wholesale incorporation into the white administrative and economic system. These battles brought to an end a century of resistance by the Xhosa people, the longest and most persistent fighters against colonial domination on the African continent. British Imperial troops accomplished what Boer commandos and Cape Volunteers had been unable to achieve. Their main strategy was "to drive the Xhosas out of the bush and mountains into the open rolling country further to the east, where their cattle could be captured and their food supplies cut. The possession of comparatively good firearms by the (Africans) made each succeeding campaign more difficult, but the result was the same–the tribes gave in when their food stocks were exhausted or their great chief killed" (Tylden). In Natal, too, it was the British Army that finally vanquished the powerful Zulu regiments, although only after suffering the heaviest reverse known to Imperial troops for a century. The Basuto under the leadership of their warrior-statesman chief Moshweshwe were never finally conquered, and in other parts of southern Africa tribal groups fought long and hard to play off Boer against Briton and to retain their independence.

During this period of conflict there continued to be extensive trade and diffusion of ideas between different groups, and when wars took place both sides invariably entered into complicated alliances that cut across lines of race, tribe, colour and language. Yet at the end of the century the main tendency had become quite clear: white power in military, economic and political terms had effectively been established throughout southern Africa. Opinions amongst those in authority differed, and, as Sir James Rose-Innes pointed out, the standpoints of the various groups changed with the passage of time, so that the 'repressionists' who favoured a policy of dispersion in the nineteenth century altered their slogan to one of segregation in the twentieth. Yet with the exception of a small minority of persons, almost all whites believed in one form or another of white overlordship in South Africa, differing only on whether brown and black South Africans should have marginal representation in political institutions or none at all. Those favouring total exclusion went so far as to quote both Darwin and the Bible as authorities for their views: one Transvaal legislator declared that the Negro races occupied the lowest position in the evolutionary scale, and that it would be flying in the face of Providence to give them the franchise (Loveday).

It might be thought that the stronger the whites became in military terms, the less need there would have been for them to take severe punitive measures against dissident tribesmen. Yet the participants in the last and most reluctant of tribal rebellions, who adopted an almost entirely defensive strategy, were punished with an aggressiveness that was never employed against their more dangerous and independent forebears. These late rebels were the Zulus of Natal who in 1906 took to the bush with arms in hand to demonstrate their opposition to expropriation of their land and the imposition of a poll tax.

A recent thoroughly researched study of the rebellion has demonstrated that there existed in heightened form in Natal all the socio-psychological forces already seen to have been manifest in the Cape (Marks). Early on in the study it is pointed out that the fantasies of white Natal about black Natal were a combination of wishful thinking, which underestimated the actual power of the African population and their hostility to the oppressive features of white rule, and fear, which exaggerated its irrational nature and evil intentions. The fear took the form of "a strong, enduring and at times almost pathological anxiety" about an African uprising, and hostility was specifically directed at

Christian Africans and the Paramount Chief, who respectively represented the new and the old forms of African independence. Coupled
with the fear and hostility was a strong determination to impose
exemplary punishments which would "instil a proper respect for the
white man" (commander of colonial troops). The perpetration by
colonial troops of what would today be considered atrocities, and what
was even then criticised as such, was justified on the grounds of the
alleged barbarism of the victims. Thus dum-dum bullets were stock-
piled in anticipation of the disturbances because of their greater stopping
power against "members of savage races who it must be remembered
are not creatures of nerves" (Governor). The protection of white
women and children from barbarous attacks which never materialised
was one of the justifications for punitive operations which included the
flogging of African women and children. The response of the authorities to the danger apprehended went far beyond rationally based legal
or military requirements. As against a total of 24 whites killed, some
3,000 to 4,000 Africans were shot dead, including many unarmed men
lying on the ground and fugitives hiding in trees. A further 700 Africans
had their backs 'lashed to ribbons', while a total of 4,700 sentences
including lashings were inflicted before the Government called a halt
to punishments. Africans were also publicly shot after brief courts-
martial, and several were hanged for murder after conviction by a jury
(though a white man who during that period had admitted castrating
an African was acquitted by a jury).

When Winston Churchill, then Under-Secretary for Colonial
Affairs, was asked to authorise the striking of an Imperial medal for
whites who had died in action, he wrote sardonically that he would
hesitate to press an Imperial medal upon the survivors of the dozen men,
four or five of whom had even died in battle, in view of the distaste
which the Colony had so strongly evinced for outside interference of
all kinds. M. K. Gandhi, who accompanied the Colonial forces as an
ambulanceman, was even more scathing. "This was no war", he wrote
in his autobiography "but a manhunt. . . . To hear every morning reports of the soldiers' rifles exploding like crackers in innocent hamlets
. . . was a trial." Amongst the wounded African prisoners whom he
treated were a number of men who had been detained as suspects and
flogged on the order of the general in command, a prominent Natal
farmer; white medical officers refused to attend to the festering
wounds which had resulted from the whippings, and when Gandhi
began to clean and bandage them he was nearly pulled away by white

volunteer soldiers "who became enraged and poured unspeakable abuse on the Zulus".

Police and military historians writing some years after the event recorded that many of the colonial troops regretted the slaughter, even though they recognised its value in shortening hostilities. Some suffered unpleasant psychological effects from shooting men at close range, and at least one was haunted by the experience for a long time. Nevertheless, it was "known that on many of the farms the natives were beginning to turn sour, when the news of a heavy repulse to the rebels brought them to their senses", and in the years since, the Africans of Natal had been "more tractable and peaceably inclined than ever before".

Disarmament of the tribes and the stern repression of rebellion should therefore be seen not simply as the expression of pathological drives, but as part and parcel of a disciplinary process whereby Africans were reminded of their subordination to the whites in what was becoming an increasingly interdependent society. The extensive shooting of rebels was not as some critics maintained part of an exterminatory process whereby white settlers attempted to clear the land of indigenous peoples. Extermination as a deliberate end had been pursued in an earlier period against the San hunting groups, whose mode of life and culture, like that of the indigenes of Australia and North America, revolved so completely around hunting and collecting, that they could not easily be impressed into service as farm labourers or herders. Being unable to postpone the killing of animals for meat, these San hunters could not regard cattle as breeding animals, and when their supplies of game diminished, they began to attack the farmers' stock for food. This in turn led the farmers to hunt them in special exterminatory commandos, more or less as if they were animals themselves; frequently they were in fact likened to vermin which had to be wiped out. The first true 'bitter-enders' in South Africa, the San were almost entirely annihilated. Thus in 1957 it was estimated that only 20 survived in South Africa, although over 50,000 lived in the semi-desert of South West Africa and Bechuanaland. By contrast, the 'rough handling' to which rebellious African tribesmen were subjected, was not intended primarily to reduce their numbers, but rather to act as a punishment. Its objective was disciplinary rather than exterminatory, and related to the process whereby independent African farmers were converted into subservient African labourers.

The placing of white dominance on a secure foundation was not followed by any reduction in hostility towards Africans. On the contrary, it eliminated the practice of dividing Africans into loyalists and enemies, and converted them all into a homogeneous group of 'natives'. The ideal African in the minds of most whites was one who remained sufficiently tribal in culture to justify his exclusion from citizenship, yet became sufficiently involved in modern society to be able to serve the white man cheerfully, obediently and well. Any African who departed from this stereotype became an object of ridicule and censure, such as was expressed by an English-speaking member of the Transvaal Legislature, who complained that an African wearing a new suit or riding a bicycle was 'advanced'.

The end of the nineteenth century saw the achievement of colonial self-government coincide with the final destruction of tribal power and the sudden development of industrial communities at Kimberley and on the Rand. The era of rapid industrial expansion was about to begin, and the colonial-type relationships which had formerly existed in the frontier regions were now carried into the towns. Africans were no longer viewed primarily as an immature but perfectible section of humanity to be Christianised and traded with, nor as competitors for possession of land and cattle, but as a mass of potential labourers to be lured, recruited and cajoled away from their land on to white-owned mines, railways and farms. "They are people whom we have to teach", said Sir Sidney Shippard, formerly a Cape judge and later a leading administrator, "to teach them the dignity of labour." If properly used, he continued, they supplied the whites with a magnificent source of labour, and his idea was that that was the best thing that could be done with them. Any idea of imagining that they could be on an equality with whites was absurd, they were thousands of years behind. "But today they should be treated with humanity and justice, and they are most useful in supplying us with labour, at any rate such labour as the white man can hardly perform in such a climate." The development of the goldfields on the Rand intensified the need for Africans to learn the dignity of labour. The Royal Colonial Institute, which once had been dominated by explorers, administrators, and philanthropists, one of whom had asked what dignity there was in forced labour, now heard one of its Fellows report after a tour of South Africa that 200,000 Africans were needed on the mines and only 50,000 had volunteered – the rest would have to be compelled to work, otherwise Chinese labour would have to be imported. He agreed with the colonists that the South African native "was altogether an inferior animal to the white man", he was treated too leniently, and was insolent, lazy and immoral; philanthropic sentiment in Britain had influenced legislation permitting liberties to Africans which was fast making life for white women and children well-nigh intolerable. He had personally had numerous experiences of the increasing insolence of the Africans and "for a very long time yet there must be one law for the white man and another for the black. At present," he concluded, "the law is in favour of the black man. The position must be reversed until at least he becomes more industrious, cleanly and moral."

With the decline in the authority of the chiefs and the massive involvement of Africans in the white-run industrial-agrarian economy, new kinds of African leaders began to emerge, men who could guide their compatriots along the highways and byways of the developing multi-racial society. Many of these men were mission-trained clerks, teachers, missionaries and journalists, others were industrial workers who had learnt through bitter trial and error how to adapt to urban life; all had acquired skills not imparted by ordinary tribal education. Although the Cape Colonial educational system was heavily weighted in favour of the whites, the literacy rates in 1894 being approximately 65 per cent for nearly 400,000 whites, 20 per cent for 300,000 coloured people and 5 per cent for 800,000 Africans, there were nevertheless tens of thousands of Africans officially regarded as literate and thousands who qualified as voters for the Cape Parliament. The novelist, Anthony Trollope, described how even in the Free State in the 1870s he had come across an African chief who had the gait of a European and dressed like a European, with a watch and chain at his waistcoat, a round flat-topped hat, and cord trousers; inside the chief's hut was a large iron double bedstead with mattress which he was sure had come from Mr Heal's establishment in Tottenham Court Road (Sapena).

Modern-style education was almost entirely in the hands of the missions, and a number of promising pupils were sent abroad by the Churches for advanced education. The bulk of white colonists, however were never able to reconcile themselves to the existence of what they called 'the educated native'. Recipients of traditional tribal education were accused of being backward and superstitious, but when some of them adopted the more advanced superstitions of the whites and in addition became more learned than most of their detractors, they were received with even greater hostility. This antagonism was sometimes disguised as concern. A Cape educationist addressing the Royal Colonial

Institute in 1883 said that despite twenty-five years of educational legislation there were hardly any well-educated Africans in the Cape,

> though certain men like Tiyo-Soga have gone as far as to be educated in Scotland and to take a Scotch degree, and more than this, marry a scotch wife – at least Tiyo-Soga did; but unfortunately the strain of doing all these great things is too heavy for even an exceptional Kafir. It is frequently the case that the too suddenly and too highly trained Kafirs fall victim to consumption and die an early death.

The one exception he was prepared to allow was John Jabavu, who was "very good at repeating a Greek noun", and who survived for three score years. Fifty years later Jabavu's son, the professor, found that prejudice against well-educated Africans had become more not less intense. "If I am stranded in the rural areas," he wrote in the 1930s, "I dare not go to a Boer farm speaking English and wearing boots and a collar without inviting expulsion with execration; but if I go bare-footed and collarless and in rags I shall enjoy the warmest hospitality." A leading member of the Cape Bar corroborated this view and indicated that it was not only Boer farmers who were hostile. White employers would rather have illiterate non-Christians working for them than educated Christian Africans, he said (Tamplin). A spokes-man for the Cape Farmers Congress endorsed this opinion, saying that he did not think that the civilised native was a success. A mine manager declared that he would rather make a Kafir useful than learned.

Among the justifications which had earlier been advanced in support of annexation of tribal lands was that this would facilitate the spread of Christianity among the heathens. Yet by the end of the century African Christians were being regarded with greater enmity than were non-Christians, this despite the stress laid by some missionaries on the Gospel of work: "six days shalt thou labour". The Natal Directory for many years stated bluntly that the so-called 'Christian Kaffir' had been a fail-ure, and according to a police historian the Zulu was not a success as a criminal either (Holt). As one writer recently remarked, the whites commonly believed that the education provided by missionaries simply produced lazy good-for-nothings, and that secular agents for change, especially a spell of work on the farms or mines or in the cities, had a far more wholesome effect (Marks). In support of this proposition she quoted the remarks of a Natal official, himself the son of a missionary, on the characteristics of Christian Africans: "They are comparatively few in number and very many of them . . . have by no means improved by having become civilised; they are as a rule less truthful, less honest, and less trustworthy; they have as a rule adopted more of the vices and few of the virtues of the superior race; and are not an element that it should be desirable to intrude into the midst of a loyal native population."

The acquisition of new skills and the adoption of an urban style of life by hundreds of thousands and then by millions of Africans, further narrowed the cultural gap between black and white, but gave rise to the erection of official colour bars which had been deemed unnecessary in the Boer Republics and unconstitutional in the Cape. Once again, the more alike Africans and whites became, the more necessary was it felt to emphasise their differences. In the 1880s the *Law Journal* fought vigorously for the retention and extension of the voting rights possessed by Africans in the Cape ("they suffer the worst form of government, namely government by the representatives of others"). It constantly stressed how adaptable Africans were, as were all people, and warned that a policy of deprivation and oppression must lead inevitably to violent resistance (1884, 1887). Yet fifteen years later the *Law Journal* defended the earlier departure in the Cape from the principle of manhood suffrage on the grounds that it was impracticable in South Africa and would probably have led in time to the white vote being swamped by that of untutored savages (1902). In the following decades Africans were virtually excluded from mention in the pages of the *Journal* and when they reappeared in a series of sketches in the 1930s they did so not as claimants for citizenship but as foolish bumpkins bewildered by the sophisticated ways of the white men. At a time when Africans were being imprisoned in their scores of thousands for infractions of the pass and liquor laws, the *Journal* carried allegedly humorous articles with titles such as 'Npongo and his Sixpence' telling of the tribulations of stereotyped elderly tribesmen caught up in a formalised court system. In 1949 the editor of the *Law Journal*, who was later to become a Judge of Appeal, wrote of the disasters which threatened to arise from "the sudden contact of infant souls with the temptations of the white man's civilisation" (Hall). More recently the *Law Journal* has dropped all such generalised references to Africans, but in another legal publication the *Journal*'s editors have rationalised differentiation in a more modern way. While stressing that differentiation can be justified only if based on objective and logical grounds, they allege that to treat all persons the same, adult and child, the sane and the insane, the raw savage and the civilised man, would be the height of injustice (1968).

The Administration of Justice in a Tribal Area— the Post-Conquest Position

As long ago as 1887 the *Law Journal* pointed out that the chiefs had become little more than government police. The effective repositories of power in the tribal areas were the white magistrates—'fathers of the people'—whose wide-ranging functions extended from hearing law-suits to advising local tribesmen of the approach of a comet. The destructions of the tribal armies and the subsequent disarmament of the African people meant that the white-officered police had a monopoly of force in the tribal areas. The chiefs were no longer spokesmen for independent communities, but rather low-ranking officials in the governmental hierarchy, expected to do the bidding of the magistrates and the Native Affairs Department. As part of the administration they were answerable to the white government rather than to their fellow tribesmen, and their vestigial judicial authority was ultimately enforceable by the police rather than the general body of tribesmen. A retired Chief Magistrate of the Transkei declared explicitly that his instructions had been to undermine the authority of the chiefs.

As the tribal areas developed into politically quiescent reservoirs of migrant labour, the sons of great chiefs became minor functionaries receiving government stipends subject to good behaviour; the sons of warriors trekked to the towns and wielded pickaxes instead of spears and guns; and the sons of diviners invoked the spirits of the forefathers to aid men going to work rather than to war, and to win victories in court rather than on the battlefield.

The last major tribal area to lose its independence and be incorporated into the boundaries of what is today South Africa, was the region between the Cape and Natal known as Pondoland. The changing pattern of jurisprudence in the area has accordingly been relatively well-documented, and may usefully be referred to by way of example to illustrate the complex interrelationships which have developed between the ordinary and the tribal courts in South Africa's various tribal areas, as well as the changing relationships between the chiefs and the white Government.

Stereotypes are notoriously contradictory, and Africans have frequently been charged with being both over-litigious and lawless. Shortly after carrying an article which described in most enthusiastic terms the refinement and skill characteristic of tribal litigation, the

Cape Law Journal made its contribution to the campaign for the annexation of Pondoland by deploring the state of lawlessness which it claimed existed there. "It is unnecessary in these pages", it declared, "to depict any of the refinements of cruelty in which 'chiefs' and 'petty chiefs' so constantly indulge". It added that if a European desired to get a hearing at the chief's court he had first to present the chief with several bottles of spirits, an oblation which was "the indispensable preliminary, the equivalent of our stamp on a summons". A few years later troops were massed upon the border; the Cape Prime Minister, Cecil John Rhodes, demonstrated the efficacy of a Maxim-gun, and the Pondo chiefs capitulated without rattling a spear. Though this bloodless annexation was widely attributed to the charisma of Rhodes, Innes observed that the persuasive power of the machine-gun was great, and the *Law Journal* claimed that the example of justice being done in the neighbouring Circuit court was decisive. Without an escort the judge had calmly gone on with his work, and "fortunately the legal profession and the public were spared the pain of realising that a vacancy on the bench had been created as a consequence of (his) capture and massacre. . . . There can be no doubt that it is precisely this cool *sangfroid* and indifference to any suggestion of danger, which appeals most strongly to the minds of native people, as they do to the minds of all nationalities." The *Journal* pointed out that during the previous few years it had been a common thing to see Pondo Councillors crowding the Circuit court and witnessing the conviction and sentence by colonial judges of their own people for crimes committed within the colonial border. ". . . It is gratifying to reflect that in great measure the present happy consummation is the result of the faithful discharge of their duties by the magistrates and judges of this country" (1894).

Like other annexed territories, Pondoland was placed under the aegis of the Cape Native Affairs Department. The chiefs were not deposed, but, after the pattern of the rest of the Transkei, converted into low-level government functionaries. From a formal point of view there was no change in their relationship with their tribesmen, but in substance they were now as much representatives of white authority as of their own people. In particular, control of armed force passed from their hands into the hands of white police and magistrates. Although the tribal courts continued to hear a large number of cases, particularly those relating to family disputes, the extension of the Circuit court area to Pondoland and the division of the territory into magistracies meant that overriding judicial authority lay with the white authorities outside of the tribal system.

Not all the chiefs submitted tamely to the new regime, and Paramount Chief Sigcau was eventually placed by a proclamation of the Governor in indefinite detention for obstructing a magistrate in the course of duty. Acting on the legal advice of a local white attorney, Sigcau "elected to avail himself of his rights as a British subject" and appeal for liberty to the Supreme Court. The Cape Attorney-General opposed the application, for which he was criticised by the *Law Journal*, which declared that he should have been only too pleased that a troublesome native chief had demonstrated his submission to the laws and tribunals of the land. On the other hand Chief Justice de Villiers "worthily maintained the best traditions of judicial office"; in a landmark judgement he forthwith ordered the release of Sigcau, and emphasised the civil court's duty to administer the laws without fear, favour or prejudice. Holding that the proclamation was *ultra vires* because it did not purport to be a general law but was aimed at a particular person, de Villiers said:

> to my mind it is a good symptom if a native of this country applies to the Supreme Court for redress ... but I hope that his advisers will tell him this, that although this Court is open to him when an injustice has been done to him, ... if it be made known to this Court that he has been guilty of transgressing the law, just as much as the Court would support him in the one case, the heavy hand of the law will be laid upon him in the other (1895).

This was the bargain being offered in the Cape to the conquered African people. They must lay down their assegais and guns and submit to the authority of the whites; in return they would have full access to the courts and the right to demand that they be treated according to law. Although they had no direct say in the enactment of the laws whereby they were judged, a section of their community could qualify for the franchise and thereby influence the selection of legislators. (The limited non-racial franchise was not simply a concession to liberal ideology–black and brown voters helped to counterbalance the numerical preponderance of Afrikaans-speaking whites in the Colony.) Similarly, although they were in practice excluded from the Bench and Bar, they could rely upon what were regarded as the strong traditions of the legal profession to ensure that justice was done to them.

As a result of the *Sigcau* judgement, the Cape Parliament placed government of Africans by proclamation on a firmer statutory foundation, and also expressly provided that Africans deemed to be dangerous might be detained for three months without trial. In practice, however, proclamations were generally issued only after extensive consultation with elected and hereditary leaders of the African people, while the detention provision appears to have been used only once in thirty years.

Restricted though they were, civic rights for Africans in the Transkei must be regarded as generous when compared with those available to Africans elsewhere in the country. In Natal the assumption of Supreme Chief status by the Governor placed him at the head of an authoritarian administration that treated Africans as colonial subjects rather than as citizens. The Transvaal adopted a similar policy to that of Natal, but implemented it with less success, while the Orange Free State adopted no special policy for governing its African inhabitants save to regard them all as members of a servile group. It was only in 1927 that a consolidated scheme of African control was worked out for the whole of South Africa. The Native Administration Act of that year combined the Cape technique of rule by proclamation with the Natal doctrine of an absolutist Supreme Chief to produce a colonial-type structure of rule by the white Government acting through the decrees of the Governor-General. As the Minister of Justice explained when arguing in favour of the widest powers being granted to the Governor-General, such powers were needed not only to control Africans living in the tribal reserves, but "also . . . detribalised and exempted natives . . . who in many cases, are the principal agitators in South Africa today" (Tielman Roos). In keeping with the theory of tribal despotism – which has been said to have been as characteristic of tribal government as Fascism was of European government (Welsh) – the Governor-General was declared to be the Supreme Chief of all Africans and invested with the power to rule them by proclamation and banish them by edict. None of the sanctions which could have been used to check a tyrannous chief, however, could be applied against the avowedly dictatorial Governor-General, since the source of his power lay outside of the tribe. Nor could dissatisfied Africans bring constitutional pressure to bear upon him because their franchise rights were so limited that they had no chance of voting the Government out of power. As one commentator neatly observed, the powers of the Governor-General were more characteristic of colonial rule than of tribal society; when eventually chiefs were given autocratic powers of banishment which most of their forefathers had not possessed, the Supreme Chief doctrine was seen to turn full circle and re-create chieftainship in its own image. Although various historians and jurists in South Africa have criticised the 1927 Act as being against the Rule of Law and granting powers similar to those possessed by Henry VIII, the trend has been for the scope of control by proclamation over Africans to be enlarged and for the limited supervision exercised by the courts to be curtailed.

On the judicial side, the 1927 Act created a segregated court system to hear civil cases in which Africans were the sole litigants, as well as to handle appeals from the tribal courts. African customary law was granted statutory recognition only when its social base had been considerably undermined, and the magistrates and Native Commissioners who constituted the new courts were given a judicial discretion as to whether in any particular case to apply Roman-Dutch or customary law. (In its modern form the latter is often referred to as 'Native law' or 'Bantu law'.) The chiefs continued to exercise limited local jurisdiction, but tribal litigants could appeal from their decisions to the local magistrate or else by-pass the chiefs and go straight to the local magistrate. Shortly after the passage of the Act, a correspondent wrote to the *Law Journal* that the bitter experience of innumerable Africans showed conclusively that very many chiefs were venal, biased and deliberately dishonest, and entirely lacking in judicial probity (1929). On the other hand the modern-minded Chief Luthuli, whose probity has never been questioned, wrote that he derived great pleasure from trying cases, and enjoyed both the debate and the reconciling of people at variance with each other. "I love the impact of mind upon mind", he added, "and I love thrashing things out in the attempt to get at the truth. The procedures of the court give these things orderliness, and getting at the truth is worthwhile for its own sake. The dying arts of exposition hold great attraction for me." The procedures in his court remained essentially unaltered from the days preceding the advent of the white man, with the exception that the modern tendency was to exclude witnesses when they were not giving evidence.

As far as Pondoland was concerned, the passage of the 1927 Act brought about few immediate changes. Because of its geographical position and late annexation the area attracted fewer mission stations, fewer schools and fewer stores than other parts of the reserves; it was also more fertile and less overcrowded. Accordingly, although thousands of men and women were forced each year by taxes, land shortage and a desire for manufactured goods to go as migrant labourers to white-owned centres of production, Pondoland was less affected by white rule than any other portion of the Transkei. In 1936 a social anthropologist summarised the main changes which had been brought about in its administration of justice during 40 years of white rule (Hunter). The territory was divided into magistracies, she wrote, in each of which was a police prosecutor, a small detachment of police, and a jail, which was often the most conspicuous building in the village. The most revolutionary effect of the new criminal code–which was enforced by the ordinary courts against all Transkeians, black and white–was that it refused to entertain charges of witchcraft and sorcery. The practice of witchcraft was not punished but the imputation of witchcraft to another was treated as a serious offence, while those who killed alleged witches or sorcerers were tried for murder or culpable homicide. No figures were available for the number of civil cases heard in the traditional manner by the chief's courts, but 'a number' of such cases were tried before the district chief each week. These cases could be taken on appeal to the local magistrate, who would re-hear the matter *de novo* and not be bound in any way by the chief's verdict. 'School people' who wished to advance civil claims tended to go directly to the magistrate, and only the magistrate had jurisdiction to try criminal cases, while serious cases went to the Circuit court. Professional lawyers could not appear in the chief's courts, but there was enough other work to keep two attorneys in each of the seven magistracies. As throughout South Africa, all magistrates and judges were white.

In a foreword to the above mentioned study, J. C. Smuts, who claimed to have been 'in contact with the native mind' all his life, observed that the Pondo were unusually conservative and tenacious of their own culture. More recently an African political writer commented that the Pondo had been well known in South African history for their allegiance to authority, and that missionary-trained chiefs had led their people with vigour, and enhanced the institution of chieftainship; in two main parts of Pondoland, they had erected modern offices and conducted cases on the pattern of a magistrates' court, complete with officers, a dock, a fairly good method of recording proceedings and a proper system of filing (Mbeki).

Thus on the surface Pondoland would seem to have been the ideal territory for the reception of the new tribal authorities which the Government established in the 1950s pursuant to its policy of encouraging Africans to develop towards self-rule along traditional lines. Yet in fact the introduction of the new authorities and the concomitant extension of powers to the chiefs, brought about a greater social upheaval in the area than even annexation had done. The chiefs and head-men found it more difficult than ever to mediate between their tribes-men and white officials, and in eastern Pondoland their action began to arouse considerable opposition.

As their statutory power increased, so did their traditional authority wane and the consensual basis of the justice which they administered disintegrate. Their courts were regarded by their opponents as instru-ments of partiality and coercion rather than as the means of reconciling parties and asserting tribal unity; they enforced the white man's policies without the restraints which operated on the white man's courts, and their judgements generated rather than reduced social friction. By the end of 1960 civil war broke out in the territory; pro-Government chiefs and informers were forced to flee and many were killed. Defiant tribesmen set up their own authorities in opposition to those of the chiefs and Government, and established popular courts to replace the chiefs' courts.

According to the African political writer quoted earlier, justice, not money, became the criterion; people did not have to pay to have their cases heard. Those who were found guilty of 'greed or selfishness' were fined and the money was used later to pay for the defence of persons charged in the ordinary courts. Appeal from the popular courts lay to the 'Pondoland High Court' which sat on the hill where peasant resistance was organised. As area after area joined the opposition, in-formal courts were set up in each locality to administer popular justice. People withdrew their cases from the chiefs and magistrates' courts, and gladly paid their fines to the popular courts "knowing that their money was not going to be used to line the pockets of a corrupt tyranny ..." The setting up of these peoples courts probably did more than any-thing else to show the peasants what a difference it would make to run their own machinery of administration in keeping with the democratic goals that they had set themselves (Mbeki).

Eventually the Government reasserted its authority by means of deploying thousands of specially trained military and para-military forces. Nearly 5,000 Africans were taken into custody and more than 2,000 put on trial; the authority of the chiefs' courts was re-established and their jurisdiction extended to punishing disobedience. It was at this stage that the full impact of the 1927 Act was first felt in Pondoland, because a special proclamation was issued to authorise the detention of suspects without trial, to compel Africans to obtain permission to hold meetings, and to empower certain chiefs to impose banishment orders on tribesmen within their jurisdiction. This proclamation made the declaration of martial law or a state of emergency unnecessary, and facilitated the mass round-up for screening of all able-bodied men found in dissident areas. The magistrates' courts and the Circuit court were not entirely by-passed, but only brought into operation at a relatively late stage, when mass trials were held at which thousands of tribesmen were sentenced to imprisonment or fines and a score were sentenced to death.

The revolt in eastern Pondoland encouraged the Government to accelerate the programme of tribal self-rule and give it a more modern character. In 1963 the Transkei was granted a Legislative Assembly with power to pass laws over a wide number of topics ranging from agriculture to education. Two-thirds of its members were *ex officio* chiefs, its statutes were subject to veto in Pretoria, its budget was dependent on subventions from Pretoria, its civil service was dominated by officials 'on loan' from Pretoria, and it had no authority to override bans and proscriptions issued by Pretoria. Similarly, the far-reaching proclamation of 1960, which applied to the whole of the Transkei, was not repealed. Thus a team of American scholars who observed the Transkei constitutional experiment for two years concluded after an extended analysis that it was more likely to remind Africans of imposed restrictions than of widening opportunities (Carter, Karis and Stultz).

Nevertheless, the Transkei Assembly became the one place in South Africa where Africans could with some safety debate political questions, and a policy of gradual Africanisation of the civil service was begun. After six years of office the Transkei Government pointed out proudly that the first black magistrates in South Africa had been appointed in the Transkei–one in Pondoland and one elsewhere. They were full district magistrates, save that they had no jurisdiction to handle matters in which white persons were litigants or accused. Some police stations and prisons were placed under African command, but subject to the control of the South African Police and Prison forces respectively, and not of the Transkei Government. A number of small villages were also zoned fully for African occupation, though the territory's only port was declared a 'white spot', and the capital remained largely in white hands.

In some areas, pro-Government chiefs were given squads of home-guards to protect them from attack. This was the first time in nearly a century that chiefs had been armed rather than disarmed by white authority, and it showed how central the maintenance of tribalism had become to those who wished to perpetuate white control in southern Africa. Now it was Africans rather than whites who attacked the arming of tribesmen; one anti-Government spokesman remarked that as there were only two guards outside Buckingham Palace, he could not see why there should be more for pro-Government chiefs in the Transkei.

Just as the destruction of tribal independence had once been regarded as essential to the disciplining of Africans on the farms and in the towns, so now paradoxically the permitting of some political activity focusing on the chiefs was being offered as justification for the repression of Africans in the towns and on the farms. During the 1960s the tribal reserves were constituted into nine separate 'homelands' occupying about 13 per cent of South Africa's surface area and containing approximately 40 per cent of the country's African population. The Transkei was the largest and most compact, but its sub-subsistence economy compelled it to export labour in order to import no less than half its staple food requirements.

The revival of the chief's power has led to some decline in the authority of the magistrates. Provision has been made for appeals from the chief's courts to be heard by regional chief's tribunals rather than by magistrates, and the indications are that questions relating to tribal law and discipline will be determined exclusively by the chief's courts, while all other matters will continue to come before the magistrates.

A white professor of law at the tribal College for the North insisted recently that "it is not for the whites, who are for the time being teaching law to the Bantu, to determine their future law. This must be done by the Bantu themselves–not only by their trained lawyers but by Bantu from all walks of life" (R. Verloren van Themaat). Yet in the same article he reported that two experts, presumably white, had been appointed by the Government in 1961 to enquire into the future of African courts, both in the towns and in the tribal areas. By 1969 they had not yet made known the results of their researches, and had worked so quietly that none of their activities appeared to have leaked out to the press or penetrated to the pages of the many legal journals in South Africa. The issue was regarded as one for semi-secret investigation rather than public debate, and if Africans were consulted at all no indication of their attitudes found its way into the professor's survey. His main thesis was that there had been considerable growth in the number of African law students and a new willingness on the part of the Government to create institutions for the administration of justice among Africans; accordingly it was imperative that legal education for Africans be adapted to train them "for the realities of practice in modern Bantu society". Whereas previously he had argued that all law students in South Africa, whether black or white, should study African customary law in a scientific way because of its importance to the legal profession as a whole, now he seemed to be contemplating a differential type of education for Africans to equip them for the practice of law in a separate court system. Legal education for white students has been dominated by the positivist approach, which has tended to accept the decisions of the courts as correct simply because they have been the decisions of the courts. Few attempts have been made by law faculties to introduce moral or sociological criteria into the evaluation of legal rules, and the only substantial critique has been that advanced by Afrikaner jurists who have used historical and nationalist jurisprudence in an attempt to expunge English influence from the common law. The professor of law being quoted here was himself the son and grandson of two of the most prominent of these Afrikaner jurists, and to some extent he can be seen as transferring their approach to the training of African law students. The 'realities' he had in mind were ideological and administrative rather than practical, inasmuch as they related to the tribal and separatist aspects of law affecting Africans, rather than to the more pressing problems that arose from their having the disabilities of being both poor and black. Granted there was sufficient realism, by which he meant acceptance of separate institutions, he thought that the possibilities for African advance in the field of the administration of justice were limitless; he could even envisage that one day in the Transkei, long after the rest of Africa had produced many outstanding jurists, there might even be an African judge.

Part Two

THE MODERN MACHINE

Judicial Attitudes towards Race in South Africa

THE UNIFICATION OF THE COURTS–THE SUPREME COURT OF SOUTH AFRICA

The setting up of a Court of Appeal for the whole of southern Africa was frequently mooted in the 1890s, both for its own sake and as a suggested precursor of political union. The judges and advocates in the Cape, the Orange Free State and the Transvaal had sufficient in common to regard themselves as belonging to the Brotherhood of the Bar: nearly all were Cape-born, where they had studied at one or two selected schools before proceeding to Universities in Holland and England. In general they were agreed on the need to maintain Roman-Dutch law as the common law of South Africa, they supported the use of English styles and procedures in court, and favoured co-operation between Englishman and Afrikaner in all walks of life. They were also at one in believing that justice should be done to dark-skinned South Africans, preferring, however, not to define the term justice too precisely.

The *Cape Law Journal* claimed that it could not but be a gain to South Africans to possess a small society of men of guaranteed qualifications for taking part in public affairs, generally with the time and opportunity for reflection on subjects legal, social and political. The occasion for this observation was the holding of a Bar dinner in Cape Town in honour of the Free State President, a former member of the Cape Bar and one time Chief Justice of the Free State. Amongst the assembled guests were judges and advocates from all parts of South Africa (1890).

Yet this barristerial bonhomie was unable to survive the bitter tensions generated by British attempts to secure control of the Transvaal and when in 1899 the Boer Republics finally declared war on the British Empire, the man who signed the final proclamation was the former guest of honour at the Cape dinner. In fact he went even further and fought with a Boer commando until the bitter end (F. W. Reitz).

The Anglo-Boer War (1899-1902) divided the legal profession just as it divided the white population of all South Africa. This was no ordinary war, wrote J. C. Smuts, but a vast tragedy in the life of a people. Judges and advocates in the Boer Republics rode with the commandos as legal advisers, and then became involved in the fighting, during which some died, some were captured and others emerged as famous guerilla leaders. Amongst the prominent jurists in the Boer forces were two future Prime Ministers of South Africa, Smuts and Hertzog, both of whom distinguished themselves as resourceful and daring commando generals. After an outstanding career at Cambridge, Smuts had joined the Kruger Government as State Attorney, and during the war he changed from "a slender, slightly built man, clean-shaven with the pallor of a student, to a broadened, hardened person with the bronzed face of a seasoned guerilla and a small beard". Frequently during the war he was said to have been seen with a gun in one hand and a book on international law in the other. Hertzog resigned as a judge a week before war was declared, and after organising courts martial and explaining the rules of international law to the soldiers of the Orange Free State, he gradually assumed military command and became a trusted and skilled leader. On the Boer side there were also three future Chief Justices of South Africa; one was wounded in action and sent as a prisoner of war to Bermuda (J. de Villiers), another fought to the end in the Transvaal (N. de Wet) and the third acted as military censor (Curlewis). Three Transvaal judges rode to the front, while Transvaal prosecutors suffered particularly heavily. One senior prosecutor was killed in action, another died in a prisoner of war camp, a third was executed by the British for distributing illegal pamphlets, while a fourth was imprisoned and disbarred in England for urging that an anti-Boer lawyer in Johannesburg be disposed of (Krause). Amongst the younger volunteers in the Boer ranks were three newly qualified lawyers recently returned from Holland who twenty years later were to establish the first Afrikaans-medium law faculty in South Africa, and so pave the way for the ultimate Afrikanerisation of the Judiciary (Bodenstein, Malherbe, H. Verloren van Themaat).

Thus a whole generation of Boer lawyers were profoundly affected by the war, although it is interesting to observe that they later tended to be far less hostile to the British than subsequent generations of Afrikaner lawyers tended to be (Roos, Pirow, Vorster).

Lawyers in the Cape and Natal were not as directly involved in the fighting as their counterparts to the north but much of their work in court related to problems raised by the war. One judge was caught in the siege of Kimberley where he administered martial law during a period of what the *Law Journal* called "vigorous shelling and repeated attacks by unreasoning enemies" (1899). Another judge proceeded nervously on the Western Circuit, where the guerillas were very active, encouraged, he observed sarcastically by the assurance of the Lord High Chancellor in London that it was "only a sort of a war" ("true this was in the course of an after-dinner speech and therefore not quite as binding as an utterance from the woolsack or in the Judicial Committee" (Laurence).

About a sixth of reported judgements in the Cape dealt with problems that arose directly or indirectly out of the war, many of them about the status of captured rebels and the relationships between ordinary and martial law courts. Chief Justice de Villiers was so distressed by the conflict that he came close to nervous collapse; in his judgements he favoured the supremacy of the civil over the military courts in areas away from the battle, and he also adopted a softer attitude than one of his colleagues towards Cape rebels, holding that they should be treated as belligerents rather than as criminals.[1] An eastern Cape judge, William Solomon, who was also destined to be Chief Justice of South Africa, was placed at the head of a special Treason Court to try leading rebels – the rank and file were amnestied – and he imposed sentences ranging from a fine to two years' imprisonment.[2] The British Army were dissatisfied with these lenient sentences, and set up martial law courts of their own, which sentenced hundreds of Cape rebels to death, thirty-five of whom were executed.

A case of a different sort which it fell to Solomon to decide was one in which a British soldier was tried for murdering an African prisoner, and in which the defence was raised that the accused had merely been obeying orders. Solomon acquitted the accused on the facts of the case but held that obedience to a superior's command did not automatically relieve a soldier of liability for his acts; if the command was manifestly illegal in that it was obviously opposed to the law of the land and to well-established army customs, then the soldier obeyed it at his peril.[3] This judgement which was given *ex tempore* and without the aid of notes, subsequently became internationally known and was used as a precedent in the trials of Nazi war criminals after the Second World War. There were at least three other matters heard in South Africa

[1] R. v. Louw, 1904 SALJ, 387; criticised in *Rebels as Belligerents*, 1904 SALJ, 119, 318.

[2] *Cape Treason Trials*, 1901 SALJ, 164.

[3] R. v. Smith, 17 SC, 561; 1904 SALJ, 192; discussed in R. v. Werner, 1947 (2) SA, 828.

during the Anglo-Boer War period in which similar problems arose. One was the 'Calvinia Flogging' case in which the Cape Supreme Court upheld the conviction and imprisonment of a rebel who had whipped a number of captives, on the grounds that even if he had been obeying orders, as he claimed, such orders had not related to ordinary acts of warfare, and could not excuse his conduct.[4] The other two cases were heard in the Transvaal by a special criminal court set up by the British to administer justice in the period before a proper Supreme Court bench was established, and both involved the killing of unarmed Africans by members of Boer commandos. In the one case, the killing was held to have been gratuitous and unrelated to military considerations, and the accused was sentenced to death, with a strong hint that he would be reprieved, while in the other the shooting of a man erroneously suspected of having been a British scout was held to have been justified. The court said in this second case that brutal and repugnant as the act was, it had been performed pursuant to an order "to further military operations, namely to allow of farms being cultivated to provide food while the owners are away fighting, to terrorise the natives so as to retain their services in the war and prevent them from deserting to the British or from giving the British any information or assistance".[5] (The relevant order of the Republican Commandant was that Africans who left their place of residence without a pass should receive twenty-five lashes, while Africans found in possession of a pass issued by the British should be executed. Many Africans were in fact shot by the Boers in terms of this latter instruction.)

The sufferings of the Boers during the latter part of the war, and the bitterness caused by the execution of the Cape rebels, left lasting memories in the minds of the Afrikaner people. A contributor to the *Law Journal* justified stern actions by the British on the grounds that it became a military necessity to lay waste the country and remove non-combatants to safety; in terms of this policy, thousands of Boer homesteads were burnt down, and 100,000 Afrikaner civilians were concentrated into camps – hence the term 'concentration camps' – where 20,000 women and children died because of insanitary conditions.

The entry of British troops into Bloemfontein and Pretoria and the defeat of the Republican armies, shifted the centre of South African legal activity from the Cape to the Transvaal. The *Cape Law Journal*

[4] R. v. *Louw*, 1904 SALJ, 387, discussed in 1904 SALJ, 119, 318.

[5] R. v. *Bodenstein*, 30 Sept., 2 Oct., 1901; R. v. *Bekker* 23, Sept., 1901, reported in 1901 SALJ, 426.

was in the van of the move, announcing in 1900 that it would move to Johannesburg and be called the *South African Law Journal*. In Pretoria the British Army occupied the High Court building, where it renamed each court-room after a British general and converted the advocates' robing room into a mortuary.

After peace was concluded in 1902, the authorities placed great emphasis on reconciliation between Englishmen and Afrikaners, hoping thereby to create a united South Africa under white control within the British Empire. The *Law Journal* observed that henceforth the flag of Britain floated over all of South Africa, and added that ungenerous recriminations would be unworthy of the gallantry with which the war had been conducted on both sides and "unworthy of the English boast that those who fought the hardest could shake hands the most cordially afterwards" (1900, 1901). Sir James Rose-Innes, who was appointed as head of a strong Bench in the Transvaal, wrote that from his serene vantage point he witnessed that step unique in history by which Great Britain handed over to the men, but lately her gallant foes, the control of the territories she had conquered.

The policy of reconciliation was reflected in the new court systems established in the conquered Republics, and most of the Boer lawyers became active supporters of this policy. Two exceptions were ex-President Steyn and General Hertzog, both of the Orange Free State, who felt that the practical effect of reconciliation was the sacrifice of Afrikaner national sentiment on the altar of British Imperialism.

In the end the main losers from the war were not the Boers, who forfeited their independence, nor the British, who paid a heavy toll in lives and incurred expenses of £200 million, but dark-skinned South Africans. Before the war, the British had complained that the Kruger Government was guilty of oppression towards coloured persons, and during the war they had made extensive use of Africans for scouting and non-combatant duties. The war bore heavily on African and coloured persons in the rural areas, 70,000 of whom were placed in concentration camps, and they hoped that a British victory would lead to an improvement of their status. Yet they discovered that the new British regime in southern Africa maintained a colour bar not only every bit as rigid as that exercised by the Boers, but considerably more efficient. Whereas British occupation of the Cape a century earlier had led to the abolition of slavery and of official race differentiation, British occupation of the Transvaal and the Orange Free State led to a consolidation of white constitutional overlordship. *The Times*

History of the War observed that "many of the Kafirs looked for the millennium with the arrival of the British and expected not only that the black man would be treated as an equal but that all those in the public employment would receive their pre-war rate of pay, with arrears". When such pay was not forthcoming, some of the Africans went on strike, but the military compelled them to return to work by arresting their leaders. "The majority of the natives, however, accepted continuance of the old system under the new administration."

As far as Indian South Africans were concerned, they experienced the same expectations of better things to come followed by the same disappointments. Gandhi had sympathised with the Boers, but out of loyalty to the Empire had organised a team of Indian ambulancemen to assist the British. He wrote later that the friendliness of the British troops was encouraging, but the harshness of British officers most disconcerting. After the war he discovered that the military administrators in the Transvaal–he called them the autocrats from Asia–were ruder to Indians than the Republican officials had been. Attempts to expose corrupt persons in the Asiatic Department were invariably frustrated, and when two such administrators were eventually put on trial they were set free by a white jury.

Yet the racism of the new colonial administration in the Transvaal was to some extent tempered by the Supreme Court which was established there. The new Orange Free State and Transvaal judges were selected with great care, especially those in the Transvaal, where a strong court was required to encourage a resumption of mining and commerce and to provide a focus of stability in a divided and ravaged land. At the local level magistrates played a key role in effecting transition from military to civilian government; English was now firmly established as the dominant language of the courts, not only in the Cape and Natal, but throughout the whole of South Africa.

The Transvaal Supreme Court proved to be especially well constituted for the functions it had to perform, and earned a reputation as perhaps the best Bench South Africa ever produced. In many respects it was to become the model for all future courts in South Africa. Reconciliation in the political sphere was matched by a form of reconciliation in the juridical sphere, whereby Roman-Dutch common law was fused with English constitutional doctrine. British dominance, however, was reflected in the preponderance of English-speaking persons on the Bench and the use of English as the main language of the courts.

Part of the strength of the Transvaal Bench was derived from the wide range of temperaments and interests of its incumbents, four of whom were later to become Chief Justices after Union in 1910; Rose-Innes, Solomon, Wessels and Curlewis. Rose-Innes and Solomon had both acted as Attorney-General at the Cape, where they had been liberal and pro-British without being militantly anti-Boer. Wessels was a Cape Afrikaner who had migrated to the Transvaal and become the leading barrister there; during the Anglo-Boer War he had returned to Cape Town, and criticised the 'Kruger oligarchy' and those young Afrikaners who made a Mauser into a holy symbol and thought they were omnipotent because they could hit a bottle at two hundred yards (1905 SALJ). Curlewis, on the other hand, was an English-speaking immigrant from the Cape to the Transvaal who had supported the Boer forces during the war and acted as one of their military censors. In personality these four judges differed markedly. Innes was stern and honourable ("he is so upright that he bends backwards"), Wessels was scholarly but explosive ("Juniors, dying and bleeding, lay strewn all over the place. Stentor with an Oxford accent . . . if he was short of material he turned on his brother judges"). Curlewis was painstaking ("He was never wrong, but took an eternity being right. I'd sooner lose a case before anyone than win one before him"). Yet all three of them, as well as the conscientious and lucid Solomon, were strong jurists and staunch proponents of Roman-Dutch law. Innes was a master of compact exposition and Wessels an outstanding legal historian, so that although this was a period of British domination when Dutch was eclipsed as a legal language and at least half of the Johannesburg Bar as well as some of the judges were men straight out from England, it was also a period when Roman-Dutch law was consolidated and invigorated as the common law in South Africa. In 1904 Smuts, who then enjoyed a flourishing practice at the Bar, was able to state in the *Law Journal* that "our venerable jurisprudence has been justified of her children in the most gratifying manner".

In their approach to questions of race, the Transvaal judges applied the Cape point of view, which asserted the general equality of all before the law as laid down by English and Roman-Dutch common law, but upheld the validity of statutes which were clearly discriminatory. Thus when the Transvaal Registrar of Deeds refused to register a transfer in favour of an African on the grounds that Africans were incapable of acquiring real rights, the court declared that there was no express statutory support for this view and that accordingly the transfer had to be registered, since all inhabitants of the country enjoyed equal rights.[6] Similarly the Court overruled as manifestly wrong the earlier decisions of the Republican Court which had obliged Indians not only to live in proclaimed areas but also to trade there.[7] Innes said that a power to compel Indians on sanitary grounds to live in special locations did not include the power to prevent them from trading elsewhere, and expressed surprise that the government of what was now a British Colony should put forward a claim which the British Government had for years strenuously resisted. The Court was also willing to give a hearing to a Chinese association which had collected funds for the illegal purpose of organising passive resistance (about 1,000 Chinese had joined a passive resistance campaign led by Gandhi), and granted damages to a Chinese whose premises had been forcibly entered pursuant to a general warrant to search for Asiatics illegally in the Transvaal, and not a specific warrant to search his premises. On the other hand, the Court showed its readiness to be bound by the terms of discriminatory statutes when it held that Asiatics fell within the expression 'coloured persons' as used in Town Regulations of 1899, and were accordingly prohibited from using the sidewalks of streets.[8]

In 1910 the four British Colonies of South Africa – the Cape, Natal, the Transvaal and the Orange River Colony – were brought together into the self-governing Union of South Africa. The separate Supreme Courts of the four territories were also fused into a single Supreme Court of South Africa, divided into Provincial Divisions and headed by an Appeal Court in Bloemfontein. Chief Justice de Villiers of the Cape was made a Baron and appointed to preside over the Appeal Court as Chief Justice of South Africa. He was joined in the Court of Appeal by another Cape judge (Maasdorp) and by Innes, Solomon and Wessels from the Transvaal. All five of the Appeal Court judges were thus former members of the Cape Bar, and it was the Cape legal tradition, as modified during the period of Colonial rule in the Transvaal, that was to predominate in the new court.

The Appeal Court was seen as the embodiment of all that was fine and honourable in South African judicial life; it introduced uniformity into South African law, laid down guidelines for its future develop-

[6] *Tsewu* v. *Registrar of Deeds*, 1905 TS, 155; cf. Tsewu, SANAC (4), pp. 787-8; 798.

[7] *Habib Motan* v. *Transvaal Government*, 1904 TS, 404.

[8] *Chairman* v. *Treasurer, Chinese Association*, 1909 SALJ, 597; *Ho Si* v. *Vernon*, 910 SALJ, 308; *Salujee* v. *Rex*, 1903 TS, 13.

ment, and established standards which were to be followed by later courts. When the judges were housed in a new building (1929), the then Chief Justice declared that the Temple of Justice, like justice itself, was beautiful in its severe simplicity.

In its majesty and strength it is itself a symbol of the majesty and strength of the law to which all alike, the judiciary, the Executive Government, Parliament, even the King himself, must bow. Above the main entrance you will not have failed to observe the emblem in sculptored stone: the Helmet of the armour of Faith, symbolical of the nation's fast faith in the justice and power of the law; the keys of Emancipation from Tyranny, where there is no law; and the Lamp and the Torches of Truth (De Villiers, 1930 SALJ).

At a bust-unveiling ceremony a short while afterwards Sir James Rose-Innes, then in his retirement after having served as Chief Justice for thirteen years, stated that the character, integrity and efficiency of its Judiciary were a priceless asset to any country, and especially a young nation such as South Africa. The confidence of all races and all sections of the people in the Bench was a sheet anchor, he declared, equipped with which the Ship of State could safely ride out storms which otherwise might overwhelm it, and people of all races realised that when a man took a seat on the Bench he stripped himself of all predilections and endeavoured only to do right to all manner of men according to law (1931 SALJ).

Other judges frequently made the point that the Judiciary stood aside from political questions and sought merely to carry out the law without fear or favour. It was claimed that in multi-racial South Africa legal positivism had rightly characterised judgements in matters of public law. Undoubtedly, this was how the judges themselves saw their role: Englishmen and Afrikaners, foreign-trained and home-educated, monarchists and republicans, liberals and conservatives, all worked together in pursuit of what they considered to be the law, a set of rules which they felt could be objectively ascertained by recognised juristic techniques in a politically neutral manner. A legal decision was to be arrived at purely by reference to established juridical criteria, which excluded all privately held political views or ethical beliefs. This has been an enduring tradition in South Africa, and when a Canadian jurist stated that South African judges in the 1950s had checked and delayed the government's apartheid programme (McWhinney), he was rebuked by the *South African Law Journal* for suggesting a policy behind what had simply been the dispassionate application of generally accepted rules. The *Journal* also criticised what it called the futile attempt to place judges in legal or political pigeonholes (1958).

Yet the various pronouncements of the Judiciary on questions of race have indicated that the positivist tradition in South Africa has in fact incorporated a number of different philosophical and sociological standpoints, and that the courts had on some occasions deliberately rejected the dominant racial attitudes of white South Africans, while at other times they had consciously accommodated themselves to such attitudes, even when not compelled by statute to do so. The range of judicial oscillation in this area has been narrow, since the dominance of Parliament over the courts has been accepted as clear constitutional doctrine. South Africa has had no Bill of Rights and save for clauses which entrenched language rights and the non-racial franchise in the Cape, any provision in the founding South Africa Act could be amended by a simple majority. Far from guaranteeing civic equality, this Act provided for an overwhelmingly white electorate and expressly restricted membership of Parliament to white persons only. The courts did not challenge their submission to Parliament: as one Chief Justice put it, Parliament could make any encroachment it chose on the life, liberty or property of any individual subject to its sway, and it was the function of the courts to enforce its will.[9] Nevertheless there was a narrow but not unimportant field in which the courts could influence the character of public life, primarily by their control over the way statutes were implemented. The courts were frequently called upon to interpret ambiguous provisions in racially differential statutes, and to review the regulations of statutory bodies and the actions of administrative officials. There was also an area of common law unaffected by statute where the courts had to consider whether or not the question of race had any legal relevance in itself. Finally, judges and magistrates often made remarks, both on and off the Bench, which indicated their general attitudes to race and revealed how thinking along racial lines influenced their judicial behaviour.

JUDICIAL ATTITUDES TO RACE

The new Appeal Court was soon confronted with a question in which racial attitudes were crucial. In 1905 the Cape Parliament had for the first time provided that special schools should be established which by law were to be restricted to children of "European parentage or extraction or descent". A white man married to a woman whose father

[9] *R. v. Sachs*, 1943 AD, 11 (Stratford).

was white and mother was not, entered his children at such a school, but after complaints from other parents, the School Board ordered his children to leave. He contended that he was obliged to pay rates towards the school, that no other school in the district existed for his children, and that since three out of their four grandparents were of European extraction they should themselves be classified as such and readmitted to the school. His counsel was W. Schreiner, leader of the Cape Bar and former Cape Prime Minister, who stressed the far-reaching consequences of the School Board's decision, and emphasised that the statute nowhere referred to colour but only to origin. The Appeal Court, however, unanimously rejected the application, and in their reasoning revealed how sensitive they were to dominant white attitudes in the country.[10] Chief Justice de Villiers conceded that the statute nowhere mentioned colour, but said that the Court could not ignore the universal meaning attached to the term 'European' in South Africa, according to which a white citizen of the United States who had never been to Europe was a European, whereas a black man born and bred in Europe was other than a European. In construing a vague expression in a statute, he said, the Court should place itself as far as possible in the position of the authors.

> As a matter of public history we know that the first civilised legislators in South Africa came from Holland and regarded the aboriginal natives of the country as belonging to an inferior race. . . . Believing as these whites did that intimacy with the black (slaves) or yellow races would lower the whites without raising the supposed inferior races in the scale of civilisation they condemned intermarriage or illicit intercourse between persons of the two races. Unfortunately the practice of many white men has often been inconsistent with that belief, but the vast majority of Europeans have always condemned such unions. . . . These prepossessions, or as many might term them, these prejudices, have never died out. . . . We may not from a philosophical or humanitarian point of view be able to approve this prevalent sentiment, but we cannot as judges . . . ignore the reasons which induced the legislature to adopt the policy of separate education. . . . It is regrettable that there should be this social chasm, but undoubtedly it exists. . . . It is fortunately unnecessary to decide how far back in a person's pedigree it would be allowable to go in order to decide whether his European extraction is unmixed.

[10] *Moller v. Keimoes School Committee*, 1911 AD, 635.

It may be mentioned in passing that de Villiers's comments must have been read with a strong feeling of irony by many coloured people in the Cape, who were convinced that along with a number of Cabinet Ministers, de Villiers himself was not of European descent in the meaning he gave to the phrase. Judge Innes said that the court could not be influenced by the social and political consequences of a decision adverse to the applicant. The question was whether the expression 'of European extraction' meant wholly of European extraction or partly of European extraction. In his view the former was the natural meaning of the term, and in any event if one looked at the defect which the legislation was intended to remedy, it was clearly to prevent white and coloured children from associating in school. Whether the policy was wise or whether it could be effectually carried out were points on which it was not desirable to express an opnion; but clearly it could inflict great hardship on deserving members of the community, and he wished to express his individual view that the machinery for the education of children of other than European extraction seemed inadequate.

The third judge (Laurence), who had been co-opted to the court from the Cape, stressed that restrictive or disabling provisions should be construed in a liberal spirit, but that the logical effect of the applicant's contention was that children with any amount of white blood should be admitted to public schools. "It seems obvious that any attempt to carry out such a theory, bringing together pupils of all shades, would in the present state of our Society, disorganise the whole system and render it practically impossible for the educational authority to perform its statutory duties." He regretted the hardships to persons like the applicant, but only the Legislature could resolve them.

The word European as commonly used in South Africa, said the fourth judge, Japie de Villiers of the Transvaal, had no geographical meaning. Apart from the races inhabiting the continent of Europe it included an American, a Canadian, an Australian, a New Zealander and a South African. Admittedly, the term was often used in contrast with Asiatics, but even then the Jew was considered to be a European while a Turk was an Asiatic. "Although colour is not the only it is usually the chief factor in determining whether a particular person is of European descent or not. But other traits such as type of feature, hair, etc., cannot be ignored." In his view the meaning of the Act was plain.

Judge Kotze, now back on the Bench after some years in the wilderness, agreed that the statute was plain and unambiguous–the word

European meant pure European. The affidavits showed that the admission of the children to the European school would be most disastrous so far as the interests of the school were concerned. "A certain amount of sympathy must naturally be felt for the innocent children, but the appellant has no one but himself to blame in this matter. It is true he married his wife before the Act was passed, yet he could hardly have been ignorant of the conditions of life and of race existing in a country like South Africa." He agreed that the prejudice of a section of the community should not be adopted as indicative of the law, but said this proposition carried the matter no further.

From the above it can be seen that some of the judges found the crucial phrase to be ambiguous, others found it to be plain; most sympathised with the applicant, but one felt that he had only himself to blame. Yet what underlay all the judgements was acceptance of the social reality of race differentiation and an acknowledgement that the purpose of the legislation, though not expressly stated, was to prevent any mixing in a public amenity between children generally accepted as white and those generally accepted as coloured. The judges could in fact have found for the applicant without in any way straining the language of the section. Had they adopted the test of 'preponderance of blood', which was used several decades later by the Appeal Court in determining whether or not a person was 'of aboriginal descent', the application would have succeeded, since three out of four of the children's grandparents were 'of European descent'. It was thus the Court and not the Legislature which imported the element of colour into the matter.

A similar style of reasoning was adopted in a case heard two years later, in which the Appeal Court had to decide whether Syrians were debarred from owning property in the Transvaal by the terms of a statute which discriminated against persons "belonging to one of the native races of Asia, including the so-called Coolies, Arabs, Malays and Mohammedan subjects of the Turkish Empire".[11] Overruling the decision of the lower court, the Judges of Appeal held that the phrase 'native races' was intended to be confined to coloured native races; Syrians, though natives of Asia, belonged to a white race and were accordingly not excluded from owning property. The Chief Justice stated that the whole tenor of laws relating to locations was such that the Legislature would have been horrified at the idea of confining white men, even if they came from Asia Minor, in locations like those set

[11] *Gandur* v. *Rand Townships Registrar*, 1913 AD, 250.

aside for other Asiatics. Innes, in concurring, said that if the word 'native' was not confined to coloured races, even a Jew from Palestine would be liable to be relegated to a location, compelled to carry a permit and subjected to other stringent restrictions.

Lord de Villiers died in 1914, having been Chief Justice, first in the Cape then in South Africa, for nearly forty years. His successor was Sir James Rose-Innes, who presided over the Appeal Court for thirteen years before retiring in order to make way for his close friend and colleague, Sir William Solomon. Innes has been honoured by lawyers in South Africa primarily because of his contribution to the development of Roman-Dutch law, and many persons regard him in this respect as the greatest judge South Africa ever produced. Yet he was Chief Justice at a time of war, rebellion and insurrection, and delivered a number of strong judgements on questions of public law, though relatively few which dealt directly with matters of race. Before his elevation to the Bench, Innes had been well known as a liberal in Cape politics, and after his retirement he spoke out strongly against attempts to deprive Africans of their limited franchise rights in the Cape. His dismay at the increasing racism of public life in South Africa was matched by his horror of racism in Nazi Germany, where his grandson, Helmut von Moltke, also a lawyer trained in the English tradition, was to play a leading role in the anti-Hitler opposition. Even while Chief Justice, Innes found occasion to make his liberal views known. In an address reported in the *Law Journal* in 1924 to mark the unveiling of a bust of W. Schreiner, he spoke in moving terms of the vision and honesty of Schreiner and his sister Olive, the famous novelist. "They belonged to that band of men and women," he declared "who had consistently maintained that racial problems can never be satisfactorily solved on lines of oppression and injustice, and that a policy which is morally wrong can never be politically right. Such persons are sometimes called cranks and visionaries by those who are irritated by their idealism, but . . . those men and women are the salt of our public and social life."

On the Bench, however, Innes stuck more rigidly than most to what he regarded as his duty in carrying out the law regardless of his personal feelings. His extra-curial statements were not repeated in court, though they did help to maintain a liberal tradition in the legal profession, which to some extent was reflected in the judgements of a later generation of Appeal Court members. In constitutional matters, Innes stressed that the courts would come to the aid of any person, whether high or low, who was injured other than by the due process of law; but where the jurisdiction of the courts was excluded, either by the clear terms of a statute or by the operation of martial law, he accepted such limitations though not without expressing disapproval.[12]

In two matters concerning disabilities imposed on South Africans of Indian descent, Innes found himself siding with the section of a divided court that favoured the construction more favourable to the Indians.[13] In the one case, the Minister of the Interior had issued a notice declaring all Indians to be prohibited immigrants 'on economic grounds'. Innes and Kotze held that the Minister's notice was invalid because it applied what was in fact a racial rather than an economic test. The majority of the court held, however, that in view of the peculiar economic conditions in the country, the Minister's opinion that Asiatics as a class were unsuited on economic grounds to the requirements of the country, was not so unreasonable as to be invalid; they also held that the expression 'Asiatic person' in the notice was intended to include only members of the coloured races of Asia. In the second matter Innes was part of the majority which held that a company had a legal personality that existed quite apart from its shareholders and directors, so that a company could not be classified as an Asiatic even if its shareholders and directors were of Asian descent.

In general, Innes was not given to making cultural generalisations about population groups, but when it came to the question of liquor he abandoned his normal restraint. Like many liberals of all racial groups, he supported withholding supplies of liquor from Africans on temperance grounds, and as Attorney-General in the Cape he had sponsored a prohibition law operating on a racial basis, which had become known as the Innes Act. In fact the enforcement of the liquor laws by means of police raids, fines and imprisonment, was to add to rather than diminish the hardship caused by drink. In an Appeal Court judgement, Innes stated that a reference to the tribes and groups referred to in the relevant statute made it clear that the intention behind the law was that liquor should not be made available to "a section of the community who from want of training and civilisation were unable to refrain from excess".[14]

[12] Cf. *Shidiak v. Union Govt.*, 1912 AD, 642 at 643; *R. v. Fakir*, 1923 AD, 46; *Krohn v. Minister of Defence*, 1915 AD, 196.

[13] *R. v. Padsha*, 1923 AD, 281; see 1927 SALJ, p. 17; *Dadoo v. Krugersdorp Municipality*, 1920 AD, 530.

[14] *R. v. Kogan*, 1918 AD, 521.

After Innes's retirement, Chief Justices came and went with great rapidity, since they were chosen on a basis of seniority in the Appeal Court, and like all other judges, had to retire on reaching the age of 70. In the 1930s, veterans of the Anglo-Boer War period were joined by a new generation of judges, most of whom had distinguished themselves as accomplished legal technicians at the Cape and Transvaal Bars, rather than as lawyer-politicians of the old type. When two semi-retired Nationalist Party leaders were appointed directly to the Appeal Court, considerable dissatisfaction was expressed in legal circles. One of these men soon resigned to re-enter the political arena (Tielman Roos), while the other made his mark not so much by the quality of his judgements as by being the first South African judge after Union to write his judgements in Afrikaans (Beyers, in 1932).

The question of whether local authorities could impose segregation without express authority from Parliament only reached the Appeal Court in 1934. The Provincial Divisions of the Supreme Court had for a number of years dealt with the question, generally on the basis that differentiation authorised by an Act of Parliament was valid but differentiation not so authorised was invalid. In this respect, the courts followed a well-known English case of the end of the nineteenth century,[15] and may be said to have adopted a viewpoint considerably more liberal than that held by the bulk of white legislators and administrators in South Africa. Thus the Transvaal Division of the Supreme Court declared invalid regulations which penalised coloured persons for walking on the pavements, as it did regulations which prohibited coloured persons from riding in trams and regulations restricting skilled jobs to white persons only.[16] In this last case, the regulations were declared *ultra vires* by the very judge who had drafted them, on the grounds that he could not imagine greater unreasonableness! These three sets of regulations all fell within the category of differentiation coupled with total exclusion, but the judges accepted that 'class discrimination' in itself was unlawful in the absence of express authority. In the Cape, the Supreme Court held that the reservation of a bathing place for whites only was *ultra vires* even if another swimming place was available for coloured persons.[17] Thus by the time the matter was

---

[15] *Kruse* v. *Johnson*, [1898] 2 Queen's Bench, p. 91 at 99.

[16] *Mphahlele* v. *Springs Municipality*, 1928 SALJ, 142; *Williams and Adendorff* v. *Johannesburg Municipality*, 1915 TPD, 106; *R.* v. *Hildick-Smith*, 1924 TPD, 69; see too 1936 SALJ, 447.

[17] *R.* v. *Plaatjes*, 1910 EDL, 63.

raised in the Appeal Court, the balance of authority in the Provincial Divisions was in favour of striking down unauthorised discrimination as being in itself unlawful, whether or not coupled with inequality. The Appeal Court, however, overruled these decisions, expressing a variety of social philosophies in so doing.

The test case considered by the Appeal Court arose out of a direction by the Postmaster-General that post offices in the Transvaal be segregated along colour lines. An Indian who was refused service at a 'whites only' section of a post office, applied to court for an order declaring the direction invalid, on the grounds that the statute which gave the Postmaster-General his powers did not authorise him to impose differentiation on racial grounds. The Transvaal Supreme Court upheld the application, but the Appeal Court, by a majority of three judges to one, overruled the lower court's decision and declared the direction to be valid.[18]

Two of the Appeal Court judges held that the mere fact of differentiation on the grounds of race, colour or religion would not serve to invalidate an instruction or by-law, in the absence of proof by whoever chose to object, that the discrimination was coupled with an inequality. Acting Chief Justice Stratford, who before his elevation to the Bench had been regarded as the most outstanding barrister in the Transvaal, said that it ran counter to principle and common sense to suggest that a by-law was invalid purely because it divided the community into White and Coloured.

> The division must not be absurd or obviously designed to serve no useful purpose, as for example a classification depending on the colour of one's hair. . . . But a division of the community on differences of race or language for the purposes of postal services seems, *prima facie*, to be sensible and make for the convenience and comfort of the public as a whole, since the appropriate officials conversant with the customs, requirements and language of each section will conceivably serve the respective sections.

A similar line of reasoning was adopted by Judge Etienne de Villiers, a former member of the Cape Bar for whom politics were said simply not to exist. In his view, discrimination *per se* was not unreasonable on the mere ground of being made on lines of race or colour, no more than a discrimination on the grounds of initial letters of names would be unreasonable. Only when a discrimination was coupled with inequality

[18] *Minister of Posts and Telegraphs* v. *Rassool*, 1934 AD, 167.

would it be unreasonable. Alternatively discrimination even though coupled with equality could be *ultra vires* if it were gratuitous, "for instance . . . instructions that all persons with blue eyes should do their postal business in one building and all other persons in another building. . . ." Such instructions would involve a gratuitous and oppressive interference with the rights of those subject to it. The position was quite otherwise in the case of discrimination on the grounds of initial letters of names or on the grounds of race or colour, "for many reasons may be conceived upon which such discriminations might justly and reasonably be made".

The other two judges adopted quite different approaches to the matter. Judge Beyers, the former Nationalist Party Cabinet Minister and pioneer of Afrikaans, expressly doubted whether the principle of equality before the law had any application in the Transvaal, which, like the Orange Free State, had known a long historical division between Europeans and non-Europeans. Legislation applicable to the Transvaal should be construed with this in mind, he said.

> The statement that all are equal in the eyes of the law cannot be unreservedly accepted. It is undoubtedly subject to considerable qualification; and as far as the Transvaal is concerned, it is a fact that Europeans and non-Europeans were never equal in the eyes of the law. Segregation runs right through our society in the Union, for example, hospitals, burial grounds, public baths and facilities, playgrounds, trams and countless other examples could be given. . . . Classification is also a marked feature of our society, e.g. smokers and non-smokers, men and women, adults and children.

He was not prepared to accept that discrimination could rest only upon express authorisation or necessary implication. Accordingly, he too felt the appeal should succeed and the validity of post office separation upheld.

The fourth and only dissenting judge (Gardiner) was a former Attorney-General at the Cape and co-author of the country's leading textbook on criminal law. The son of a bank manager, he had been an enthusiastic agitator for international socialism in his student days at Oxford, and at the Cape Bar had a reputation for championing lost causes, sympathising with the oppressed and criticising conventional policies. In his view the history of statutory discrimination created one status for the European, another and inferior status for the Asiatic, and another and more inferior status for the native. A part of a man's status was his *dignitas*, which varied with his status. *Dignitas* derived from the inborn right of every person to enjoy tranquil peace of mind, secure against degrading and humiliating treatment; it carried a corresponding obligation on others to refrain from assailing that right.

> To my mind this relegation of Indians to a non-European counter is humiliating treatment. Lord de Villiers . . . declined to ignore the colour prepossession or prejudice which exists in South Africa, and I cannot shut my eyes to the fact that the instruction in question is actuated by the circumstances that a large number of Europeans object to being brought into contact in public offices with non-Europeans, and that they regard the latter as being of a lower order of civilisation.

The argument that separation could be justified by language convenience had not been advanced by the Postmaster-General himself, and could not have been, because it was far more likely that an Indian would be understood at a counter where English or Afrikaans was spoken than at one where a Bantu language was used. The same applied to an African if the clerk were chosen because of his familiarity with Indian languages.

> In view of the prevalent feeling as to colour, in view of the numerous statutes treating non-Europeans as belonging to an inferior order of civilisation, any fresh classification on colour lines can . . . be interpreted only as a fresh instance of relegation of Asiatics and natives to a lower order, and this I consider humiliating treatment. Such treatment is an impairment of the *dignitas* of the person affected, and it is the Legislature only that can cause that impairment.

He quoted cases from the Cape, Natal and the Transvaal which held that race distinction *per se*, apart from inequality, was invalid, and concluded by expressing his satisfaction that his view was in accordance with what had hitherto been the trend of judicial opinion in South Africa.

A contributor to the *Law Journal* criticised the majority view in this case, and especially the contention that discrimination against persons with blue eyes or brown hair would be gratuitous and invalid whereas discrimination on grounds of race was not unreasonable and therefore not invalid (1936). He pointed out that had the two senior judges of the Court (Wessels and Curlewis) not been absent, the result would probably have been different, since in their days as judges in the Transvaal they had consistently held that race differentiation *per se* was unreasonable unless expressly authorised. Nevertheless, he accepted that the majority view was binding and must be taken to set out the law.

The doctrine of 'separate but equal', or, as it was sometimes expressed, separate but not substantially unequal, was thereafter followed by the courts in a number of cases, the main juristic problem being to determine what was substantially unequal in any particular case. When the Nationalist Government under Dr Malan came to power in 1948 it intensified segregation measures, particularly in the Cape where they had previously not been so rigidly applied, and this led to extensive counteraction in the form of civil disobedience. The civil disobedience campaigns in turn produced a number of prosecutions, which prompted the accused to challenge the quality of facilities made available to them. The law reports for that period contain a number of cases in which the courts reaffirmed the 'separate but equal' doctrine, the leading one being a decision by the Appeal Court that railway regulations which provided the same number of coaches for white and black, but penalised blacks for entering white coaches and not *vice versa*, were invalid, because their effect was to allow whites the run of the whole train whereas blacks were confined to half the train. The Natal Supreme Court, on the other hand, held that the provision in a bus of soft seats for whites and hard seats for blacks did not constitute sufficient inequality to render the demarcation invalid.[19]

One important consequence of these court cases was the enactment by Parliament of the Reservation of Separate Amenities Act, 1953, which expressly and in general terms authorised persons in charge of public amenities to reserve such amenities wholly or partially for members of any race. The effect of this Act was to give blanket authority for the provision of separate and unequal facilities. Thus at a time when the United States Supreme Court was about to strike down the 'separate but equal' doctrine as invalid, the South African Parliament entrenched not only separation but inequality. South African law had accordingly moved in the opposite direction to that followed by American law. In the early part of the century, South African law was the more 'liberal', in the sense that it forbade the provision of segregated facilities unless expressly authorised by an Act of Parliament. Later both South African law and American law accepted the doctrine of 'separate but equal'. Finally, both systems moved away from that doctrine, the American towards non-differentiation, and the South African towards separate but unequal.

[19] R. v. *Abdurahman*, 1950 (3) SA, 126 (AD); R. v. *Mozumba*, 1953 (1), 235; R. v. *Zihlangu*, 1953 (3) SA, 871; R. v. *Lusu*, 1953 (2) SA 484; R. v. *Lepile*, 1953 (1) SA, 225. See too R. v. *Carelse*, 1943 CPD, 242.

The Reservation of Separate Amenities Act applied to public amenities, but left the common law untouched with regard to administrative actions not relating to public amenities. Thus the question arose as to whether licensing boards could be influenced by racial factors in the issuing of licences, and the Appeal Court held that discrimination to a substantial degree in this field was invalid.[20] The question flowed from the refusal of a Road Transportation Board to issue a licence to an Indian taxi driver to carry white passengers. The Transvaal Supreme Court upheld the action of the Board, stating that what the courts of one country would regard as unreasonable was not necessarily what the courts of another country would so regard. "Conditions may be different and public opinion is not necessarily the same in all countries." On appeal, Chief Justice Centlivres said he could not understand the reference to public opinion. "I do not see how public opinion is relevant to the subject under enquiry," he stated, "nor do I see, if it were relevant, how the court is to ascertain the opinion of the public which consists of Europeans and non-Europeans."

The question of the courts and public opinion was soon to arise again in the famous Coloured Voters' cases, which led to a constitutional conflict between the Appeal Court and Parliament.[21] The issue was whether Parliament, now completely sovereign, was still bound by the entrenched clauses of the South Africa Act which provided that coloured voters in the Cape could not be removed from the common voters' roll except by a two-thirds majority of both Houses of Parliament in a joint sitting. The Government claimed that Parliament as the voice of the electorate was supreme and could by a simple majority repeal any law, including the South Africa Act. A coloured man who objected to being placed on a separate voters' roll contended that the 'entrenched clauses' were still binding, and the matter eventually reached the Court of Appeal.

The five Appeal Court judges and one additional Judge of Appeal at the time were diverse in background, training and political inclinations. Chief Justice Centlivres was a conservative liberal from the Cape Bar, who was not particularly active in politics before he became a judge but who on his retirement was to be a vigorous critic of the effects of apartheid on the Rule of Law. Judge Fagan had been more politically engaged in the Cape, generally in the ranks of Afrikaner Nationalists,

[20] *Tayob* v. *Ermelo Road Transportation Board*, 1951 (4) SA, 440 (AD), Centlivres at p. 446. See 1952 SALJ, 16.

[21] *Harris* v. *The Minister of the Interior*, 1952 (2) SA, 428 (AD).

though later he broadened the range of his political activities. Judge O. D. Schreiner, the son of W. Schreiner, had during his years of practice at the Johannesburg Bar been a supporter of liberal causes, while Judge Greenberg, the only Jew to sit in the Appeal Court, also came from the Transvaal where he had shown himself to be rather more conservative. Judges Hoexter and van den Heever were both Orange Free State men; van den Heever was a well-known Afrikaans-language poet, who had been a government law adviser under the first Nationalist Government, and who sometimes wrote his judgements in Afrikaans and often resuscitated old Roman-Dutch authorities so as to avoid reference to English law.

Had the voting been on strictly party lines, the Court might have divided three to two against the Government, but in fact it was unanimous in holding that the entrenched clauses of the South Africa Act were still valid. It also rejected a subsidiary argument advanced on behalf of the Government that the coloured voters on the separate roll would have more rights than they had had on a common voters' roll. The Chief Justice, in whose judgement the other judges concurred, declared that the entrenched clause contained a guarantee of defined rights, not of their equivalent; "the argument suggests that a spoliator may deprive me of my property if he is prepared to give something of equal or greater value in return."

When Parliament thereafter constituted itself into a High Court of Parliament with power to overrule decisions of the Appeal Court on constitutional matters the Appeal Court again unanimously rejected this as a device to by-pass the entrenched clauses, and stated that the High Court of Parliament was no court at all, but a legislative body.[22] At this stage the sharpest critic of the Government's legal manoeuvres and the strongest defender of the independence of the judiciary was Judge van den Heever, who on any simplistic view of the correlation between past political and current judicial behaviour should have been the most sympathetic to the Government.

The Appeal Court's firm stand in defence of its limited testing right gained it an international repute but hastened its demise as a small body of venerated jurists. The Government not only enlarged the Senate so as to give itself the required two-thirds majority, but also enlarged the Appeal Court to eleven judges, all of whom were obliged to sit in any constitutional matter. This gave rise to the jibe that having failed to turn Parliament into a court, the Government was now seeking to turn

[22] *Minister of Interior* v. *Harris*, 1952 (4) SA, 769 (AD).

the Court into a Parliament. In the event, the required two-thirds majority was obtained for the removal of coloured voters from the common roll, and the Appeal Court held by ten votes to one that the enlargement of the Senate did not vitiate the procedure; Schreiner was the sole dissentient.[23]

The enlargement of the Appeal Court was seen by some critics as a packing, and by others as a dilution of the Bench, but on any view it changed the complexion of the Court and introduced to it a number of persons whose thinking on constitutional, race and security matters was closer to that of the Government. When Centlivres retired as Chief Justice, Schreiner was passed over as his successor, and eventually in 1959 one of the new and relatively inexperienced judges, L. C. Steyn, was appointed as head of the Court. Eight years earlier, Judge Steyn had been appointed to the Transvaal Bench straight from his position as Government law adviser, and the Johannesburg Bar had been so incensed that it had organised a temporary boycott of his court sittings. His rapid judicial advancement made him Chief Justice at a relatively young age, so that he has had a longer time than any other Chief Justice except Innes to make his influence felt on the Court. The author of the first legal textbook to be published in Afrikaans (1946), he had long criticised the undue influence which he believed English law had had on Roman-Dutch law in South Africa, and the impact of his stewardship of the Court was felt in the field of private rather than of public law. The strongest criticisms of the Court under his leadership have been that it has neglected considerations of social utility, carried jurisprudential worship of authority and purity of descent to an extreme, and been unduly executive-minded in questions involving fundamental issues of civil liberties. Relatively little has been written about the Court's stand in racial matters, though it has delivered judgements in at least two matters bearing directly on the question of race differentiation.

In the one case, an African attorney's clerk appealed against a sentence for contempt of court imposed on him by a magistrate after he had refused to obey the magistrate's directive that he seat himself at a segregated table.[24] The clerk had wished to address the magistrate on the legality of the order from the formerly unsegregated table, and the Appeal Court held that in insisting on arguing from his customary position, the clerk had committed contempt of court. Chief Justice

[23] *Collins* v. *Minister of Interior*, 1957 (1) SA, 552 (AD).

[24] *R.* v. *Pitje*, 1960 (4) SA, 709. See criticism in 1961 SALJ, 152.

Steyn said that the magistrate's order, although not actually promulgated in terms of the Reservation of Separate Amenities Act, was nevertheless consistent with the spirit of the Act, and that the clerk could have been as well seated at the one table as at another. Segregation in the courts was in fact so thorough that a visiting Chief Justice from New Zealand was led to observe that he could hardly see the purpose of separate witness boxes for whites and blacks, since only one witness could testify at a time (Wild, 1971).

If this case demonstrated the Court's support for apartheid in the court-room, the other case showed its support for apartheid in the social field. The latter case was especially significant because it established that the Court was willing in certain circumstances to support the doctrine of 'separate but unequal' even when it was not obliged by the Reservation of Separate Amenities Act to do so. In terms of the Group Areas Act, 1950, as amended, the Government was empowered to issue proclamations setting aside areas of land for occupation and ownership by specified racial groups, and disaqualifying members of other racial groups from living or owning property there. One such proclamation was challenged on the basis that it discriminated in gross fashion against Indians and in favour of whites. This challenge was excepted to in the Natal Supreme Court on the grounds that it could not be the foundation of a legal action, even if true in fact. The Natal Supreme Court rejected the exception and held that proof of substantial inequality would invalidate the proclamation. The matter was taken on appeal, and the Appeal Court reversed the lower court's decision, and held that substantial inequality could not invalidate the proclamation.[25] The Appeal Court reiterated support for the principle that the power to discriminate with substantial inequality would not be attributed to the Government unless the relevant statute gave it expressly or by necessary implication.

> No such power is given in the Group Areas Act, but it seems ... to be clearly implied. The Groups Areas Act represents a colossal social experiment and a long term policy. It necessarily involves the movement out of Group Areas of numbers of people throughout the country. Parliament must have envisaged that compulsory population shifts of persons occupying certain areas would inevitably cause disruption, and within the foreseeable future, substantial inequalities. Whether all this will ultimately prove to be for the common weal of all is not for the court to decide.

[25] *Minister of Interior* v. *Lock hat,* 1961 (2) SA, 587 (AD).

The underlying premise of this judgement, which was a unanimous one of the Court, was that the judges should apply a benevolent rather than a critical scrutiny to a measure which involved wholesale interference with existing rights. From one point of view it may even be argued that the inequality was condoned precisely because it was so substantial, and accordingly could be justified as falling within the expression 'a colossal social experiment'. This case may be regarded as representing the highwater-mark of judicial support for segregation coupled with inequality, and is in keeping with the long-term trend which has been away from the English common law doctrine of assumed equality towards an acceptance of race discrimination, not merely as something harmless and neutral, but as something positively beneficial. This later position is not an unrealistic one for the courts to adopt, inasmuch as it attributes to an all-white Legislature the intention that it wishes to promote the interests of an all-white electorate; it does, however, diminish the role of the courts as self-constituted upper guardians of the large section of the population unrepresented in the Legislature. The earlier approach of declaring *ultra vires* unauthorised discrimination, was based on English legal doctrine which might have had some basis of fact in England but was largely fictional in South Africa. Adherence by the South African judiciary to this doctrine, however, was not due merely to slavish acceptance of English precedent, but to a desire on the part of the South African courts to play the role of "striking a balance between the interests of all sections of the population". The decision in the Group Areas Act case, therefore, marked a movement towards greater harmonisation than hitherto between the racial policy of the Legislature and the racial attitudes of the judiciary.

This development has not meant that the judges are no longer willing under any circumstances to interpose themselves between the administration and the victims of differential legislation. In a recent address to students, a Cape judge said that in the case of controversial political legislation the courts frequently had to deal with cases of hardship. "The rules of interpretation are elastic," he commented, "one sugars the pill, one says politely that Parliament could never have intended to create an injustice of that nature. What is the result? The Act goes back to Parliament, and Parliament and the Bench become involved in a sort of legal ping-pong. In the next session Parliament patches up the loopholes and fills the gaps" (Diemont). This legal ping-pong has in fact been played in relation to a number of statutes, particularly those which purport to define what a 'white man' actually is; the Legislature may lose a few points, but it always wins the game.

The Transvaal Court thus held in 1967 that an order requiring an Indian to remove to a Group Area in which no accommodation was available to him was unreasonable and therefore invalid,[26] and both the Transvaal and the Cape Courts, more especially the latter, have leaned heavily in favour of constructions favouring individuals adversely affected by the Population Registration Act, 1950. The principles of statutory interpretation have thus been applied in such a way that the courts have been more willing to help individuals than communities. A cynic may well amend the maxim to read *De maximis non curat lex*. Thus the Appeal Court rejected an argument that a Group Areas Proclamation was void for vagueness because, according to the uncontradicted evidence of a social anthropologist, its definition of 'Indian' made no sense scientifically and was an unsafe description of any individual or group ("member of a race or tribe whose national home was in India or Pakistan"). The Court held that the definition substantially reflected conventional language and would be reasonably clear to the ordinary citizen affected by it.[27]

The concept of the 'colossal social experiment' has subsequently been used to justify massive discrimination, such as the setting aside of all the beaches in a particular area of Natal for whites only. An Indian who was convicted of going on to one of these beaches in order to swim in the Indian Ocean, appealed to the Natal Supreme Court, which upheld his conviction, observing that South Africa had a long coastline, and that the particular allocations complained of had to be seen as part of a colossal social experiment which might, unfortunately, lead to substantial immediate inequality.[28] The charge sheet in the above-mentioned matter gives a good indication of how strong the legal underpinning of race discrimination has been, and refutes the notion that the mere observance of legal forms in itself provides some guarantee of equality. The charge alleged that the accused was guilty of

> contravention of regulation 19(a) read with regulations 18(b) and 23 of the regulations made by the Minister of Lands published on 2nd February, 1962, in Government Gazette No. 169 under Notice No. R. 168, further read with Government Notice No. 1090 dated 6th July, 1962, published in Government Gazette No. 285 of 1962,

[26] *S. v. Variawa*, 1968 (1) SA, 711 (T).
[27] *S. v. Bhoolia and another*, 1970 (4) SA, 692 (AD).
[28] *S. v. Naicker*, 1963 (4) SA, 610 (N). Per Kennedy, J.

further read with Provincial Notice No. 37 of 1946, dated 1st August 1946, such regulations being made under section 10(1) of the Sea-shore Act, No. 21 of 1935, as amended, and as read with regulation 424 of Government Notice No. 201 published in the Government Gazette of 16th March, 1962.

The judge commented adversely on the 'bewildering array of references' which were used to indicate to the accused that as an Indian man he was prohibited from entering a beach reserved for Europeans, but leaned in favour of an approach to the regulations which upheld their validity.

The above discussion of the case-law and of judicial attitudes should not detract from the fact that in South Africa it has been the Legislature rather than the judiciary which has been primarily responsible for giving the force of law to race discrimination. The role of the courts in maintaining race domination will be discussed in a different context at a later stage, but some attention should first be given to the attitudes of the courts to race in matters where questions of public law were not involved.

In theory South African jurisprudence has had an integrated character in the sense that, save where statute provided otherwise, the law imposed the same duties on and required the same standards of conduct of all South Africans, whether rich or poor, black or white. Limited recognition was given by statute to African customary law in matters where Africans were the only litigants, but otherwise the principles of civil and criminal law applied equally to all inhabitants of the country. Whether or not this equality was achieved in practice has been a matter of dispute. The great wealth differentials between white and black and the very limited character of legal aid in themselves reduced the opportunities for the poorer and darker sections of the community to avail themselves of what rights existed for them. Defenders of the South African legal system have maintained that within the limitations imposed by statute and by poverty, the courts have meted out a fair measure of justice to all litigants and accused, irrespective of race; critics have alleged that the prejudices which affected social life generally operated, even if in modified form, in the judicial arena as well. The present discussion will concentrate largely on the official judicial attitudes to race, though some attention will be paid to whether or not in practice formal equality has given way to actual differentiation.

In the field of civil law, the most important example of the courts' stand in favour of equality has been in relation to the assessment of damages for pain and suffering for personal injuries received. In a Supreme Court trial heard in the Transvaal in 1948, the judge awarded an African £16 damages for pain and suffering after he had been shot in the penis by the (white) defendant. The judge stated that he would certainly not award the African plaintiff the same amount for pain and suffering that he would have awarded for the same pain and suffering to a person who had had more culture. Thus he would award a far larger sum of damages in the case of an injury to a 'European woman' than he would to a 'native male'. The Appeal Court emphatically rejected this line of reasoning, and said that the assessment of pain and suffering could not be determined by whether or not the injured person was rich or poor, and most certainly not by reference to his race.[29] In raising the award to £200 and granting the appellant costs on the highest scale, the Court stated that the fact that he was an African earning only £2 per week was not evidence that he was insensitive to pain.

For African litigants the consequences of this judgement were considerable, since almost the only cases in which Africans appeared in the ordinary courts as plaintiffs in private law matters were those that resulted from personal injuries received by them. Occasionally such cases flowed from assaults, but usually they arose out of running-down cases. The existence of compulsory third party insurance in respect of all motor vehicles meant that African pedestrians, cyclists and motorists frequently brought actions against insurace companies for injuries received at the hands of negligent motorists, and the assertion of a non-racial judicial attitude towards pain and suffering meant that such Africans could acquire a capital sum through being knocked down which they could never have accumulated through a lifetime of toil.

The question of whether a man's race was part of his good reputation for the purposes of defamation actions caused South African courts considerable difficulty. There do not appear to have been any cases in which dark-skinned persons have claimed damages for being called 'coloured', 'African', 'coolie', 'Kafir', 'black', 'Hottentot', 'Bushman' or any such name, or for being called 'white', but there were a number of cases in which white persons sought to protect their fair name against statements implying that they were not white. Thus the courts held that it was defamatory to call a white woman 'a white Kafir', and to call a white man a coloured man.[30] The allegation that a white farmer

---

[29] *Radebe* v. *Hough*, 1949 (1) SA, 380 at 385-6.

[30] *McDiarmid* v. *Spence*, 1909 EDC, 143; *Louw* v. *Kielblock*, 1911 CPD, 209.

was a Hottentot was held to be defamatory in its ordinary meaning without any special innuendo, and the court commented that there was an impairment of reputation when imputation was made of poverty, leprosy, bastardy or anything else which, according to the standards prevailing in the country, was calculated to bring a person into contempt, even though it might not reflect on his character. In another case an attorney who was called a 'messenger boy' claimed that these words meant that he was a youth or native or coloured person, and the court held on exception that the phrase was in fact capable of bearing these innuendoes and as such was actionable. Similarly a statement that a Labour Party candidate wished the electors to give their daughters' hands in marriage to coloured persons was held to be defamatory of him. On the other hand it was held not to be defamatory of a bus owner to say that he plied for hire amongst coloured persons.[31]

Thus until recently there was a considerable body of authority from the various Divisions of the Supreme Court in favour of the view that to call a white man coloured was in itself defamatory. The correctness of this view was, however, called into doubt by an *obiter dictum* of Judge Schreiner in the Appeal Court.[32] In Schreiner's opinion it was reasonable to suppose that to say of a person he was of a particular race would be defamatory of him, if in the circumstances he would be guilty of a crime or dishonourable conduct if he were of that race. Thus it might be defamatory of a coloured man to say that he was white if he was discovered having connection with a coloured woman, or if he were living in an area in which it would be a crime for him to live if he were white. Unless some such accusation could be inferred from the circumstances, however, he was not prepared without full argument to hold that to say of a white man that he was coloured was *per se* defamatory. Some support for Schreiner's viewpoint was offered in a recent case in which a white woman sued attorneys whose typist had inadvertently referred to her in a summons as a 'non-European female'. The plaintiff stated that after reading this description of herself she wept bitter tears for several nights, but the trial judge doubted whether her sorrow was genuine, and dismissed the claim on a technical point. The judge expressly left open the question whether calling a white person a

---

[31] *Pitout* v. *Rosenstein*, 1930, OPD, 112; *De Wet* v. *Morris*, 1934 SALJ, 269 (EDL); *Brill* v. *Madeley*, 1937 SALJ, 238; *Carelse* v. *van der Schyff*, 1928 SALJ, 101 (CPD).

[32] *Maskowitz* v. *Pienaar*, 1957 (4) SA, 195 (AD) at 197.

non-European was in itself actionable, but said that future would-be plaintiffs would do well to bear in mind Schreiner's *obiter dictum* before embarking on litigation.[33]

As far as land law is concerned, restrictions relative to race have mainly been imposed by statute, but restrictive covenants forbidding dark-skinned persons from acquiring title have frequently been inserted into title deeds and accepted as valid. In interpreting conditions in title deeds, the courts have taken cognisance of the fact that it is universal practice in South Africa for whites to employ African domestic servants, and that domestic service is only rarely performed by whites. In an early Natal case, residents in a 'white' suburb of Durban, successfully applied for an interdict restraining the erection of a hospital for Africans in their midst, one of the grounds being that such a hospital would cause their property to depreciate.[34]

It is generally claimed that in South African law racial factors play no part in determining whether or not at common law a criminal offence has been committed, though they might influence the question of punishment. The one recognised exception is, significantly, in the field of sexual crime, where it has been held that in regard to the offence of *crimen injuria* a difference in colour between the accused and the complainant may be sufficient in itself to convert a trifling *injuria* not in itself meriting punishment into a criminal offence. Thus an African domestic servant who had written to a young, unmarried white woman that he loved her and asked for a reply was held to have been correctly convicted, even though the same letter from a white person would not have been sufficient for a conviction.[35] Had the declaration of love been purely Platonic, the African would not have been convicted; had the advances taken the form of physical interference, then on that evidence a white man too would have been convicted.

In other cases, the courts have tended as a matter of principle to exclude racial factors from the determination of whether or not an offence has been committed. The standard of conduct required of all South Africans has been that of a 'reasonable man', to whom is attributed the general cultural beliefs of the white community. Thus a genuine belief in witchcraft, which in traditional African society might have excused the killing of a suspected witch, was held not to excuse

[33] *Taljaard* v. *Rosendorff and Venter*, 1970 (4) SA, 48 (O).
[34] *Norwood Land Co.* v. *North Eastern Districts Association*, 1929 AD, 32; *Epstein* v. *Avenstein*, 1942 WLD, 52; *Brown* v. *McCord*, 1907 SALJ, 320; 1908 SALJ, 78.
[35] *R.* v. *Olakwu*, 1958 (2) SA, 357 (c).

homicide in modern South African law, though it did reduce the gravity of the crime.[36] Similarly, the special customs of the San people, in terms of which a man was said to be justified in killing his wife's paramour, could not be pleaded as a defence in a murder trial, though they were accepted as providing extenuating circumstances.[37] When judicial officers took notice of what a writer on the law of evidence has called facts established only in racial mythology (Hoffmann), their convictions were frequently upset on appeal: for example, convictions were quashed on appeal when a trial judge said: "It is well known from the experience of this court that natives can and do recognise people they know in comparative darkness, which, for a European, would make recognition quite impossible," and when magistrates asserted without evidence that Africans could make definite identifications from spoor marks, that African women submitted to rape without protest, that African witnesses giving alibi evidence were generally liars, and that an African wife would not ordinarily support the evidence of her husband against that of her lover.[38]

The official judicial attitude with regard to the imposition of sentence has been not to differentiate on the grounds of race. Thus a judge criticised a magistrate who, after claiming that during prison inspection he had frequently watched the imposition of corporal punishment and noted what meagre effects it had on Africans, said that white standards of punishment could not be applied to Africans.[39] The judge stated that these observations were entirely without legislative, judicial, scientific or medical authority, and added: "No doubt some individuals are more sensitive than others to corporal punishment, whatever their race may be, but we cannot generalise and assume that one race is less sensitive than another. . . . The race or colour of the accused does not enter into the question in determining what number of strokes to inflict." The same judge, however, held some years later in a rape case that the fact that the accused was black and the complainant was white constituted an aggravating feature, since the shock to her would have

[36] *R. v. Mbombela*, 1933 AD, 269. More recently, however, the courts have moved towards a more subjective approach. *R. v. Mkize*, 1951 (3) SA, 28 (AD)– the love-philtre case.

[37] *R. v. Mukeirib*, 1938 SWA, 4 (applying the law of the Union in South West Africa), and *R. v. Kgau*, 1958 (2) SA, 606 (SW).

[38] *R. v. Tusini*, 1953 (4) 406 (AD); *R. v. Sitimela*, 1962 (4) SA, 60; *S. v. M.*, 1965 (4) SA, 577; *R. v. Mcunu*, 1938 NPD, 229; *R. v. Sihlani*, 1966 (3) SA, 148.

[39] *R. v. Maboko*, 1956 (3) SA, 144 (GWLD).

been all the greater and sentenced the African to death.[40] A colleague of his when sentencing a white man for raping a seven year old coloured girl, stated that peace in South Africa depended to a large extent on the men of each race not laying hand on the women of other races. He did not, however, impose the death sentence, but sentenced the accused to seventeen years imprisonment. Another judge from the same Division felt it to be a mitigating factor that a white man convicted of having sexual relations with a coloured woman, was a lavatory attendant occupying a low position in white society and therefore not possessed of the moral inhibitions or class and colour consciousness of better privileged whites.[41]

Sentencing policy has clearly been influenced by racial factors in regard to persons found illegally in possession of firearms.[42] Generally in regard to matters seen to be affecting the security of the white man, there is a considerable body of evidence supporting the contention that black murderers, rapists and rebels have been punished more severely than their white counterparts. The racial context has been all important: homicide, rape and rebellion by blacks have been treated more severely when across the colour line than when within the same racial group. The figures for executions establish clearly that black persons who rape or kill white persons stand in far greater jeopardy of being hanged than whites who rape or kill blacks.

Thus data given in Annual Police Reports in recent years for persons prosecuted for rape across the colour line indicate that in absolute terms more white men have been so prosecuted than black or brown men; in relation to the total population, white men have been charged with inter-racial rape approximately four times as often as black or brown men (1961 to 1966). Yet in the years from 1911 to 1968 only 2 out of 132 men executed for rape were white, and both of these had been found guilty of raping young white girls. The great majority of the others were African or coloured men convicted of raping white women. No two particular cases are ever exactly alike, but when white men are never sentenced to death for raping black women, and black and brown men are frequently executed for raping white women, the inference is inescapable that racial factors do operate in the minds of judges when imposing sentences. On occasions the discrepancies in sentences have been so marked that public criticism has been offered of the Judiciary.

[40] Diemont J., in *S. v. Ngubelanga*, 6/10/66, unreported (Cape).
[41] *S. v. Germishaysen*, van Zijl, J., quoted in Maister; *R. v. D.* 1960 (1) SA, 151.
[42] *R. v. Mhlauli*, 1954 (1) SA, 87 (c).

Thus a newspaper received several indignant letters from readers after it had carried two news items which revealed that a coloured man who had raped a white woman aged 52 had been sentenced to death, whereas a white man who had raped an Indian girl aged 9 had received 9 months' imprisonment. More recently, four young white men convicted of raping an African woman and assaulting her escort were each sentenced in effect only to receive six strokes with a light cane, in circumstances where, had the racial situation been reversed, almost certainly at least one and probably all four of the accused would have been sentenced to death. The leniency of this sentence was widely commented on, but it was in keeping with remarks made by the Penal Reform Commission of 1947 about a similar case. The Commission stated that the usefulness of strokes as an alternative to imprisonment for young offenders had been borne out by the case of four or five white scholars in their late teens who "finding a young native girl alone in the veld, succumbed to the sudden urge of sexual passion and raped her. They came from good homes where an adequate degree of discipline had been exercised. To have taken these youths from their homes; to have ended their course of education; to have placed them in prison with other offenders would have ruined their careers and spoiled their lives." By way of contrast, the Minister of Justice stated in 1955 that in the seven years he had been in office not a single reprieve had been granted to a non-European convicted of raping a European woman.

In cases such as these where light sentences are passed it is difficult not to infer that the whites are being punished more for having given in to temptation and disgraced themselves than for having done violence to the victim. To the extent that differential punishment of rapists is rationalised at all, it seems to be done on the assumption that the shock of being ravaged is much greater for a white woman than it is for a black woman; conversely, the shock of an execution is assumed to be much greater in respect of a member of the white community than it is in relation to a member of the black.

The figures for murder across the colour line present a similar picture of leniency towards whites and severity towards blacks. In the $5\frac{1}{2}$ years ended 30th June 1966, 189 whites were sent for trial for murdering black or brown people, whereas only 130 black or brown persons were sent for trial for murdering whites (Police Reports). In proportion to the total populations of the different racial groups, this represented white leadership in the ratio of six to one. Precise information is not available as to what the outcome of all these trials was, but in respect of the total period 1911 to 1968, only some 85 out of approximately 2,000 persons executed for murder were white, and of these 85, only 6 had murdered persons who were not white. (Two of this latter group were convicted of killing African lovers; one of killing an African during the 1922 miners' revolt; one of killing two Africans and wounding several whites; and one of taking part in a gang murder jointly with an Indian.) There do not appear to be any published figures indicating how many of the 1,900 black or brown persons hanged for murder had killed across the colour line, but such information as is available suggests that the number runs into hundreds at least. Similarly, although a considerable number of whites are prosecuted each year for housebreaking or robbery with aggravating circumstances, it would seem that none of the 57 persons hanged for these offences in the years 1958 to 1968 were white, while only one person out of seven hanged for sabotage was white.

These figures provide substantial if not irrefutable statistical evidence in support of the charge that racial considerations do play a part—whether conscious or not—in the sentencing of prisoners. In a society where all amenities are distributed on an avowedly differential basis, it would not be surprising to find all penalties allocated with equal discrimination. Any such assertion, however, is made in South Africa at the peril of prosecution. A senior lecturer at the Witwatersrand University was prosecuted on the initiative of the Transvaal Judge-President for having published an article in the *South African Law Journal* in which he reported as part of a survey he had conducted that a substantial number of advocates believed that judges consciously discriminated on racial grounds when imposing capital punishment (Van Niekerk). The lecturer was eventually found not guilty of the charge of contempt of court, but the judge passed adverse comments about him and did not reaffirm in clear language the right of jurists and the public to investigate and discuss the workings of the Judiciary.[43] One of the curious consequences of this prosecution has been the subsequent appearance of a learned and lengthy article on the death sentence in South Africa, in which the author establishes by statistics what appears to be an incontrovertible pattern of discriminatory punishment, and yet is at pains to deny that the judges could possibly be capable of the very differentiation revealed in his figures.

[43] *S. v. van Niekerk*, 1970 (3) SA, 655.

The disparities on racial grounds with regard to the punishment of murderers and rapists can also be discerned in relation to persons convicted of crimes against the security of the State. Here, however, the greatest source of differentiation has been the action of the Executive rather than of the Judiciary. In general, white rebels have been treated with considerable leniency. The Reformers found guilty of treason after distributing guns and seizing Johannesburg at the time of the Jameson Raid in 1895 were all released within months of their conviction; four were formally sentenced to death, but the judge knew that the Executive had aready agreed to commute the sentences. The rebels in the Cape and Natal who joined the invading Boer commandos at the time of the Anglo-Boer War were all either amnestied, sentenced to short terms of imprisonment or else released shortly after the war's end. The British Army officers were so incensed at what they regarded as the dangerously lenient attitude of the Colonial Treason Courts that they insisted on imposing their own courts martial, as a result of which thirty-five Cape rebels were executed by firing squad. After the 1914 Afrikaner rebellion, during which hundreds of Government troops were killed and generals in the Union Defence Force led whole battalions over to the Germans, one officer who had fought against the Government to the bitter end was court-martialled and shot, but all the other rebels were released within eighteen months. After the 1922 Rand revolt of white artisans, in which more than 100 Government troops and police and dozens of non-combatant civilians were killed, 4 strikers were hanged, but all the others were released within two years. All persons convicted during the Second World War of crimes against the State, including persons found guilty of treason, murder, sabotage, spying and broadcasting for the enemy, were released within three years of the war's end. One of these men was a boxing champion who had gone to Germany to fight Max Schmeling and had later returned by submarine to lead a pro-Nazi rebellion;[44] another two had killed a bystander when attempting to blow up a post office.

The harsh treatment meted out to black rebels in the nineteenth century and during the 1906 Zulu 'revolt' have already been alluded to. In the first few years of the 1960s more Africans were executed for offences with a political background than were whites executed for treason in all the major rebellions referred to in the previous paragraph.

[44] R. v. *Leibbrandt and others*, 1944 AD, 253.

Estimates place the figures at over fifty, which would seem to exceed the number of persons who died during the course of their campaigns. In addition hundreds of Africans were sentenced under the security laws to periods of imprisonment ranging from ten years to life, and now nearly a decade later the Government is adamant in refusing to grant them an amnesty or even the normal remission of sentence for good behaviour. At the beginning of 1970 more than 800 persons were in prison under four security laws, of whom 15 were Asian, 14 were white, 11 were coloured persons, and the rest were Africans.

There are other figures which suggest that the courts are influenced by racial factors in the course of criminal trials. Thus in recent years the acquittal rate for whites charged with serious offences has been significantly but not substantially greater in every one of the six major categories of crime used by the Bureau of Statistics. Between 1949 and 1962 the rate of acquittal for both whites and Africans increased by approximately 10 per cent to approximately 30 per cent of all prosecutions; looked at in relation to each group of crimes, however, it can be seen that the white acquittal rate exceeded that of Africans by from 4 to 12 per cent (*Penal Statistics*). As far as sentences were concerned, a sociologist wrote in 1948 that in proportion to the total number of convictions for each racial group, ten times as many Africans as whites went to prison each year, either because of heavier sentences or because of greater inability to pay fines (Simons). By 1962 a total of 43,000 whites were convicted of more serious crimes, yet only 6,000 whites were received into prison. In the same year 230,000 Africans were convicted of more serious crimes, and approximately 260,000 Africans were received into prison (*Penal Statistics*). Thus a large number of Africans convicted of non-serious crimes (called 'law infringements') must have paid heavier penalties than many whites convicted of serious crimes.

Most of the above discussion on judicial attitudes towards race has related to judgements of the superior courts, which have laid down the law and set standards of procedure and decorum for all courts. It should not be forgotten, however, that the great majority of cases have been heard in the magistrates' courts, and that members of the public were far more likely to appear before magistrates than before judges. There has been no system of reporting judgements in the magistrates' courts, so that the attitudes of magistrates to race cannot be determined by reference to law reports, except where they have been quoted in cases on appeal. It has frequently been pointed out, however, that magistrates were civil servants lacking the legal training and sense of independence of the judges, and as such more amenable to departmental pressures and less likely to fly in the face of white public opinion. Their court rolls were longer and their tempers often correspondingly short. One magistrate recommended in his memoirs that new judges should spend a year in the magistrates' courts, mucking in with the rough and tumble, getting the good old smells of a fetid atmosphere, seeing the riff-raff pass before him day after day in almost endless procession, and having to punish, punish, punish (Corder). On questions of race this particular magistrate was relatively liberal, and asked in his memoirs what justice there could be, what respect for the sanctity of human life, when a white man could merely be fined £10 for striking an African dead with his fist. Another magistrate who succeeded in finding a publisher for two sets of memoirs adopted a quite different approach to race relations, and offered his readers the following advice: "There is but one way to treat a South African aboriginal—perform your promise whether it be a tip or a thrashing, and avoid familiarity at all costs" (Devitt). Examples could be quoted to show similar variations of attitudes amongst magistrates in cases where Africans have taken action to remedy grievances. Whereas one magistrate went out of his way to emphasise that all persons had the right to take action to improve their conditions, provided they did not break the law, another magistrate was at pains to castigate African bucket-workers who had gone on strike to get their monthly pay raised from £3 to £4. This latter man was the Chief Magistrate of Johannesburg, who was later to head a committee for the defence of white strikers, and he told the African workers that they would have to serve two months hard labour doing the same work as before, without pay and under armed guard; if they tried to escape, they would be shot, and if they refused to work they would be flogged. The race consciousness of magistrates is likely to increase rather than diminish, if the attitudes of the head of the training section of the Department of Justice are any guide (Ferreira). In a standard textbook on criminal procedure in the magistrates' courts, he lists eighteen characteristics of African witnesses for the benefit of those, who unlike the author, 'do not know the Bantu'. He also suggests that magistrates should impose heavy sentences in political trials, and refrain from criticising the police or legislation.

In concluding this chapter, it is fitting to quote the remarks of ex-Chief Justice Centlivres who after his retirement from the Bench became a vigorous critic of statutes which he felt offended against the

Rule of Law. In a discussion of the motto 'Equal Justice under the Law' which appears on the pediment of the United States Supreme Court, he wrote that such words would be out of place on the pediment of the South African Appeal Court, for the simple reason that the courts in South Africa were bound by law to apply or enforce legislation under which the rights of individuals differed according to the colour of their skins. Apart from discriminatory legislation which was binding on the courts, he felt that it could be said that South African courts were colour-blind, with the possible exception of some punishments. "It is discriminatory legislation which prevents our Courts from dispensing equal justice under law; if that legislation were to be repealed our Courts would dispense equal justice . . . for our common law is colour-blind."

Whether or not black South Africans were as ready to absolve the courts from responsibility for race differentiation will be discussed in a later chapter. Before dealing with that question, however, it will be convenient to consider, by means of reference to statutes and judicial statistics, the extent to which the courts, as the centre of penal apparatus in South Africa, have been involved in the maintenance of colonial-type relationships between white and black in South Africa.

CHAPTER SIX

The Administration of Justice in a Racially Stratified Society

Rapid industrialisation and modernisation of South Africa in the twentieth century accelerated the integration of all sectors of the population into a common society. In a few decades great cities sprang up on what had formerly been stretches of open veld, and quiet colonial towns on the coast burgeoned into busy ports and manufacturing centres. The demand of the urban areas for food and labour soon destroyed whatever economic autonomy the rural regions had once possessed, and an extensive system of internal communications brought all the inhabitants of the sub-continent into contact with each other. Millions of black, brown and white farmers trekked by road and rail into the towns, whilst a reverse flow of manufactured goods proceeded into every nek and krantz of the countryside.

In this setting it was hoped by some and feared by others that increasing industrialisation and cultural assimilation would undermine colour consciousness and erase legal disabilities based on race. Some would have argued then, as many maintain today, that an industrial economy was essentially colour-blind, and that its labour requirements and marketing needs would inevitably subvert archaic racial attitudes. Liberal investors, politicians and lawyers anticipated that the growth of industry would promote the spread of skills and education throughout the population and pave the way for the extension of the franchise, the removal of the colour bar, the softening of law enforcement and the liberalisation of race feelings. The test of citizenship would be civilisation and not race. The British Parliamentary system as adapted to the Cape and then transferred to the North was seen to have implicit in it an intrinsically democratic character and inherent virtue, which, in the benign atmosphere created by industrial advance, would become increasingly attractive even to the most race-conscious members of the South African population. Finally, it was assumed that the existence of a court system modelled on British lines and staffed by a Judiciary imbued with a sense of independence and justice, would ensure to every individual irrespective of colour freedom under the law.

This chapter will examine the extent to which in the sixty years after Union all these expectations were contradicted.

In the constitutional sphere, the limited Parliamentary franchise of black and brown was progressively eliminated and in its place a variety of racial and tribally constituted bodies were created. At the same time, the entire surface area of the country was racially zoned, with the result that by 1970 approximately 85 per cent of the land was reserved to the whites, who made up less than 20 per cent of the total population. Legal machinery was created to enforce large-scale removals of black and brown; discriminatory notices proliferated until no public amenity was left unsegregated; penalties were attached to an ever-widening range of sexual contact between white and black or brown. An elaborate race register was created in order to ensure that every individual was allocated to a defined racial group and thereby made entitled to certain legal privileges and subject to specified legal disabilities. Controls over the movement, residence and labour of Africans were constantly extended, while exemptions from the operation of restrictive laws were continually removed. Job reservation was increasingly under-pinned by statute, and such 'mixed' trade unions as emerged were compelled by law to divide along racial lines. Segregation in schools and universities was intensified. All the lawcourts save one were segregated, as were the prisons and police stations. What had formerly been regulated by geographical separation or social practice now became enforced by law, and the courts became more not less active in penalising breaches of differential statutes.

Thus in the sixty years after Union in 1910, the number of blacks charged under avowedly racial statutes rose elevenfold from 90,000 per annum to 1,000,000 per annum. In 1928 fewer than 50,000 Africans were charged under the pass laws, while forty years later nearly 700,000 were charged under these laws. The number of prosecutions for illegal occupation of land in the same period rose from 10,000 to more than 150,000.

Partly as a result of this growing enforcement of discriminatory legislation, the number of persons received into prison each year rose from less than 100,000 in 1911 to nearly half a million in 1967. A comparison with countries that had a similar penal, though different social, system, reveals that in the early 1960s more than twice as many Africans were received under sentence in the prisons of South Africa (total population 18 million) as persons of all races were received under sentence into the prisons of England and Wales, Tanganyika, Kenya and Ghana combined (total population 69 million). So great has been the recent incarceration of Africans in South Africa that if the level at the end of the 1960s is maintained, more than one African man in two can expect to be jailed in the 1970s.

Racial factors have also played a part in the continuing and in some respects increasing severity of punishments handed down by the courts. Thus in the first forty years after Union a total of 100,000 offenders were sentenced to 900,000 strokes, while in the next twenty years 200,000 offenders were ordered to receive 1,200,000 strokes; although the average number of strokes per offender nearly halved, the total number of strokes actually inflicted each year more than doubled. Similarly, the number of persons executed rose from less than thirty per annum in the first decade after Union to nearly one hundred per annum in this last decade. The number of crimes carrying the death sentence increased from three to nine in the same period, and in the early 1960s South Africa was responsible for 47 per cent of all judicial executions reported to the United Nations for a five-year period.

The remainder of this chapter specifies the statutes and sets out the statistical data on which the above propositions are based. It may accordingly be of special interest to criminologists, academic lawyers, sociologists and social historians, but of less interest to the general reader, who may prefer merely to glance at Tables 2, 7, 8, 9, 12, 15 and 20 and to pick out the passages which quote the rationalisations advanced by those in authority for the increased use of imprisonment, whipping and the gallows.

THE FRANCHISE

At the time of Union in 1910 some 20,000 or 15 per cent of all Parliamentary voters in the Cape were black or brown. Although they had never managed to elect one of their number to the Cape Legislature they constituted a considerable force at election time, especially since the rest of the electorate was fairly evenly divided between Englishmen and Afrikaners. The South Africa Act, 1909, which established the Union of South Africa, entrenched their voting rights, but did not extend such rights to the North. A special section of the Act provided that none should be removed from the voters roll on account of race except by a law passed by a two-thirds majority of the House of Assembly and the Senate sitting together.

In 1930 the voting power of Africans and coloured persons in the Cape was effectively halved when the vote was extended to white women in South Africa.

In 1936 African voters were by the requisite two-thirds majority removed from the common voters roll and placed on a special roll which entitled them to elect three white persons to the House of Assembly and four to the Senate, which between them had a total of nearly two hundred members.

In 1956 coloured voters were placed on a separate voters roll which entitled them to elect three white persons to the House of Assembly. The necessary two-thirds majority was obtained after a long constitutional battle culminating in the reconstitution and enlargement of the Senate.

In 1959 African representation in Parliament was abolished altogether.

In 1968 coloured representation in Parliament was abolished altogether.

Thus the Parliament elected in 1970 contained no representation, either direct or indirect, of black or brown South Africans. Pursuant to the policy of apartheid or separate development, the 80 per cent of South Africans who were disfranchised were provided with various councils. Nine separate tribally-based authorities were established in the rural reserves with varying degrees of local autonomy to represent the African population of South Africa; a Coloured Representative Council was created to act as official spokesman for the coloured people; and an Indian Advisory Council was appointed to consult with the Government on matters affecting people of Indian descent.

RACIAL LEGISLATION

At the time of Union differential pass, liquor and tax laws already existed throughout most of South Africa. One of the first enactments of the new Parliament was a law which regulated recruitment of African workers and made breach of service contracts by Africans a criminal offence. This was soon followed by a statute which prohibited Africans from acquiring an interest in land outside of the tribal areas; the eventual effect of this law as amended was to prohibit Africans from owning or leasing property in 87 per cent of South Africa's surface area.

In the 1920s Africans living in the urban areas were obliged by statute to live in locations subject to the control of white superintendents. The Governor-General was declared to be Supreme Chief of all Africans with power to rule by proclamation. A special court system staffed by white officials was established to hear civil disputes involving

African litigants and to try Africans under differential legislation. Taxation of Africans on a capitation basis was made uniform throughout the country, and the failure to produce tax receipts on demand was made a criminal offence. Sexual intercourse between black and white was made illegal throughout the country.

In the 1930s African voters in the Cape were removed from the common voters roll.

In the 1950s pass laws inherited from the pre-Union period were consolidated and extended to African women; exemptions from the operation of these laws were cancelled and Africans in the Cape were subjected to the same controls as Africans in the rest of the country. The education of Africans was taken away from the missions and placed under total Government control. The authorities were given extra powers to evict Africans from land and to compel them to live in designated areas. Africans were prevented from belonging to registered trade unions, and strikes by Africans were made unlawful.

In the 1960s Government officials were given extra powers to control the residence and employment of Africans. The African National Congress and the Pan African Congress were declared unlawful organisations.

During these decades Africans were also adversely affected by a number of laws which discriminated generally between white-skinned and dark-skinned persons. These will be mentioned below. The only disabilities to be repealed during all this time were those relating to possession of liquor. The Government contends that the creation of tribal authorities in the 1960s opened the way to the exercise of full citizenship rights by Africans in their separate tribal homelands.

General colour bar laws were passed from time to time to enforce segregation between whites on the one hand and Africans, coloured persons and Indians on the other. In the early years after Union these statutes referred mainly to employment; in the 1950s statutory authority was given for the reservation of public amenities on a separate and unequal basis; a national race register was compiled in terms of a race classification law; intermarriage and any form of sexual activity between white persons and black or brown persons was prohibited; black and brown students were excluded from the Universities of Cape Town and the Witwatersrand; all urban and rural areas were racially zoned for purposes of ownership or occupation; the reservation of jobs on racial lines was extended, and 'mixed' trade unions were split on racial lines. In the 1950s and 1960s major African political organisations were proscribed, the non-racial Communist Party and Liberal Party were forced to disband or go underground, and the multiracial Progressive Party was compelled to shed its black and brown members.

Thus by 1970 legal segregation was more extensive and systematic than it had been in 1910. Instead of the Cape policies being extended to the rest of the country, the rigid segregation of the North was extended to the Cape. African women throughout the country were made subject to the same controls as their menfolk, and the class of Africans exempted from the pass laws–only partially exempted, since in practice they had to carry documents–was abolished. At the same time the legal disabilities of coloured people and Indians were considerably increased. Segregation notices appeared on buses, trains, taxis and ambulances, on park benches, beaches, sportsfields and swimming baths, in libraries, concert halls, museums and zoos, in post offices, telephone kiosks, railway stations and urinals. Interracial conception was forbidden, interracial marriage was prohibited, the sick were treated in separate hospitals and the dead were interred in separate burial grounds.

The old policy of segregation, which operated unevenly and without plan, gave way to the new concept of apartheid, which was enforced in a total and systematic fashion. There was no essential break between the old and the new, in fact it was this very continuity which was novel, since everywhere else in the world legal differentiation according to race was being formally repudiated. Apartheid was the modernised form of segregation, justified by Scripture, adapted to industrialisation, and implemented by the formidable machinery of a contemporary state.

LAW ENFORCEMENT AND RACE

The differential laws referred to in the previous section were not self-enforcing. It is not surprising, therefore, that an increase in what will be referred to as race-statutes was associated with an increase in the extent to which the courts were involved in the maintenance of segregation. This section will examine in some detail the way in which the penal scene was affected by race, and, conversely, the manner in which the Judiciary assisted in regulating race relations. In order to introduce this section, a synoptic view of some of the major areas of penal development in the years since Union is given in Table 2.

TABLE 2

GENERAL PICTURE OF PENAL STATISTICS FOR THE YEARS
1911 AND 1967

	1911	1967	Approximate Rate of Increase
Total population of South Africa	6,000,000	19,500,000	× 3¼
Total prosecutions	260,00[a]	2,300,000	× 8
Prosecutions in terms of race-statutes	90,000[a]	1,000,000	× 11
Number of prisoners admitted under sentence	96,000	486,000	× 5
Average daily prison population	13,000	80,500	× 6
Persons given corporal[b] punishment	3,500	12,300	× 3½
Persons executed[b]	28	93	× 3⅓

[a] These figures may be slightly too low–see *Prosecutions in Terms of Race-Statutes* (below).

[b] The figures for corporal punishment and executions are the averages for the decades starting in 1911 and ending in 1967 respectively.

The figures given in Table 2 will now be considered separately, in detail and with reference to appropriate sources.

(i) *Total Prosecutions*

In the years from 1910 to 1967 the total South African population increased slightly more than threefold, the authorised establishment of the South African Police increased approximately fourfold, and the number of persons charged in court increased approximately eightfold. Table 3 gives a summary of the number of police and number of prosecutions in relation to the total population for nine selected years starting with 1912 and ending with 1967.

It will be seen from Table 3 that the total number of prosecutions has risen dramatically though not regularly in the years since Union. The only two years in which a drop was recorded were 1942 and 1962; in 1942 a depleted police force was extensively engaged in security operations against pro-German Afrikaners, while in 1962 an increase in

Table 3

SUMMARY OF NUMBER OF POLICE AND NUMBER OF PRO-
SECUTIONS RELATIVE TO TOTAL POPULATION FOR SELECTED
YEARS 1912 TO 1967[1]

Year	Total Population	Numbers of S.A. Police	Police per 1,000 of Population	Number of Persons Prosecuted	Prosecutions per 1,000 of Population
1912	6,100,000	8,705	1·42	280,000	46
1922	7,055,000	10,214	1·44	346,000	49
1932	8,310,000	9,882	1·19	596,000	72
1942	10,850,000	11,139	1·03	772,000	71
1947	11,390,000	17,612	1·55	1,020,000	89
1952	13,465,000	20,742	1·54	1,329,000	99
1957	14,690,000	23,226	1·58	1,661,000	113
1962	17,200,000	28,328	1·65	1,375,000	80
1967	19,365,000	33,168	1·71	2,318,000	117

security work against rebellious Africans coincided with the cessation of large-scale liquor raids.

(ii) *Prosecutions in Terms of Race-Statutes*

The early Annual Reports of the Commissioner of Police were far more voluminous and revealing than the modern ones, but unfortunately not always complete. Thus the report for the year 1911 gave a great amount of uncollated information in relation to prosecutions brought in the Transvaal, the Orange Free State and Natal, but far less complete figures for the Cape (UG 62/1912). A collation of the information provided in relation to prosecutions or arrests for particular crimes presents the following Provincial picture:

In the *Transvaal* 120,000 persons were sent for trial, of whom 56,000 were charged with race-statute offences, 16,000 with contravention of

[1] Based on Annual Report of Commissioner of Police, for year ended 30th June 1968, RP 47/1969. The figures for 1967 relate to the year ended 30th June 1967, and those given in the last two columns for that year were calculated by the writer on the basis of information in the Report for the year ended 30th June 1967, RP 40/1968. Figures for the total population are to the nearest 5,000 and for the number of persons prosecuted to the nearest 1,000.

municipal regulations, 11,000 with drunkenness, 9,000 with offences against property, and 6,000 with offences against the person.

In the *Orange Free State* 21,000 persons were prosecuted, of whom 5,000 were charged with race-statute offences and 2,000 with theft.

In *Natal* 50,000 persons were prosecuted, of whom 16,000 were Africans charged with race-statute offences, and 4,000 were Indians charged with similar offences.

In the *Cape*, the Urban Police made 9,000 arrests, of which 500 were made under vagrancy laws and only 1 under an avowedly racial statute. The Mounted Police made 8,000 arrests, of which 1,000 were under the masters and servants laws, 500 for trespass, 500 under the liquor laws and 200 for pass offences. The Kimberley Police made 4,000 arrests, of which 200 were for pass offences and 100 for liquor offences. Thus these three separate Cape police forces were between them responsible for 21,000 arrests, of which 3,000 were for infringements of what may broadly be referred to as race-statutes. A fourth force, the Rural Police, was responsible for bringing a further 35,500 accused persons before the courts. How many of these persons were charged with more than one offence is not revealed, nor what the offences were with which they were charged. On the assumption that the Rural Police were responsible for the same proportion of prosecutions in terms of race-statutes as were other police forces in the Cape (i.e. one in seven) it may be estimated that in the Cape at least 56,000 cases were brought to court, of which at least 8,000 were based on race-statutes.

The above figures are expressed in tabular form (Table 4) together with an indication of the proportion that race-statute prosecutions formed of the total number of prosecutions in each province.

The figures in Table 4 indicate that the Transvaal led the field both in terms of the total number of prosecutions brought and in terms of charges laid under race-statutes. Not too much reliance may be placed on the Cape figures, since they are only estimates,[2] but the low figures for the largely rural Orange Free State contrast strongly with the high figures for the industrialised Transvaal. When the whole of South Africa became more industrialised, the pattern of prosecutions throughout

[2] The Cape figures were probably higher than those shown. The report for 1916 showed that the number of persons arrested in that year were: Cape 82,000; Natal 54,500; O.F.S. 23,000 and Transvaal 120,000. UG 42/1917. Although the reports for the years after 1911 gave reliable totals, they did not break down the information so as to permit a picture of the different kinds of prosecution being obtained.

TABLE 4

TOTAL POPULATIONS, TOTAL PROSECUTIONS, AND PROSECU-
TIONS FOR RACE-STATUTE OFFENCES, ON A PROVINCIAL BASIS
IN 1911

Province	Total Population	Total Prosecutions	Race-Statute Prosecutions	Column 4 as a % of Column 3
Transvaal	1,700,000	120,000	56,000	45%
Natal	1,200,000	50,000	20,000	40%
O.F.S.	500,000	21,000	5,000	24%
Cape	2,600,000	56,000	8,000	14%
Union of S.A.	6,000,000	267,000	89,000	33%

(Figures collated by the writer from the annual report for 1911, UG 62/1912. The percentages in the last column were calculated by the writer.)

the country came increasingly to resemble that of the Transvaal in 1911.

From the 1920s onward the police reports presented their information in a terse but continuous manner. Data were no longer supplied

TABLE 5

FIGURES OF ALL PROSECUTIONS AND RACE-STATUTE
PROSECUTIONS FOR THE YEARS 1927, 1947 AND 1967[3]

Year	Total Population	All Prosecutions	Race-Statute Prosecutions	Column 4 as a % of Column 3
1927	7·7 million	503,000	188,000	37%
1947	11·4 million	1,020,000	418,500	41%
1967	19·4 million	2,300,000	1,043,000	44%

[3] Based on annual reports for 1927, 1947 and the year ended 30th June 1967. From 1963 onwards the reports covered the period from mid-year to mid-year. Total figures were no longer given for statutory offences regarded as less serious, but information was supplied as to the main offences prosecuted and what percentage of all prosecutions these represented, and from this it is possible to calculate the total number of prosecutions for all offences. The last two columns in Table 5 were compiled by the writer on the basis of data in the above mentioned reports. The figures given in subsequent tables for years after 1963 refer to the 12-month period ended 30th June of the year mentioned.

on a Provincial basis, but figures were given of the main kinds of prosecution brought throughout the country, and it became possible to calculate the total number of charges for each year. On the basis of these figures the writer has calculated the growth rate for all prosecutions and for race-statute prosecutions from 1927 to 1967, as represented in Table 5.

The figures in Table 5 establish that the total number of prosecutions increased at a markedly greater rate than did the total population, and that the number of race-statute prosecutions increased at an even faster rate. Roughly speaking, during a period of forty years when the total population increased by about 2½ times, the total number of prosecutions increased by about 4½ times and the total number of specifically race-statute prosecutions increased by about 5½ times. In proportional terms, the percentage of race-statute prosecutions rose from 33 per cent of the total in 1911 to 44 per cent in 1967.

The term race-statutes has been used here to refer to five main groups of laws, namely those relating to taxes, passes, liquor, masters and servants and trespass. The tax laws penalised failure by African men to produce on demand annual receipts for poll tax. The pass laws referred to documents of identity and permits relating to work and residence, all of which had to be produced on demand, as well as to curfew laws and location regulations, the latter including such crimes as failure to pay rent. The liquor laws rendered it a criminal offence for Africans to brew or possess so-called kaffir beer or so-called European liquor. The masters and servants laws applied almost invariably to white masters and black or brown servants, and related mainly to indentured farm-workers. The trespass laws were used almost exclusively to prosecute Africans found without permission on land or premises owned by whites. Although the total figures for prosecutions under race-statutes increased rapidly over the years, the figures for each of these five main categories varied considerably. The changes in respect of each of these five groups from 1928 to 1968 are reflected in Table 6.

Table 6 demonstrates that a vast increase in the number of prosecutions for tax, pass and trespass offences was associated with a marked drop in the number of prosecutions for liquor and masters and servants offences.

A special word should be said about the decline in prosecutions under the liquor laws. These had originally been prompted as temperance measures, but they also helped perpetuate the concept of Africans as a subordinate people requiring special controls. Whereas the drop in the

TABLE 6

THE TOTAL NUMBER OF PROSECUTIONS BROUGHT UNDER
FIVE MAIN GROUPS OF RACE-STATUTES IN 1928 COMPARED
WITH 1968

	Tax	Pass	Liquor	Master and Servant	Trespass
1928	60,000	44,000	33,000	43,000	10,000
1968	243,000	670,000	26,000	23,000	166,000

(Based on annual Police Reports)

number of prosecutions brought under the old and cumbersome masters and servants laws was gradual and steady, the decline in prosecutions under the liquor laws in fact only took place after there had first been a steep rise not reflected in Table 6. Liquor law prosecutions rose from 33,000 in 1928 to over 200,000 in the late 1950s, but plummeted when the liquor laws were amended in 1961 to permit Africans to buy liquor in bottle stores. Thus prosecutions under the liquor laws rose from 7 per cent of all prosecutions in 1927 to 11 per cent in 1948 and dropped to 2 per cent in 1967. For decades the prohibition of liquor for Africans had been regarded as fundamental to the maintenance of social peace and the combating of crime in South Africa, yet the eventual abandonment of such prohibition brought about no noticeable change in either the social picture or the crime situation in the country. The police had long felt uneasy about the administration of the liquor laws, partly because of the corruption they had engendered in the police force itself. Thus, the Police Commission of Enquiry of 1937 commented that although the prohibition laws did much "to save the natives from the disaster which unrestricted liquor supply would inevitably have brought about, and preserved other races from appalling resultant dangers . . . thousands of Europeans, natives and coloured persons were degraded and ruined in the process of putting the law into force" (UG 50/1937). A strong wine farmers lobby had also long urged the ending of prohibition, but it was only after the shootings at Sharpeville in 1960 that the law was actually changed.

The drop in prosecutions for liquor and master and servant offences was small in comparison with the increase in prosecutions under the other race-statutes. Thus prosecutions for tax offences rose 4 times in the forty years, for pass law offences 15 times and for trespass 16 times.

Prosecutions under the pass laws in fact rose so steeply that they increased in average from less than 1,000 per week to more than 2,000 per day. Thus statutory controls over the African people were intensified rather than weakened with the growing economic progress of the country. The archaic masters and servants laws which had served a predominantly rural economy were superseded by modernised pass laws designed for an industrialised society, and the liquor laws which were irrelevant to the economy or the administration were jettisoned.

It has already been mentioned that by 1967 prosecutions for race-statute offences amounted to approximately 44 per cent of all prosecutions brought. For purposes of comparison the figures given in the annual report for the other main offences prosecuted in that year, namely traffic offences, drunkenness and drugs, assaults and common theft, are given in Table 7.

TABLE 7

MAIN OFFENCES PROSECUTED IN YEAR ENDED 30TH JUNE 1967

			% of Total Prosecutions
Total prosecutions		2,300,000	100%
Race-statute offences		1,043,000	44%
Other main offences		715,000	31%
Motor vehicles	420,000	(18%)	
Drunkenness and drugs	120,000	(5%)	
Assaults	110,000	(5%)	
Common theft	65,000	(3%)	

(Based on annual Police Report)

Table 7 demonstrates that prosecutions for race-statute offences substantially exceeded the combined figures for motor vehicle offences, drunkenness and drugs, assaults and common theft. The pass laws alone accounted for approximately five times as many prosecutions as assault, and nearly ten times as many as common theft, the two most significant common law offences.

By way of comparison, approximately 2 million persons were prosecuted in 1969 for all offences in England and Wales, which have a population about 2½ times that of South Africa. One million of these prosecutions related to motoring offences, 200,000 to common theft,

85,000 to drunkenness, 65,000 to assaults, and 60,000 to violent theft. Thus more persons were prosecuted in South Africa for race-statute offences than all persons were prosecuted for non-motoring offences in England and Wales (*Criminal Statistics*).

(iii) *Race Laws and Sex*

The increase in race-statute prosecutions has been brought about through the more rigid enforcement of old statutes rather than through the creation of new offences. Penal sanctions were invariably attached to new segregation measures, but they were invoked relatively rarely. Thus prosecution under the Group Areas Act, 1950, and for breach of segregation rules relating to public amenities are not frequent. Nevertheless, the social significance of the new race-statutes was considerable, and the ultimate threat of penal sanctions ensured general compliance with them.

One field of increasing intervention by the law was in sexual relationships between persons of different colour. In general, pre-Union statutes prohibited sexual intercourse between white women and black men, the severest penalty being in Natal where 25 years' imprisonment could be imposed (Simons–*African Women*). Prosecutions appear to have been rare, and in the first years after Union official attention was focused on unwilling interracial intercourse rather than on intercourse by consent. Thus the police report for 1911 gave figures for sexual assaults committed by black or brown men on white women (Natal 52, Transvaal 40, Cape 27 and Orange Free State 3), to which the term Black Peril was applied. The Commissioner for Police observed that the Black Peril should be most prevalent where Africans were the most numerous, and yet in fact in the populous Cape Province, "where the coloured men and the native who is a registered voter is in most respects on terms of equality with the white man (and where) consequently far more cases of the kind under discussion might be expected", the prevalence was the lowest. His conclusion was that Black Peril outrages were due mainly to the existence of the houseboy and the illicit liquor traffic (UG 62/1912).

Five years later a Deputy-Commissioner recommended that a Union statute be passed forbidding the sale of pictures of nude statues or paintings, "it being felt that the exposure of pictures representing nude white women incites coloured men and natives to sexual offences" (UG 42/1917). The Immorality Act of 1927, however, placed no prohibition upon pictorial nudity, but did penalise sexual intercourse between 'Europeans' and 'natives' of the opposite sex. The Immorality Act of 1950 extended the prohibition to sexual intercourse between 'Europeans' and 'non-Europeans', and the Immorality Act of 1957 further forbade sexual activity falling short of intercourse, and at the

TABLE 8

CONVICTIONS FOR INTERRACIAL SEXUAL ACTIVITY DURING
SELECTED YEARS 1928 TO 1966

Year	Intercourse between 'European' and 'Native'	Intercourse between 'European' and 'non-European'	Sex between 'White' and 'Coloured'
1928	89		
1948	78		
1949	118		
1950		265	
1951		275	
1952		313	
1953		261	
1954		360	
1955		313	
1956		305	
1957			363
1958			457
1959			551
1960			427
1961			389
1962			382
1963			364
1964			382
1965			405
1966			488

(Figures taken from annual Police Reports)

same time increased the penalties to a maximum of seven years' imprisonment.

The number of convictions during selected years from 1928 to 1966 for breaches of the colour bar provisions of the Immorality Acts is given in Table 8.

These totals are small in comparison with those for prosecutions in terms of other race-statutes, and standing on their own fail to convey the importance attached to the sexual colour bar in South African life. Whereas prosecutions under the pass, tax and trespass laws usually pass unnoticed save by those directly affected, Immorality Act trials are highly publicised. The more prominent the white person involved and the more salacious the evidence, the wider the press coverage. A secretary to the Prime Minister, a Minister of the Dutch Reformed Church, lawyers, businessmen, academics, policemen and farmers have all been hauled before court for loving their black neighbours too well, and almost every year the newspapers carry reports of whites who have committed suicide rather than face the ignominy of such a charge.

It is generally agreed that only a small amount of interracial sexual activity is detected by the police, yet the existence of the Act and the bringing of exemplary prosecutions helps to promote the concept that the maintenance of racial purity is the ultimate end of government. A sociologist has observed that when, as in South Africa, status is closely linked to racial type, any assimilation that blurs the obvious physical differences is seen as a threat to the social order. "The dominant group will apply strong pressure to prevent coition between its members and the underlying population." White tribalism, he adds, contributes its quota to the list of sexual taboos (Simons).

Yet if the preservation of white purity is seen as the primary objective of the Immorality Act, in practice it is white men who seek sexual intercourse with black and brown women rather than black and brown men who attempt intimacy with white women. Figures in Police Reports for prosecutions under the Immorality laws reveal that very few white women have been involved; thus in 1928 a total of 78 white men and African women were convicted, as compared with a total of only 11 white women and African men, while in 1966 out of 488 persons convicted only 4 were white women and 13 black or brown men.

(iv) Race Laws and Residence

One of the immediate consequences of industrialisation in South Africa was the creation of large multiracial urban centres. As industry expanded and the population of the cities increased, so did the Legislature increase its measures to segregate residential areas according to racial criteria. Far from declining with the onset of modernisation, racial zoning became more extensive and grew to involve ever greater sections of the population. In the past two decades the machinery of the law has been invoked to compel the removal of hundreds of thousands of persons from one area to another on racial grounds. The removal of Africans was accomplished by a combination of many statutes, some old and some new, and it is difficult to compile accurate figures for the total numbers of persons involved. One estimate put the figure of enforced removals of Africans during the decade 1960 to 1970 at 900,000. The enforced removal of Indians and coloured persons, however, was accomplished almost solely by one statute, the Group Areas Act, 1950, the operation of which has been more precisely documented.

TABLE 9

THE DIFFERENTIAL EFFECT OF GROUP AREA PROCLAMATIONS IN
THE PERIOD 1950 TO 1970

Race	Number of Families ordered to move	Number of Families actually Re-settled
White	1,318	1,196
Coloured	68,897	34,240
Indian	37,653	21,939
Chinese	899	64

(SAIRR 1970 p. 186)

The basic aim of the Group Areas Act was to divide the country into separate racial areas for ownership and occupation. In practice the Act was used mainly to force Indians and coloured persons living in areas close to the centre of towns and villages to remove to the outskirts; while being ideologically satisfying to the white electorate, these removals also proved to be economically advantageous to the Government and to serve its security ends. The differential manner in which the law was implemented appears from Table 9.

Table 9 reveals that for each white householder obliged by law to make way for brown people, almost one hundred brown householders have been compelled to make way for white people. On the assumption that each family consisted of five members, only 1 in 570 whites in South Africa would have received orders to move, compared with approximately 1 in 6 coloured persons, nearly 1 in 3 Indians and more than 1 in 2 Chinese.

(v) *Increase in Prison Population*

The size of the prison population in any society is an important index of the extent to which the courts are used as instruments of social control. A growing prison population indicates either an increase in conduct defined as criminal, or an improvement in law enforcement machinery, or the emergence of a sterner judicial attitude towards punishment. In South Africa all three factors appear to have operated in the years since Union to increase the size of the country's prison population. The growth in the total number of admissions each year is given in Table 10, which refers to selected years from 1912 to 1969.

TABLE 10

ADMISSIONS TO PRISON FOR SELECTED YEARS 1912 TO 1969[4]

Year	Population of South Africa	Total Admissions (including remands)	Column 3 as % of Column 2	Admissions on Sentence
1912	6,100,000	120,894	2%	95,822
1922	7,100,000	127,875	1·8%	96,722
1932	8,300,000	202,276	2·4%	172,555
1942	10,800,000	199,708	1·9%	151,922
1952	13,500,000	265,000	2%	201,000
1962	17,200,000	461,000	2·7%	347,000
1965	18,500,000	411,000	2·3%	285,000
1968	19,800,000	665,000	3·4%	486,000
1969	20,300,000	658,000	3·2%	496,000

Two comments should be made about the figures in Table 10. First, the growth in total admissions and admissions under sentence greatly exceeded the growth in total population, the ratio being approximately 5 : 3. Second, the growth in unsentenced prisoners who were subsequently not returned to prison was even greater. Thus in the late 1960s the already vast prison population was added to by more than 150,000 persons each year who were either refused or unable to raise bail, and

[4] Total populations from Police Reports; admissions to prison from Reports issued in respect of each year by the Director of Prisons; percentage calculations by the writer. From 1963 onwards the reports by the Director of Prisons related to the year ended 30th June. No allowance is made in any of the figures relating to admissions for the fact that one person might have been admitted more than once in one year in respect of separate convictions.

who were subsequently acquitted or sentenced to a non-custodial order (Prisons Reports).

A major defect in the published South African judicial statistics is that they do not relate prosecutions to imprisonment. The outcome of prosecutions is not given, nor is the cause of imprisonment. Prisoners are classified in the Annual Reports of the Director of Prisons according to race, sex and length of sentence, but not according to the offence they have committed. Figures are not even provided of the number of persons received into prison because of inability to pay fines; when the Penal Reform Commission conducted a special investigation into the question over an eighteen-month period in the early 1940s, it was shocked to find that out of more than 100,000 prisoners at eleven major urban centres, no less than 82 per cent of African prisoners, 87 per cent of coloured and Indian prisoners and 64 per cent of white prisoners were admitted because of non-payment of fines (UG 47/1947 p. 171).

A very large proportion of persons admitted to prison each year go there to serve sentences of only a few weeks or a few months. Table 11 gives a breakdown of admissions for the year ended 30th June 1969, according to race, sex and length of sentence.

According to Table 11, out of slightly less than 500,000 persons received as convicts into prison during the year, as many as 460,000 were sentenced to six months or less. Furthermore, nearly half the prisoners sentenced to less than six months were first offenders.

As long ago as 1939 the then Director of Prisons stated in his annual report that short term sentences were seldom effective, and that they had been found to be neither reformative nor deterrent. The Penal Reform Commission of 1947 made similar observations, and in 1953 the annual prisons report emphasised the uselessness of short-term imprisonment from the point of view of training of prisoners. In recent years a Cape judge has spoken out strongly in favour of reviewing penal policy in South Africa and especially of reducing the number of petty offenders being sent to prison (Jan Steyn). Despite these authoritative opinions, the annual intake of short-term prisoners shows no sign of diminishing, and in a recent interview the Minister of Justice and Prisons declared that short-term imprisonment was 'here to stay'. In his opinion there was no alternative, because "after all, the courts cannot allow people to commit offences with impunity. Once a man is convicted of a minor offence he is given the choice of either a fine or imprisonment. If he is unable to pay the fine he must go to jail" (P. C. Pelser, *Rand Daily Mail*, 30/6/1965).

TABLE II

DISTRIBUTION ACCORDING TO RACE, SEX AND LENGTH OF SENTENCE OF CONVICTED PERSONS ADMITTED TO PRISON IN THE YEAR ENDED 30TH JUNE 1969

Sentence	White Male	White Female	African Male	African Female	Asian Male	Asian Female	Coloured Male	Coloured Female	Total
Death	1	—	83	1	2	—	19	1	107
Life imprisonment	—	—	12	—	—	—	1	—	13
Intermediate sentence	105	6	838	25	6	—	233	10	1,223
Prevention of crime (5–8 years)	91	9	1,132	51	6	—	356	11	1,656
Corrective training (2–4 years)	170	9	2,444	111	13	2	645	37	3,431
2 years and over	280	18	5,680	172	25	4	1,181	49	7,409
Over 6 months under 2 years	669	23	16,092	1,562	119	3	2,850	167	21,485
Over 4 months up to 6 months	661	41	27,094	3,542	104	5	4,181	285	35,913
Over 1 month up to 4 months	1,595	97	116,746	25,719	354	27	11,631	2,312	158,481
Up to 1 month	3,613	346	181,918	40,682	850	87	30,225	7,992	265,713
Periodical imprisonment	122	—	42	2	3	1	31	—	201
Corporal punishment only	26	—	354	—	—	—	59	—	439
TOTAL	7,333	549	352,435	71,867	1,482	129	51,412	10,864	496,071
First offenders under 6 months	1,852	171	149,631	24,830	902	12	9,590	2,878	189,886

(Prisons Report)

In this connection a comparison with penal development in England provides a significant contrast. Table 12 compares the trend in relation to short-term imprisonment in England and Wales on the one hand, and South Africa on the other: the selected years are 1913, 1938 and 1968.

TABLE 12

PERSONS ADMITTED TO PRISON WITH SHORT SENTENCES IN THE YEARS 1913, 1938 AND 1968, IN ENGLAND AND WALES AND IN SOUTH AFRICA

	1913	1938	1968
England and Wales:			
Sentences up to 5 weeks	110,000	16,000	6,000
South Africa:			
Sentences up to 1 month	74,000	111,000	276,000

(Annual Prison Reports; *People in Prison, England and Wales*)

Table 12 shows that during the period 1913 to 1968 the number of short-term prisoners declined by approximately 95 per cent in England and Wales and increased by nearly 400 per cent in South Africa. It was this reduction in England and Wales that was mainly responsible for the drop there in annual admissions from 138,000 in 1913 to 36,000 in 1968.[5]

What happens to the hundreds of thousands of persons admitted to prison for short terms in South Africa each year? Their entry into and exit from prison is achieved with such rapidity that although their total numbers are great, on any particular date they account for a relatively small proportion of persons in custody, as appears from Table 13.

The last column in Table 13 shows that out of 89,000 persons in custody on a particular date, 14,000 were awaiting-trial prisoners, 55,000 were serving sentence of over 6 months, and only 20,000 were serving sentences of 6 months and under.

The Prisons Department has in fact evolved two major techniques for

[5] The problem of the short sentence has not been confined to South Africa. In the late 1950s in Australia and New Zealand an even greater proportion of prisoners seemed to have been short term (Rhoodie).

TABLE 13

PERSONS IN CUSTODY AS AT 30TH JUNE 1969, CLASSIFIED BY RACE, SEX AND LENGTH OF SENTENCE

Sentenced Prisoners	Whites		Africans		Asians		Coloured		Total
	Male	Female	Male	Female	Male	Female	Male	Female	
Death	1	—	49	—	2	—	13	—	65
Life	15	1	305	10	3	—	30	1	365
Indeterminate	609	8	5,420	65	49	—	2,102	37	8,290
Preventive	395	7	5,123	143	38	—	2,069	57	7,832
Corrective	372	21	5,258	220	39	1	2,079	85	8,075
2 years and over	640	14	13,697	356	108	2	2,983	75	17,875
Over 6 under 24 months	379	11	9,098	765	62	3	1,376	65	11,759
Over 4 up to 6 months	162	1	6,026	892	41	3	883	82	8,090
Over 1 up to 4 months	131	6	4,210	1,115	20	3	603	139	6,227
Up to 1 month	84	11	3,835	920	39	1	698	264	5,852
Corporal punishment only	—	—	2	—	—	—	2	—	4
Sub-total	2,788	80	53,023	4,486	401	13	12,838	805	74,434
Awaiting trial	454	18	10,696	1,052	74	3	1,901	164	14,362
Sundry others	8	—	7	12	1	—	11	—	39
GRAND TOTAL	3,250	98	63,726	5,550	476	16	14,750	969	88,835

RP 44/1970 p. 7. Preventive detention is from five to eight years, corrective training from two to four years. The category of 'sundry others' includes judgement debtors, mentally ill persons and detainees.

dealing with the large numbers of short-term convicts sent to prison each year. The first is to hire out such prisoners to farmers at nominal charge and the second is to release prisoners on parole subject to their working on farms and gardens at local wage rates (Prisons Reports for 1943 and 1952; UG 47/1947).

The hiring-out system was started in 1932 when the charge to farmers was 6d. per convict per day; various abuses were exposed, and the system was modified, the charge to farmers being raised to 9d. a day. In 1952 more than 40,000 prisoners serving sentences of less than four months imprisonment were hired out to farmers under this scheme, which the Department extolled for relieving pressure on the prisons "meeting in large measure the pressing need for farm labour, and providing the prisoner with a healthy out-door occupation". In the early 1950s the Prisons Department invited farmers' associations in various parts of the country to construct farm jails to which medium-term prisoners might be sent, and by 1956 the movement of prisoners from the cities to the countryside had become so extensive that the Director of Prisons was able to report that 37 per cent of all prisoners worked extramurally–mainly for farmers, in the highly productive areas where free labour was in short supply. The remaining 63 per cent were employed on State use, the hiring out of convicts to mining companies having been finally ended in 1955 (Reports for 1933, 1955, 1956).

The release of short-term prisoners on parole proved to be another boon to persons owning land in the neighbourhood of prisons, since the usual condition of parole was that the prisoner remain in the employ of a particular landowner for the unexpired portion of his sentence. Thus in the year ended 30th June 1960 more than 100,000 short-term prisoners were released on parole or probation. It should be mentioned that in practice white prisoners are not amongst those sent to perform menial tasks on privately owned farms or gardens. Segregation runs right through the prison system in South Africa, and results in black and white prisoners receiving different amenities and rations in physically separate institutions. A leading penologist explained, presumably without intentional irony, that "placing the Bantu offender in a correctional institution for people of his own group and race not only recognises existing ethnological differences but is in accordance with the national policy of differential development" (Rhoodie).

The incidence of imprisonment is not the same for all race groups in South Africa. If the figures relating to race in Tables 11 and 13, which deal respectively with annual admissions under sentence and persons in custody on a particular date, are compared with the total population of each race group in South Africa, it becomes clear that there are a disproportionately low number of white and Asian prisoners (see Table 14).

TABLE 14

THE TOTAL POPULATION OF EACH RACIAL GROUP IN
SOUTH AFRICA COMPARED WITH THE POPULATION OF
SUCH GROUPS IN PRISON IN 1969[6]

	Africans	Whites	Coloured	Asians
% of the total population of S.A.	68	19	10	3
% of admissions under sentence for year ended 30.6.1969	85·5	1·5	12·5	0·3
% of persons in prison as at 30.6.1969	78·5	3	18·5	0·3

Amongst the many criminological questions which remain unexplored in South Africa is the problem of why so many coloured persons and so few Asians find their way to prison each year. Both groups are affected by poverty, overcrowding and race discrimination; a possibly relevant factor is the extent to which strong family and community bonds amongst the Indians help to cushion the effect of adverse social and political conditions.

The high proportion of Africans in prison is interpreted by some as evidence of Government repression and by others as proof of popular lawlessness. Prosecutions brought under race-statutes are undoubtedly responsible for a large number of Africans going to prison, but common law offences also make their contribution. Thus in the early 1960s more than 70,000 Africans were convicted per annum for offences against property and approximately the same number for offences against the person (Penal Statistics, 1949-1962). Nearly a thousand murders are committed in Johannesburg each year compared with about 60 in London and about 200 in the whole of the United Kingdom.

[6] The total size of each race group was based on population estimates by Bureau of Statistics for mid-1967, quoted in SAIRR 1967 p. 19. The percentage calculations are by the writer, rounded off to the nearest 0·5 per cent, except for the figures for Asian prisoners which are to the nearest 0·1 per cent.

There are indications that many African employees regard pilfering as a legitimate means of supplementing low earnings, and the courts constantly reiterate their determination to suppress such 'betrayals of trust' with severe sentences. Thus theft from an employer, even of the most inexpensive article, is almost invariably punished with a sentence of several months imprisonment; first offenders are not exempt, and not long ago two Transvaal judges confirmed on review sentences of six months imprisonment passed on Africans who had respectively stolen a packet of matches and a toilet roll at their places of work (1964 SALJ, 113).

Hardly any sociological analysis has been attempted to explain the extent of common law crime amongst Africans. To adherents of racial theory it is self-evident that Africans have an ethnic propensity towards violence and plunder, and criminal statistics are seen merely as confirming what every white man is considered to know from common experience. In the view of such theorists, the only realistic approach towards crime in South Africa is to have strong laws, a strong police force, a strong Judiciary and escape-proof jails. A common variant of this attitude is that Africans in their tribal or 'natural' state are basically law-abiding, but that they are unable to resist the temptations of city life and collapse into lawlessness once they enter the white man's world. Thus a Deputy-Commissioner for Police declared in 1917:

> When one remembers the overwhelming majority of natives in the Division compared with Europeans, and their extensive facilities for wrongdoing, it must be confessed that the native is a wonderfully law-abiding subject. The native attitude towards the white is almost one of profound indifference, closely bordering on insolence, but usually it is only in the towns that over-civilisation jeopardises and impairs the native's uniform good conduct and obedience to the law.

A Commissioner of Police agreed that 'raw natives' were being debauched by the city environment, and pointed the moral that the answer lay in more compounds and closer controls (UG 42/1917; UG 62/1912).

Critics of racial theory, on the other hand, attribute lawbreaking to the very controls that are supposed to counteract it.[7] They point to the

[7] The Penal Reform Commission of 1947 adopted a rather eclectic approach in which all viewpoints were manifest. Cf. UG 47/1947, section on Race and Crime, pp. 3 et seq., and references to 'barbarism', p. 64. An Inter-Departmental Committee Report published in 1942 placed strong emphasis on poverty and broken homes as a causative factor in relation to crime amongst Africans.

disruption of communities and the breaking up of families by the law, and to the blatant inequalities of wealth and opportunity that attach to race in South Africa, and argue that what appears to the racist to be an inherited deficiency in the personalities of blacks is in fact a reaction to deficiencies in society. They agree that traditional African societies in southern Africa were generally fairly free of crime (whether defined in traditional or modern terms), but state that the only realistic solution to contemporary law-breaking is to allow Africans full rights and participation in a common society rather than to try to restore a past that vanished irretrievably with the destruction of the tribal armies and the dispossession of the tribal lands.

In view of the ever-increasing flow of Africans into prison it is perhaps ironical that for many years the authorities regarded the very idea of imprisonment of Africans with uncertainty. Some Cape judges were said to pass moderate sentences on Africans because "natives pine so much in captivity". More recently a prominent South African judge stated that solitary confinement bore particularly harshly on Africans because they did not have much to contemplate (Van den Heever). Other jurists, however, felt that "to natives of the class who fill our jails, to be well fed and clothed is a mild form of punishment of which they can bear a considerable amount". One writer went so far as to say that Africans positively enjoyed going to prison; entirely misconstruing this institution of Western civilisation, they proudly wore their clothing embroidered with the Queen's coat of arms, and felt themselves to be lodged in a splendid building which would give them status in the eyes of their peers (Seymour). More recently a Director of Prisons wrote that unsophisticated Africans had alarming anticipations of prison, but found their fears dissipated by reality, so that imprisonment lost its deterrent value. In his view, the answer was to keep petty offenders out of prison if at all possible, and to subject them instead to corporal punishment. "The brutalising effect of strokes at any rate on natives has been grossly exaggerated, and there is no doubt that whipping is far less harmful than a term of imprisonment, which may completely demoralise the person and give him a trend towards a criminal career" (UG 38/1932).[8]

---

[8] None of the five above mentioned statements was made by Africans or purported to be based on what African prisoners themselves had stated to be the impact of imprisonment upon them. Cf. *The East African Experience of Imprisonment* by R. E. S. Tanner, in (ed.) Milner, based on a survey conducted amongst prisoners, especially at pp. 295 and 314.

Whether or not imprisonment deters Africans from criminal careers or predisposes them towards such careers, the scale of incarceration of Africans has become very large by international standards. Table 15 provides a comparison between the annual admission rates in the early 1960s of prisoners in South Africa, England and Wales, Tanganyika, Kenya and Ghana. It should be remembered that more than three-quarters of the South African prisoners were African.

TABLE 15

PERSONS RECEIVED INTO PRISON UNDER SENTENCE IN
SOUTH AFRICA, ENGLAND AND WALES, TANGANYIKA,
KENYA AND GHANA IN THE EARLY 1960S[9]

Country	Year	Number of Persons received into Prison under Sentence	Total Population in millions
South Africa	1964	297,000	18
England and Wales	1964	53,000	46
Tanganyika	1962	37,000	9·2
Kenya	1964	29,000	6·5
Ghana	1964	16,000	8

According to the figures in Table 15, in absolute terms nearly six times as many South African convicts went to prison as convicts in England and Wales, while in relation to the total population of the country, the proportion was nearly fifteen times as many. The absolute figure for South Africa was also three times that of the combined total for Tanganyika, Kenya and Ghana, while the relative figure was four and a half times as great.

By the end of the 1960s the disparity between the South African and the English and Welsh totals had become even greater, as appears from Table 16.

[9] South Africa–prisons reports for year ended 30th June 1964; England and Wales–*People in Prison*, Command 4214, HMSO, November 1969, p. 14 (figures for Borstals and detention centres are included); Tanganyika–J. Read in (ed.) Milner, p. 130 (the latest figure given is for 1962); Kenya–J. Read *ibid*, p. 129; Ghana–Robert E. Seidman and J. D. Abaka Eyison in (ed.) Milner at page 87 (footnote 72).

Table 16 establishes that by 1968 the absolute total of South Africans going to prison under sentence was ten times that of England and Wales, while the relative figure was approximately fifteen times.

Included in the 1968 South African figure of nearly half a million convicts admitted to prison were 416,000 Africans (350,000 men and 66,000 women; a further 4,000 infants at breast were admitted, and nearly 200 children were born in prison).

TABLE 16

PERSONS RECEIVED INTO PRISON UNDER SENTENCE IN SOUTH AFRICA AND IN ENGLAND AND WALES IN THE YEARS 1961 AND 1968[10]

	Number of Persons received into Prison under Sentence		Increase in Seven Years
	1961	1968	
South Africa	289,000	486,000	197,000
England and Wales	47,000	49,000	2,000

Thus by the end of the 1960s approximately 350,000 African men were being received into prison under sentence each year, and approximately 150,000 of these were first offenders (Prisons Reports). If this level of imprisonment is maintained in the 1970s, then according to the writer's calculations within the decade one African man in three will have served a sentence as a convict in South Africa,[11] and if remand prisoners not subsequently admitted as convicts are included as well,

[10] South African figures from annual prison reports; English and Welsh figures from *People in Prison*; a subsequent jump of nearly 10,000 in the next three years has caused considerable concern in England.

[11] Calculations based on (i) Total African population in 1969 of approximately 14 million, 7 million of whom were male; expected to increase by about one-third over the whole of the decade. (ii) More than 1,500,000 African men first offenders being imprisoned as convicts in the decade; and (iii) Fifty per cent of African males being under the age of 18 at any particular time (cf. Native Affairs Department report for 1963, RP 41/1965, p. 2).

probably one African man in two will have been in jail.[12] If the 1960s rate of increase is maintained, then more than half the adult African male population will have served sentences as convicts, and well over half would have spent some time in prison.

It was mentioned earlier that the great majority of sentences served by Africans were for relatively short periods. Nevertheless the core of long-term prisoners has grown at a rapid rate, and is partly responsible for the increase in the average daily prison population in South Africa. Table 17 charts the increase from 1912 to 1969 in the average number of persons in custody each day.

TABLE 17

AVERAGE DAILY PRISON POPULATION FOR SELECTED YEARS
FROM 1912 TO 1969

Year	Population of South Africa	Average Daily Prison Population
1912	6,100,000	13,824
1922	7,100,000	17,386
1932	8,300,000	20,831
1942	10,800,000	21,483
1952	13,500,000	31,903
1962	17,200,000	62,769
Year ending 30th June		
1964	18,000,000	70,351
1965	18,500,000	72,627
1966	18,900,000	74,033
1967	19,400,000	73,030
1968	19,800,000	80,534
1969	20,300,000	88,079

(Prisons Reports)

[12] In the year ended 30th June 1969, only 97,000 out of 258,000 awaiting-trial prisoners were subsequently admitted to prison as sentenced prisoners. It is not known how many of the remaining 161,000 prisoners were African male first offenders, but the figure should not be less than that for African male first offenders amongst sentenced prisoners, namely about 30 per cent. This would add more than half a million to the total for the decade, bringing it up to more than 2 million. Persons detained in police lock-ups and not subsequently sent to prison would not appear to be included in any of these figures.

The figures in Table 17 demonstrate that during the period 1912 to 1969 the daily average prison population increased at nearly twice the rate of the total population of South Africa. The increase in daily average prison population was also greater than the increase in total admissions, in the ratio of approximately 5 : 4. This latter ratio suggests that there has been an increase in the average length of sentence served, due either to a reduction in paroles or remissions granted or to an increase in the length of sentences imposed. Since greater use seems to have been made of parole and remission in more recent years, the inference may be drawn that the courts are imposing steadily heavier sentences. It is not clear whether such heavier sentences are due to an upsurge in convictions for serious offences, or to a tendency on the part of the Judiciary to impose more severe sentences for the same kinds of offence, or to both. Reliable analysis on this score is frustrated by lack of particularity in the published statistics. One hypothesis which may be advanced as a contributory factor, however, is that just as the courts have tended to increase the level of fines in order to keep pace with monetary inflation, so they have tended to increase the lengths of prison sentences as though the value of these too depreciated over the years.

A breakdown by race and sex of the average daily prison populations for selected years from 1911 to 1968 highlights the extent to which African and coloured prisoners have increasingly contributed towards the total (see Table 18).

The figures in Table 18 establish that the increase from 1911 to 1968 was greatest for African and coloured women, and next greatest for African and coloured men. The increases for white men and women did not quite keep pace with the increase in total population, whereas the average daily total of Asian men and women prisoners actually decreased. (The totals for the years 1911 and 1913 were inflated by the civil disobedience campaigns led by M. K. Gandhi.) It is noteworthy, however, that in the period 1938 to 1968 increases were recorded for all racial groups. The upward trend in the prison population was considerably less marked in the three decades immediately following Union than it was in the next three decades, and whereas the average daily population of African and coloured prisoners increased by about 65 per cent in the 27 years from 1911 to 1938, it rose by more than 400 per cent in the 30 years from 1938 to 1968. The comparable figures in England and Wales for average daily prison populations (including Borstals and detention centres) were 18,200 in 1913, 11,086 in 1938 and 32,461 in 1968.

TABLE 18

AVERAGE DAILY PRISON POPULATION FOR SELECTED YEARS
FROM 1911 TO 1968 CLASSIFIED ACCORDING TO RACE AND
SEX[13]

Year	Combined Figures for African and Coloured Prisoners		Separate Figures for African and Coloured Prisoners			
			African		Coloured	
	Men	Women	Men	Women	Men	Women
1911	10,867	815	—	—	—	—
1913	11,515	914	—	—	—	—
1938	17,349	1,340	—	—	—	—
1968	71,160	5,757	58,415	4,914	12,745	843

	White		Asian		Total for all Race Groups
	Men	Women	Men	Women	
1911	1,286	53	519	15	13,556
1913	1,157	80	565	21	14,649
1938	859	21	109	16	19,679
1968	3,078	98	433	8	80,534

(vi) *Executions*

At the time of Union capital punishment was competent in respect of three crimes, namely, murder, rape and treason. In the case of murder it was an obligatory penalty, but for rape and treason its imposition lay within the discretion of the trial judge.

By 1967 capital punishment had become competent for nine crimes – namely: murder, rape, treason, aggravated housebreaking, armed robbery, kidnapping, and offences under the 'Sabotage' Act, the Suppression of Communism Act, and the Terrorism Act.[14] The death

[13] Annual Prison Reports. The figures for 1911 have been rounded off to the nearest 1. Until the 1960s separate figures were not kept for African and coloured prisoners. The figures for 1968 are for the year ended 30th June 1968.

[14] Criminal Procedure Amendment Act, 1958, sec. 4 (robbery and housebreaking); General Law Amendment Act, 1962, sec. 21 (sabotage); General Law Amendment Act, 1963, adding a new offence and punishment to the Suppression of Communism Act, 1950; Criminal Procedure Amendment Act, 1965 (kidnapping and child stealing); The Terrorism Act, 1967.

sentence continued to be compulsory for murder, save that since 1935, if extenuating circumstances were found to be proved, the judge could impose a lesser penalty. As far as the other eight offences were concerned, capital punishment could be imposed at the discretion of the judge.

TABLE 19

PERSONS EXECUTED IN THE DECADES 1911 TO 1920, 1939 TO 1948 AND 1960 TO 1969[15]

	1911-20 Number Hanged		1939-48 Number Hanged		1960-69 Number Hanged
1911	57	1939	11	1960	70
1912	24	1940	22	1961	66
1913	24	1941	20	1962	129
1914	23	1942	12	1963	115
1915	29	1943	17	1964	81
1916	36	1944	14	1965	113
1917	23	1945	14	1966	70
1918	23	1946	20	1967	121
1919	32	1947	27	1968	99
1920	19	1948	37	1969	84
Total for decade	290		194		948
Average per annum	29·0		19·4		94·8

The addition of the six new capital crimes took place in the decade 1958 to 1968, which was also a time of considerable increase in the number of persons executed in South Africa (see Table 19).

From the figures in Table 19 it can be seen that in the first decade after Union the average annual number of executions was 29, in the fourth decade it was 19 and in the sixth decade it was 95. Thus an

[15] Figures extracted from annual reports of the Commissioner of Prisons, which referred to calendar years until 1956, when they referred to the 12-month period ending 30th June of the year mentioned. In the past decade about 90 per cent of executions were for murder: thus in the year ended 30th June 1965, there were 100 executions for murder, 3 for rape, 5 for robbery, 1 for sabotage and 3 for murder and sabotage and 1 for murder and rape. RP 13/1966 p. 5. In the previous year 6 of the executions were for sabotage and 2 for housebreaking.

initial diminution consistent with a trend in many countries towards abolition was followed by a sudden rise inconsistent with such trend. The result has been that after being indistinguishable from dozens of other countries sixty years ago, South Africa now has the distinction of occupying first place in a United Nations survey on the rate of capital punishment throughout the world. Table 20 records the number of death sentences imposed and the number of executions actually carried out during the five-year period 1956-1960 in 32 respondent countries that still retained capital punishment.

A feature of the list is that eleven of the twelve respondent countries with the highest rates of execution were former British colonies, whilst the legal system of the twelfth (the United Arab Republic) had been considerably influenced by British administrators. It should be remembered, however, that a number of countries where capital punishment has not been abolished did not respond to the survey, and that the figures refer only to judicially imposed executions.

During the following decade a number of countries in the list below either abolished capital punishment altogether, or else suspended its operation (e.g. New Zealand, the United Kingdom, Dahomey, France and the U.S.A.). In many other countries the rate of execution declined, either because fewer death sentences were imposed or because more reprieves were granted. Thus a second United Nations survey revealed that in the next five-year period (1961 to 1965) judicial executions in Nigeria declined from 291 to 191, in the U.S.A. from 219 to 132, in Japan from 126 to 48, in the United Kingdom from 28 to 12, in Canada from 16 to 4, in France from 11 to 6 and in Somalia from 8 to 3; in Taiwan they rose from 15 to 25, and in South Africa, according to the annual Prisons Reports, they rose from 392 to 508.

The total number of executions reported to the United Nations for the period 1961 to 1965 was 1,033. During the five-year period ended 30th June 1966 a total of 508 persons were executed in South Africa, representing nearly half the world's reported total for approximately the same period.

The discovery that the hangman in Pretoria was responsible for almost half of all the world's reported judicial executions, prompted discussion on capital punishment in South African legal journals and the press. Nearly all the academic writing was abolitionist in character, and many advocates as well as a few judges declared themselves against capital punishment. Yet when in 1969 a Member of Parliament introduced a motion to request the Government to consider the advisability

TABLE 20

FIGURES FOR DEATH SENTENCES IMPOSED AND EXECUTIONS
CARRIED OUT IN 32 COUNTRIES IN QUINQUENNIUM
1956 TO 1960

Country	Death Sentences Imposed	Executions
South Africa	592	392
Sudan	547	354
Nigeria	590	251
U.S.A.	not available	219
Tanganyika	289	144
UAR	103	66
Malaya	85	56
Ghana	179	54
Ceylon	451	48
Turkey	33	32
Yugoslavia	38	31
United Kingdom	100	28
N. Rhodesia	49	26
Hong Kong	30	26
Canada	59	16
Taiwan	15	15
Morocco	43	14
France	33	11
Nyasaland	25	9
Spain	33	8
Somalia	15	8
New Zealand	10	7
Fiji	14	7
Zanzibar	14	5
Lebanon	30	4
Thailand	27	4
Chile	12	2
Mauritius	4	2
South Australia	9	2
West Australia	8	1
Ivory Coast	16	0
Dahomey	3	0

(Capital Punishment, UN 1968)

of appointing a commission to enquire into the desirability of abolition, she was unable to find a seconder, and the motion lapsed. The main argument in favour of retention has been essentially a racial one. Thus the 1947 Penal Reform Commission commented that comparisons with abolitionist countries were unhelpful, since they did not have heterogeneous populations in which the bulk of 80 per cent of the population had not yet emerged from barbarism. In 1968 the head of the Department of Criminology at Pretoria University stated in a popular weekly newpaper that the abolition of the death sentence might be regarded by the non-whites as a sign of weakness and as a licence to sow death and destruction (Venter, Landstem 1/9/1968).

(vii) *Corporal Punishment*

The incidence of corporal punishment in South Africa dropped consistently for a number of decades and then rose sharply again before recently declining once more. In the first four decades after Union a total of approximately 115,000 offenders received approximately 910,000 strokes, while in the following two decades approximately 220,000 offenders received approximately 1,220,000 strokes.[16] Thus the number of persons per decade receiving corporal punishment increased nearly fourfold, outstripping the increase in population, while the number of strokes inflicted per decade more than doubled. Table 21

TABLE 21

CORPORAL PUNISHMENT DURING SELECTED YEARS
1911 TO 1969

Year	Number of Offenders	Number of Strokes
1911	3,399	34,048
1921	2,733	24,407
1931	2,981	19,751
1941	1,617	10,164
1951	4,783	28,152
1961	17,389	80,949
1969	5,273	25,933

(Annual Prisons Reports)

[16] Rough calculations by the writer based on figures in the Annual Reports of the Director (now Commissioner) of Prisons.

indicates the number of offenders sentenced to corporal punishment and the number of strokes inflicted during selected years from 1911 to 1969.

Starting in 1911 with approximately 3,400 offenders receiving 34,000 strokes, the figures tended to drop until they reached their nadir in 1941, when 1,600 offenders received 10,000 strokes. Thereafter the figures crept up consistently until 1952, when Parliament laid down that corporal punishment should be a mandatory sentence for persons found guilty of certain specified offences. This led to a very rapid rise in the figures which reached a peak of 18,500 offenders sentenced to 94,000 strokes in 1958. The figures then stayed on a plateau before descending once more when judicial discretion was restored in 1965. By 1969 slightly more than 5,000 offenders received slightly less than 26,000 strokes.

The South African Penal Reform Commission reported in 1947 that corporal punishment as a method of dealing with crime had been abandoned by most of the civilised countries of the world, outstanding exceptions being the British Commonwealth and dependencies and parts of the United States of America. It added that the main argument for its retention in South Africa was that it was a deterrent "of special efficacy especially in a country largely populated by a people the bulk of whom have not yet emerged from an uncivilised state, and that no other penalty would be equally effective in respect of crimes of violence or those crimes which by reason of their diabolical or inhuman character gravely shock the sense of a law-abiding community". After considering the arguments for abolition, the Commission declared that while not losing sight of the ideal that a civilised community should rid itself of the obloquy of exercising a brutal means of penalty, a sensible realism should be adhered to, and corporal punishment should be retained in South Africa. It recommended that flogging be imposed only for sexual assaults, or assaults involving grievous bodily harm, aggravated cruelty to humans or animals, stock-theft or housebreaking. With regard to stock-theft, it said that the withdrawal of corporal punishment as a penalty might be gravely detrimental to the interests of stock-farmers, who were entitled to special protection. Similarly, housebreaking was on the increase and might call for special deterrent.

The notion of corporal punishment being a special deterrent was developed in Parliament in the 1950s when the law relating to criminal procedure was amended to make whipping an obligatory sentence for specified crimes.[17] Previously corporal punishment had been a competent penalty, either on its own or in addition to any other penalty, for most common law offences. Now the discretion of the courts was removed, and judges and magistrates were ordered to impose strokes on all persons found guilty of housebreaking, receiving stolen property, theft of motor cars or theft from motor cars, and the more serious crimes of violence. Defending the subsequent large-scale flogging of youths, the Secretary of Justice said in an interview: "I frequently walked around with what we regarded as honourable scars after I had had a difference of opinion with authority, and I do not think I am any the worse for it. . . . Boys being what they are there will always be some who scream and some who will not. . . . Such hidings naturally left small wounds but the same happened to boys who were caned at school" (Jansen, *Cape Argus*, 25/6/1955).

The general increase in whippings was considerable, but there appeared to be little corresponding decrease in the specified offences. Eventually, after twelve years had elapsed and a million strokes had been imposed, the failure of mandatory flogging was officially acknowledged, and the discretion of the courts was restored (Act 96 of 1965).

While there have been sharp fluctuations in the number of persons subjected to whipping since 1911, the trend towards reducing the average number of strokes inflicted on each offender has been fairly consistent. This drop was noted with dismay by one Director of Prisons, who reported in 1935 that the effect of corporal punishment had been closely watched for some time, and the definite conclusion had been arrived at that the infliction of a lesser number of strokes than six in the case of whites and eight in the case of blacks was not an effective punishment. The Penal Reform Commission, on the other hand, observed that after the eighth stroke the cane fell upon numbed flesh and was ineffective. In practice the average number of strokes inflicted on each offender fell from 10 in 1911 to 5 in 1958, and it has remained at slightly under 5 since then.

At the same time as the average number of strokes per offender was being reduced, provincial variations were also being eliminated. Table 22 sets out the changes in the incidence of corporal punishment according to province for the year ended 30th June 1958 compared with the year 1918.

[17] Act 33 of 1952 and Act 25 of 1955 brought about the changes which were consolidated in the Criminal Procedure Act 56 of 1955, Third Schedule, Part II.

Table 22 shows that Natal has lost its pre-eminence as the 'lashing colony', and that the incidence of whipping now corresponds roughly with the total population of each province. The Transvaal has moved from being third in terms of total whippings and last in terms of average number of strokes, to first in each category.

The word 'whipping' has been used here interchangeably with 'floggings' and 'corporal punishment', in the same way in which it has been used in South African legislation. The term covers both lashes with

TABLE 22

AVERAGE NUMBER OF STROKES PER OFFENDER AND
PROVINCIAL CONTRIBUTION TO TOTAL NUMBER OF
WHIPPINGS IN THE YEAR 1918 AND THE YEAR ENDED
30TH JUNE 1958

Province	Average Number of Strokes per Offender		Percentage of All Persons Whipped in S.A.	
	1918	1958	1918	1958
Natal	9·8	4·9	42·0	16·0
Transvaal	7·6	5·1	18·5	42·0
OFS	10·3	5·0	5·0	6·5
Cape	9·2	5·1	34·5	35·5

(Annual Prisons Reports. Figures in last two columns rounded to nearest 0·5%)

a cat-o'-nine-tails and strokes with a heavy or light cane. The use of the cat has in fact become increasingly rare, and the prisons reports appear to have made no mention of its administration since 1958, when four persons were whipped with the cat. A heavy cane is used for offenders over 21 years old and a light cane for those under 21.

Now that the courts have had their discretion restored as to whether or not to impose corporal punishment, the incidence of flogging has dropped considerably. It is still higher than it was thirty years ago, but proportionate to the total population it is lower than it was at the time of Union. Men who are over the age of 50 or else who are medically unfit may not be whipped, and it is never a competent punishment for women offenders. The flogging of white men and youths is relatively infrequent but nevertheless not rare, as is shown in Table 23, which sets out the race and age of persons subjected to corporal punishment in the year ended 30th June 1969.

TABLE 23

FIGURES FOR CORPORAL PUNISHMENT FOR THE YEAR ENDED 30TH JUNE 1969, INDICATING THE NUMBER OF ADULT AND JUVENILE OFFENDERS OF DIFFERENT RACES AND THE COURT WHICH IMPOSED THE STROKES

	White	African	Asian	Coloured	Total
Number of Offenders					
21 years and over	41	3,299	5	562	3,907
Under 21	15	1,055	1	295	1,366
Number of Strokes Inflicted					
21 years and over	197	16,176	23	2,713	19,109
Under 21	94	5,283	4	1,443	6,824
Sentences Imposed by					
Supreme Court	2	167	—	57	226
Inferior Courts	49	4,136	5	768	4,958
Prison Disciplinary Courts	5	51	1	32	89

TOTAL: 25,933 strokes on 5,273 offenders

A comparison of the figures in Table 23 with those in the annual report for the year ended mid-1958 reveals that all racial groups have benefited from the recent reduction in thrashings, but that white offenders have benefited the most. The judges have also tended to exercise their discretion more benevolently than the magistrates, while even in the prisons, where corporal punishment for disciplinary offences was never made compulsory, its incidence has declined.

CHAPTER SEVEN

Black Attitudes and Actions

Modernisation of the Union of South Africa did not lead to a relaxation of race domination but rather to an improvement in the techniques of control and greater sophistication in its justification. As the interdependence of black and white South Africans in a common economy increased, and as cultural differences between them diminished, so was the law used in ever greater measure to create statutory differentiation and to maintain black subordination. Thus industrialisation did not erode race distinction; on the contrary, it enabled segregation to be enforced with the powerful weapons of a modern state. The courts were an integral part of the State machine. While the higher courts from time to time delivered judgements which softened or delayed the impact of new segregatory measures, the lower courts continuously and on a massive scale punished breaches of established race-statutes.

White lawyers and judges have generally directed their attention to the occasional superior court judgements which have had great constitutional interest but little practical impact, whereas black litigants have generally been more concerned with the extensive number of inferior court cases which have had slender constitutional import but considerable practical effect.

To any litigant the character of neighbourhood law depends upon the kind of neighbourhood he inhabits. If he lives in a wealthy suburb and works in a thriving city centre, neighbourhood law signifies to him company flotations, property deals, tax avoidance, insurance claims, matrimonial disputes, embezzlement, motor offences and keeping black servants and employees under proper control. If he resides in a poverty-stricken compound or location, on the other hand, neighbourhood law denotes pass and tax raids, debtors' enquiries, and prosecutions for theft and violence. The legal profession has been overwhelmingly concerned with the welfare of the wealthy white litigant, and the bulk of legal literature has been devoted to examination of nuances of doctrine relevant to his disputes. To the half million Africans who go to prison each year, however, it matters little whether a new Chief Justice is liberal or segregationist, whether the courts rely mainly on English or Roman-Dutch authorities, or even whether the law adopts an objective or a subjective approach to the question of criminal intent. Previous chapters have considered the incorporation of Africans into the legal order, judicial attitudes to race, and the extent to which the legal system has impinged on African life. It is now appropriate to investigate African attitudes towards the law and its administration.

ATTITUDES TOWARDS LAWYERS

Was it proper that Africans should be legally represented in South African courts? This was one of the subsidiary questions investigated by the South African Native Affairs Commission, constituted by the British in 1903 to hear evidence and make recommendations on a unified 'native policy' for the sub-continent. Judging by their questions, most of the Commissioners were of the *prima facie* view that the answer was 'no', since lawyers appeared to be at best superfluous and at worst harmful to African litigants. Such a viewpoint was supported by a number of magistrates who testified that the true function of lawyers was misunderstood by Africans, whose respect for the administration was undermined by applications brought against the Government and further diminished by appeals noted against the judgement of magistrates. A police chief went further and urged that separate rules of evidence be created for Africans, so that they might be questioned more easily; he agreed fully with the suggestion from one of the Commissioners that the meaning of 'getting off' on a technicality was quite different for Europeans from what it was for Africans (Mavrogordato).

Some of the magistrates who gave evidence, however, insisted that lawyers were quite as useful in cases involving Africans as in any other cases, and almost without exception African witnesses spoke strongly in favour of retaining the right to be represented in court. One African witness went so far as to claim that every African boasted of his lawyer, while another said the African people would learn quickly enough how to make the best use of lawyers. If lawyers were so bad, he asked in effect, why did the whites use them? Questioned on whether or not the right to retain lawyers to advise them against the Government tended to teach Africans to be respectful towards authority, this last witness said that the lawyers would not advise them to bring actions against the Government if it were not the practice of the whites to do so in similar circumstances. Another witness repudiated the suggestion that Africans were accustomed only to despotic forms of rule, and told the Commissioners: "You have had your Charles and your James, and knew how to deal with them–the same with the natives" (Jabavu). Finally, an African who had worked for a white attorney dispelled the idea that there was anything peculiar or mysterious about African attitudes towards lawyers. His evidence ran as follows:

Do the natives generally speaking like lawyers . . .?–No, they do not like lawyers.

Do they not help them then . . .?–It is a matter of necessity, going to the lawyers, but they do not like lawyers.

Why do they not like lawyers . . .?–I do not suppose anyone in the world likes lawyers; lawyers are not liked on account of their fees (Umhalla).

The evidence of these and other witnesses indicated that Africans throughout South Africa had become accustomed to the use of lawyers, who, if they could not secure rights for them, could at least soften their disabilities. African witnesses complained about pass raids, curfews, rude policemen and unequal laws ("the law has only one eye"), but they did not disparage the use of lawyers. It might even be argued that the more unfavourably Africans felt towards the laws, the more well-disposed they were towards the lawyers. Racial statutes were so pervasive and the criminal law so extensive that lawyers came increasingly to occupy in relation to African society the position which doctors, moneylenders and priests occupied towards the poor of other lands. The word in everyday use amongst Africans in the Cape for lawyers was the unflattering 'igqwetha', meaning 'perverter' or 'twister', and traditionalist Africans expressed surprise that the whites who claimed to be upholders of the truth kept 'professional liars'. Yet if 'twisters' could save them from unjust (or even from just) punishments and appropriations, Africans were not averse to using them. For their part, if Africans paid their fees, lawyers were not averse to having them as clients. Many small firms of attorneys in various parts of the country began to develop lucrative practices on the basis of African clientele. Most of their work consisted of defending Africans charged with criminal offences, but they also handled civil claims, gave advice on a wide variety of matters, arranged for Africans to get permits and licences, and generally acted as intermediaries between Africans and the authorities. In more recent years the law compelling all motorists to take out compulsory third party insurance has made the humblest African pedestrian or cyclist a potential plaintiff for relatively substantial claims, and as such welcome in the offices of even the largest and most respectable firms. There has in addition developed a small but active class of lawyers willing to act for reduced or no fees on behalf of African litigants, especially in cases where civil liberties have been directly in issue. Some of this latter group have earned great popularity amongst Africans, and have on occasion been chaired out of court. If for no other reason, they would have been enthusiastically accepted because of their willingness to subject policemen to vigorous cross-examination, since the court-room was the only place where it was possible to see policemen being hectored and even humiliated.

ATTITUDES TOWARDS POLICE

Policemen and police raids have long impinged deeply on the consciousness of Africans, particularly those living in the urban areas. A social anthropologist who in the 1930s collected dreams of Africans living in an eastern Cape town, reported that the motif which occurred most frequently was that of a police raid. Several times when going round the location for the purpose of interviews, she heard a warning cry which announced the impending arrival of the police, and saw women rush to empty or hide tins of beer, while other residents gathered in groups until the police went by. In her view the continual conflict between residents and authorities over petty matters meant that in serious affairs the police did not get the support of the law-abiding section of the population. In a more recent survey of a location in Cape Town, she and an African colleague made the point that in any society the attitude towards the police varied in a well-to-do suburb from that in a slum; what was peculiar about African locations was that all the 'decent people', including the middle class, were in conflict with the police in only slightly less a degree than were the town toughs (Wilson, Mafeje).

The police raid has also featured as a dominant theme in African autobiographical literature. The first African professor in South Africa, Professor Jabavu, complained sharply in the 1930s of what he called the unnecessarily coarse treatment handed out to arrested Africans by "ruffians who merit dismissal from their jobs". It was a dreadful experience, he wrote, for an African to be caught in the streets of town after curfew hour; an inebriated white could roam safely, but a respectable African was a target for any policeman. In his view the pass laws were similar to those which circumscribed movement during martial law at a time of belligerency, and "South Africa, so far as we aboriginals are concerned, is a country perpetually in the throes of martial law from which there is no escape". Thirty years later the Professor's daughter described how her aged father pleaded with the police for the release of a cousin who had been arrested for being 'cheeky' after coming to their village to attend her brother's funeral; the Professor spoke abjectly to the sergeant, "appealing to the humanity we all know lurks behind those granite-hard, sun-tanned faces, behind those glittering blue eyes".

The writer Ezekiel Mphahlele wrote in his autobiography how after leaving a party given in a 'white' suburb to celebrate his receipt of an M.A. degree in literature, he was stopped on his way home by five different batches of policemen over a distance of fifteen miles, a ghastly reminder to him of motion pictures showing life in occupied countries during the war. His childhood in the 1930s had been dominated by the police—once he had been so terrified by the mere sight of a constable that he had hidden behind a bush—and in the 1950s he found that his children were in turn overwhelmed by their presence. His oldest boy always reminded him when he went shopping not to forget his pass; his middle son strutted around with imitation handcuffs, crudely made of wire, shouting: "Where's your pass, I'll teach you not to be naughty again"; whilst his four-year-old clung to him every time a policeman walked by and said: "Daddy, is the policeman going to arrest me, is he going to take you, is he going to take mamma?" Chief Luthuli also related in his autobiography how as a schoolboy he learnt to beware of the police. He stated that the white police were the section of the white community who had the most intimate and regular meeting with Africans; those who behaved with restraint he had applauded, but generally "they must assert and parade themselves, demanding this, ordering that and hurling abuse". For Africans "our country has been made into a vast series of displaced persons camps". He himself was gratuitously beaten by a policeman while in custody in 1960. Finally, he asked, could anyone who read in the press a routine announcement of a pass raid by police possibly imagine "the fear of the loud, rude bang on the door in the middle of the night, the bitter humiliation of an undignified search, the shame of husband and wife being huddled out of bed in front of their children and taken off to a police cell?"

The theme of the police raid figured prominently too in the autobiography of the writer Bloke Modisane, who as a child saw his mother insulted, sworn at and bundled into a police van so often that it began to seem to him part of their way of life. The hero image he had had of his father was destroyed when a policeman demanded his father's pass. Location residents never knew whether a loud hammering on the door heralded the police or gangsters, nor of which group to be more afraid. He recalled a pre-dawn police raid conducted to check on residents' permits; the police burst into his home, shining a torch into the eyes of his wife and frightening his child. "When the police drove off ... people emerged from out of the dark yards, out of the ruin of demolished houses, out of the dark alleys; they were dressed in scanty garments: blankets, bed-sheets, towels, table spreads, in almost anything which was handy at the time of fleeing ... from the processes of the law which required them to have a permit to live in the peace and security of their homes." The passes, officially called reference books, assumed such importance in the eyes of authority that they seemed to develop a life of their own. He suggested that marriage ceremonies could well be conducted as follows: "Do you, reference book no. 947067 take reference book 649707 as your lawfully documented wife?" Africans were expected to be eternal students at the school of good manners, he added, but the law was white, and in the location in which he lived heroism was measured by acts of defiance against the white man's law and order.

BROWN AND BLACK LAWYERS IN ACTION

(i) Passive Resistance–Advocate M. K. Gandhi

The first dark-skinned professional lawyer in South Africa was M. K. Gandhi, and the difficulties he encountered have already been referred to. Initially he was a strong believer in constitutionalism, the power of reason and the fairness of British rule, and this led him to adhere strictly to constitutionally acceptable forms of action, such as appearing in court on behalf of indentured labourers, drawing up petitions, organising public meetings and protesting through the press. Yet however persuasively he argued, the white colonists were always able to find a suitably phrased formula to oppose him, and in the end arguments were won on the basis not of pure reason, but on who had the ear of the Colonial Office. Thus the disfranchisement of Indian voters in Natal was effected by a measure which, purporting to be free of colour restrictions, allowed the vote only to those persons who had come from countries which had known Parliamentary institutions.

All the while, Gandhi was being prepared in a very personal manner for the kind of life style that was later to be associated with his name.

His abandonment of the splendid habits of a barrister in favour of the spare accoutrements of an ascetic was not precipitated by any sudden moral conversion. He adopted the philosophy of self-reliance partly because of the refusal of white barbers to cut his hair when he was due to go to court; he decided to renounce sexual pleasure and dedicate all his passion to public life after wandering in the hills of Zululand during the crushing of the Zulu 'rebellion'; and he vowed to refuse all food that gave pleasure to the palate after receiving the tasteless food given to black prisoners in South African jails.

If the first decade of his sojourn in South Africa was dominated by years of practice as a lawyer and months in the field as an ambulance-man, the second decade was devoted almost entirely to leading his people in campaigns of civil disobedience against the law. His loss of faith in the British Empire coincided with what he regarded as a betrayal of hopes after the British victory in the Anglo-Boer War. During the war he had frequently been at the battlefront, and had carried the son of the British Commander, Lord Roberts, from the field. The British tommies had been so friendly towards his ambulance corps that despite his feeling that the Boers were the victims of an unjust war, he looked forward to a British victory, inasmuch as it promised to usher in a new era of civil rights for brown South Africans. Instead he found that the British Army officers were harsher than the Boer officials had been. His disillusionment was complete when power was handed over in the Transvaal to an all-white legislature, which promptly reversed a court decision which had been favourable to Indians and imposed trade restrictions and pass laws on Indians (1907). Under Gandhi's leadership, the angry Indian population in the Transvaal refused to register for passes, whilst hundreds of traders defiantly plied their wares in areas forbidden to them. Thus South Africa, recently the birthplace of commandos and concentration camps, now became known as the birthplace of passive resistance, or, as Gandhi preferred to call it, satyagraha. (In fact the term passive resistance had been used previously in England in connection with educational struggles.) By the time the first campaign of passive resistance came to an end, more than 2,000 Indians had been imprisoned for periods of up to six months each, 700 for non-compliance with the registration laws and 1,300 for illegal trading. Many of those convicted of illegal trading were workers and professional men who deliberately pushed barrows to court arrest. One of the latter was a Natal-born barrister and graduate of Cambridge who, according to Gandhi, left his law books, took up a basket of vegetables, and was arrested as an unlicensed hawker. Gandhi now found himself placed in the dock, and he wrote later that it was an embarrassing experience standing as an accused in the very court where he had often appeared as counsel, but he considered that the former role was far more honourable than the latter, and willingly accepted his imprisonment. Later he was marched through the streets of Johannesburg wearing convict's clothes and carrying his bundle as any convict would.

Gandhi's principal individual antagonist at this time was Smuts, the brilliant lawyer, turned guerilla leader, turned politician. The Mahatma and the General were diametrically opposed to each other on many issues, but they also had much in common. Both were barristers trained in Britain, both belonged to communities aggrieved by British Imperial policy, both were activist politicians with a philosophical turn of mind, and both were noted for their simple habits and lack of personal ostentation. Yet whereas Gandhi was now entering a period of opposition to Empire, Smuts had just begun to follow the road of collaboration with the British, and whereas Gandhi was later to spend many years in prison for leading campaigns on behalf of a colonised majority, Smuts was to exercise power on behalf of a dominating minority. Gandhi is said to have spent some of his time during his first spell in prison fashioning a pair of sandals for his opponent Smuts, and Smuts is said to have remarked later that it was difficult to walk in the shoes of such a man. Yet at the time the two men were to indulge in bitter exchanges. Gandhi was brought from his prison cell to negotiate a settlement with Smuts; they were both lawyers and expert in the art of compromise, yet they did not keep notes of the agreement they arrived at, and each subsequently accused the other of dishonesty. The passive resistance campaign flicked to life once more, and the flames of civil disobedience spread to Natal. Indians in Natal were incensed by two issues: one, a poll tax recently imposed on them, and two, a Supreme Court decision that customary Indian marriages were legally invalid because they were potentially if not actually polygamous. A general strike of Indian workers was called, and Gandhi led 2,000 strikers and their families in an illegal march across the Natal-Transvaal border. A thousand of the marchers were sentenced to imprisonment, and Gandhi was ordered to spend a year in jail. The uproar that followed the killing of ten strikers by the army and police coincided with a simultaneous but unconnected threat of insurrection by white artisans on the Rand, and compelled Smuts once more to seek a negotiated settlement with Gandhi. Once again Gandhi was brought from his prison cell to

Smuts' office, and for a second time agreement between the two men was reached. Eventually legislation was passed which relieved Indians of the specific disabilities against which they had campaigned, but did not grant to Indians any further civic rights. Twenty years earlier Gandhi had arrived in South Africa as a well-mannered, elegantly attired and shy young barrister; now he departed as a lean, simply-dressed and resolute political campaigner. "The Saint has left our shores," Smuts observed, "I sincerely hope forever."

Gandhi did not in fact return to South Africa, though he continued to take a close interest in South African affairs. One of his sons remained behind, and took part in two further passive resistance campaigns after the Second World War. The first of these campaigns was launched at a time when Smuts and Gandhi were both elderly men at the height of their fame and approaching the end of their careers. Smuts had been Prime Minister of South Africa for a total of nearly fifteen years, and Gandhi was the elder statesman of newly independent India. The campaign of South African Indians against what they called Smuts' ghetto laws, focused international attention on South Africa, and led the Indian Government to charge in the United Nations that South Africa was ill-treating her citizens of Indian origin. Smuts had helped to draft the Charter of the United Nations, and now he suffered the indignity of finding his own Government amongst the first to be stig-matised for breach of its provisions. In this connection, however, he was not without honour in his own country, and he received strong backing from the two law journals published at the time. The then editor of the *South African Law Journal*, who was later to become a Judge of Appeal, noted the strange turn whereby the coloured races of the world could dictate to the European how to conduct his own white civilisation, and he rejected the charges of ill-treatment as being based simply on a refusal to give the Indians, who were mostly of the coolie class, political and social equality with the Europeans (Hall, 1949). Similarly, a senior government law adviser who was later to become Chief Justice used the columns of the *Tydskrif* to denounce the charges against South Africa, though he did so in more dignified language (Steyn, 1949). The major difference between the two articles was that whereas the former implied that the Indians were too poor to be entitled to have the franchise, the latter hinted that they were too rich to need it.

At this time there were very few Indian lawyers in practice in South Africa, but many of the younger supporters of the passive resistance campaign were now becoming legally qualified, and in the 1950s a new generation of young and politically radical Indian lawyers emerged. By 1962 out of 26 Indian attorneys and four Indian advocates in the country, nearly half had been subjected to banning orders by the Government because of their support for joint campaigns by the Indian and African Congresses against apartheid. Later in the decade even stronger action was taken against them, and one Indian advocate was sentenced to several years imprisonment for illegal political activities, and two were struck off the roll for being on a list of former members of the Communist Party. Many of the others were able to establish successful practices, but nevertheless they still had to endure the kinds of social indignity suffered by Gandhi seventy years earlier. Thus the first Indian barrister to appear in the Appeal Court was commended by the judges for his eloquent pleading, but when the tea-break arrived he was refused the customary cup of tea offered by the court staff to counsel, and when lunch-time came he was obliged to eat sandwiches in his motor car because there was no restaurant or hotel in Bloemfontein which would serve him (1959).

(ii) *Active Resistance – Attorneys Mandela and Tambo*

At the beginning of the twentieth century more than a hundred Africans were sent to Britain and the United States of America by various missions in South Africa to receive higher education. Most qualified as missionaries and teachers, but a few returned as lawyers and set up practice in South Africa. The pioneer of this latter group was Alfred Mangena (1879-1924) who after being called to the Bar in London, returned to the Cape and then decided to practise as an attorney in Johannesburg. At this stage a conference was being held to unify the Bars of the different parts of South Africa, and Mangena's arrival on the scene highlighted the conflicting racial attitudes of the Transvaal and Orange Free State Bars on the one hand, and the Cape Bar on the other. The northern advocates, whose delegates included Smuts and Hertzog, insisted that only white persons be allowed to join the proposed new union of advocates, whereas the Cape barristers, led by W. P. Schreiner, were determined to have no colour bar; in the end the conference broke down on the issue. The Transvaal Law Society, which represented attorneys in the Transvaal, followed the lead given by the Transvaal Bar, and when Mangena formally applied to the Supreme Court to be admitted to practise in the Transvaal, the Society opposed his application. The matter featured briefly in the Law Reports, which stated that the applicant "possessed the statutory qualifications, but was a native"; the President of the Law Society declared in an affidavit that in the existing state of society in the Transvaal there was no possibility of a native finding work as an attorney among white people, and that the applicant would have to practise among the natives; that the policy of the Government was to discourage litigation among them and to encourage them to have their grievances settled by the native affairs department or by means of native courts: that it would not be in the interests of natives of the Transvaal to create among them a class of native practitioner, and that the Law Society would find it difficult to exercise discipline over him. The judge held, however, that the Court would not be justified in refusing the application merely because the applicant belonged to one of the native races, or because there was no precedent in the Transvaal, nor would the Court assume that the applicant was going to encourage litigation amongst natives or behave dishonourably.

A short while afterwards two more Africans set up practices as attorneys in Johannesburg, R. W. Msimang, who had qualified as a solicitor in Somerset, and P. K. Seme, who after a distinguished career at Columbia University had gone on to Oxford and been called to the Bar in London. Seme's academic distinctions made him a respected figure in the African community, but did not save him from indignities in the course of his work, such as having to walk up five flights of stairs to consult with counsel because he was forbidden to use the lift. Although Seme was to remain in practice for many decades, these early African lawyers became better known for their political activities than for their legal work. In particular they were remembered for having convened the first conference of the African National Congress (ANC) and for having drafted its constitution (1912).

For the next forty years very few Africans entered the legal profession. The obstacles were social, educational and economic–bursaries were available for African matriculants intending to work for Church bodies or for the Government, but not for those desirous of becoming self-employed, and especially not for those who might become political agitators. Probably the biggest single barrier was the unwillingness of white attorneys to take on Africans as articled clerks. One African managed to qualify as an advocate by means of a correspondence course, but he did not go into practice, and instead became a respected academic figure and Vice-President of the ANC (Professor Z. K. Mathews). Yet just as at the time of Union embarking on a legal career had impelled young Africans into politics, so after the Second World War an interest in politics drove young Africans into law. Oliver Tambo and Nelson Mandela both discontinued their studies at Fort Hare University College after they had come into conflict with what they had regarded as excessively paternalistic authorities, and then served articles in Johannesburg with a view to becoming independent professional men. While in Johannesburg they met up with A. M. Lembede, who was articled to the now ageing and conservative Seme, and the three young men formed a new trio of ardent African nationalists determined to advance African claims. Lembede died at an early age, but Tambo and Mandela qualified as attorneys, set up in partnership, and became popular both as lawyers and as political leaders. They encouraged a friend and political colleague of theirs, Duma Nokwe, to study for the Bar, and in 1956 he became the first African to practise as an advocate in the Transvaal. At about this time the Government was using the provisions of the Bantu Education Act, 1953, to purge the ranks of African teachers of men who believed in equal rights, and a number of dismissed teachers thereupon qualified as lawyers. Yet the accretion of Africans to the legal profession was slow, and by 1962 there were only 13 African attorneys in practice in the whole country, and no advocates. Thus out of a total of approximately 3,000 attorneys in South Africa, only 44 were not white: 13 Africans, 26 Indians and 5 coloured persons. Africans constituted 70 per cent of the country's population but accounted for less than 0·3 per cent of the legal profession: their share of the £17 million income earned in that year by all attorneys amounted to only £15,000.

During the 1960s a number of African lawyers were imprisoned or placed under banning orders, while others slipped over the border into exile. Prominent amongst those who went into exile was Duma Nokwe, who during his few years at the Bar had been put on trial for treason, detained without charge, assaulted by a policeman (for which he was awarded damages), and prosecuted for carrying on the activities of the banned ANC. While some of his colleagues at the Bar had been friendly towards him, others had been hostile, such as the advocate who on being formally introduced to him looked at his outstretched hand and said: "No money today . . . out!" At the Supreme Court a special robing room had been set aside for him, in case, as he put it, he contaminated his white colleagues by donning his gown in front of them. Eventually he had gone over to full-time political work under cover of a dry-cleaning business, before finally leaving the country.

Yet despite the enforced departure of many African lawyers from practice, the 1960s saw a relatively rapid increase in the total number of Africans pursuing legal careers. By the beginning of 1969 the total was 44, two of whom were at the Bar; most of the attorneys were concentrated in Durban, Johannesburg and the Transkei. As far as the legal profession as a whole was concerned their numbers were tiny and their influence correspondingly small. Not a single African was in practice in the Orange Free State, not one in the Transvaal outside of Johannesburg, and not one in any of the tribal areas other than the Transkei. Those practising in the cities were faced with the threat of having to give up premises in the vicinity of the courts, and all were subject to the general restrictions imposed by law and practice on Africans. Nevertheless, they could hope to receive an income considerably greater than that available to all but the wealthiest Africans, and to have a relatively large measure of independence in their work.

For the few lawyers who chose the path of active collaboration with the Government, the rewards were even more substantial: Kaiser Matanzima became Chief Minister in the Transkei Parliament, and his brother George (no longer in practice after having been struck off the roll for irregularities) became Minister of Justice, while the Leader of the Opposition, K. Guzana, was also an attorney. Kaiser Matanzima expressed his enthusiasm for working with Pretoria in the following words:

> Summarised, our policy in the Transkei embraces a wholehearted acceptance of the policy of separate development; gradual and evolutionary progress in the Transkei towards greater autonomy; a firm rejection of the policy of multi-racialism; the preservation and development of our father-land by all means at our disposal; the promotion of the welfare of our people in all fields of human endeavour; the preservation of our own traditional system of chieftainship; the establishment in the Transkei of a state founded on justice, law and order; and finally a policy of intimate friendship with our mother-country, the Republic of South Africa (TLAD 1965, 1, 120).

When a motion was moved in the Transkei Assembly that the Pretoria Government be asked to release political prisoners who had come from the Transkei, George Matanzima moved an amendment which expressed full appreciation towards the Pretoria Government "for taking suitable and timeous steps against communist infiltrations into South Africa and the saboteurs who have no respect for life and property" (TLAD 1965, 2, 271). The man whose name cropped up most frequently in the debate on the above question was Nelson Mandela, and it is appropriate now to examine the history of the partnership of Mandela and Tambo to see how the attitudes of radical African lawyers towards the legal order were expressed, and with what consequences.

In the early 1950s Mandela and Tambo practised as attorneys in Johannesburg in a shabby office across the street from the magistrate's court. Theirs was the best known African legal partnership in the country, and they occupied premises in one of the few buildings in central Johannesburg where Africans were permitted as tenants. Tambo later described the scene as follows:

> To reach our desks each morning Nelson and I ran the gauntlet of patient queues of people overflowing from the chairs in the waiting room into the corridors. . . . Weekly we interviewed the delegations of grizzled, weather-worn peasants from the countryside who came to tell us how many generations their families had worked a little piece of land from which they were now being ejected. . . . Our buff office files carried thousands of (similar) stories (from the towns) and if when we started our law partnership we had not been rebels against South African apartheid, our experiences in our offices would have remedied the deficiency. We had risen to professional status in the community, but every case in court, every visit to the prisons to interview clients, reminded us of the humiliation and suffering burning into our people.

Even in their years of apprenticeship they had been given constant reminders of their status as Africans. Mandela had been articled to a relatively liberal firm of attorneys, yet he had been given a special cup from which to drink his tea; one day a white typist had been so embarrassed at having been seen taking dictation from him, that she had given him a sixpence and asked him to fetch her some shampoo from the chemist.

When in 1952 the ANC and the South African Indian Congress launched a passive resistance movement, known as the Defiance of Unjust Laws Campaign, Mandela was named as Volunteer-in-Chief. It was he who wrote the code of discipline for the defiers, and when the campaign came to an end (more than 7,000 persons had been convicted of participation) he was one of the leaders given a nine months suspended prison sentence for promoting what the judge called 'statutory communism'. The Minister of Justice also imposed a series of banning orders on him, and the Transvaal Law Society moved the Supreme Court to have him struck off the roll of attorneys. The Society's main argument was that any person who incited others to break the law was not a fit and proper person to act as an attorney, but the court vigorously rejected the application and declared that nothing had been placed before it which suggested in the slightest degree that Mandela had been guilty of conduct of a dishonest, disgraceful or dishonourable kind. ". . . In advocating the plan of action," the judges said, "the respondent was obviously motivated by a desire to serve his fellow non-Europeans."

The firm of Mandela and Tambo carried on in practice, but did so precariously. Permission for them to occupy premises in central Johannesburg was withdrawn, and they did their work under constant threat of eviction and prosecution. In December 1956 both partners were amongst the 156 persons of all races arrested and charged with High Treason.

South Africa has known many treason trials but the one brought against supporters of the ANC had the distinction of being both the longest and the least successful (1956-1961). Unlike the previous trials, this one was not a sequel to war, rebellion or insurrection. It was based on a document called the Freedom Charter which had been adopted at a public congress held in the presence of the police. Mandela and Tambo associated themselves with the demands of the Charter, which called for the creation of a non-racial democratic state assuring equal rights to all citizens. One section of the Charter declared that All Shall Be Equal Before The Law, and specified that no one should be condemned or restricted without fair trial; that the courts, the police and the army should be open to all and serve as the protectors of the people; that imprisonment should be for serious crimes and be aimed at re-education not vengeance; and that all discriminatory laws should be repealed. The prosecution case in essence was that these goals could be achieved only by violence, which was implicit in the ideology of all the accused and explicit in the language of some of them.

The legal profession was well represented amongst the accused, who included four African and two Indian attorneys, and one African and two white advocates. One of the advocates conducted his own defence, and was allowed to sit with defence counsel (Slovo), while another spent his time in the dock writing a book about the trial, which was published well before the trial was over (Forman, 1957). A composite photograph of all the accused appeared on the cover of the book, and standing out as certainly the tallest and possibly the most independent-looking of all the accused was Mandela.

Tambo later described Mandela as passionate, emotional, sensitive and quickly stung to bitterness and retaliation by insult of patronage. "He has a natural air of authority. He cannot help magnetising a crowd: he is commanding with a tall handsome bearing; trusts and is trusted by the youth, for their impatience reflects his own, appealing to the women. . . . He is the born mass leader."

During the early part of the trial, Mandela took little or no part in the proceedings other than to sit in the dock and listen to the evidence. A number of leading Johannesburg counsel handled the defence at reduced fees, and a special Treason Trial Defence Fund was established under the auspices of liberal clergymen, Members of Parliament and trade unionists; eventually the Fund raised more than £200,000, much of it from abroad. A vigorous opening address by one of the country's leading criminal lawyers ended with the assertion that the case was "a political plot of the type which characterised the period of the Inquisition and the Reichstag Fire Trial" (Berrangé).

The trial dragged on for four and a half years, causing great personal inconvenience to the accused, but also giving them the opportunity during adjournments to plan further campaigns of the kind which had brought them to the dock. During the trial, some of the accused became parents, some died and some got married; on one day Oliver Tambo and two other of the accused were respectively wed, causing advocate Forman, accused number 83, to write that "never in the history of South Africa have so many people accused of high treason gathered together to celebrate the wedding of so many people accused of high treason".

The bulk of the prosecution evidence consisted of documents found at the homes of the accused and transcripts of speeches made by the accused. Compared with the grim trials that were to take place in the 1960s, the Treason Trial frequently assumed the character of farce, particularly when detective witnesses were tested on their capacity for taking accurate notes in longhand. One detective admitted that he had been unable to understand the language used by the speakers at a meeting allegedly part of the treasonable conspiracy, but added that the chairman had provided him with a special interpreter. His cross-examination proceeded as follows:

> *Counsel*: Do you hold your notebook in one hand? – Yes.
> Do you hold your pencil in the other hand? – Yes.

Then where do you keep your pen? – In my mouth.
There are two different colours of ink in your notes? –
Yes, I can manage with two pens in my mouth.
Do you always carry your pens in your mouth?
Magistrate: Well, his mouth is big enough.

In the case of another detective witness the entire cross-examination occupied three lines:

When you go to meetings, do you go with the object of seeing if any offences are committed? – I don't understand.

No further questions. I just want the court to appreciate how much you do understand.

On one occasion the court adjourned early in order to enable the accused, who were out on bail, to take part in a street collection on behalf of the Treason Trial Defence Fund.

Until 1960 the accused played an entirely passive role in the proceedings. A number of them were discharged at the end of the preparatory examination, whilst the others were split up into three groups, only one of which was actually brought before the Supreme Court. Mandela belonged to this latter group, but Tambo did not and was able to carry on with his legal work. It was at this time that apartheid notices were being put up in court-rooms throughout the country, and in Johannesburg a magistrate ordered Tambo to take his seat at a table reserved for non-white lawyers. Tambo tried to argue from the table he had always used, that the magistrate's direction lacked lawful authority, and after a prolonged dispute involving several appearances in court first by Tambo and then by a clerk from his office, the clerk was fined for contempt of court, on the ground that he had refused to argue the invalidity of the magistrate's order from the separate table. The finding of the Appeal Court, namely that the accused would be as well seated at the one table as at the other was therefore in contempt of the magistrate, has already been dealt with (Chapter Five).

Graver issues than this, however, were to bring Tambo's legal career to an end. During the crisis which followed the shootings at Sharpeville early in 1960, Tambo was sent out of South Africa to campaign for the ANC abroad. Mandela, on the other hand, was one of thousands of persons placed in preventive detention under special emergency regulations; the Treason Trial continued, but under difficult circumstances, and eventually the accused decided by way of protest to dispense with counsel and conduct their own defence. Mandela had already emerged as the leading personality amongst the accused. He voiced their protests in prison and in court, and now he and his co-accused Duma Nokwe formally took over the running of the defence, their task being facilitated by the fact that after four years in the dock all the accused were thoroughly familiar with court-room styles and tactics. Several months later as the State of Emergency approached its end, counsel were re-engaged, and Mandela entered the witness box for the first time. His evidence and cross-examination lasted four days, during which he adamantly insisted that the ANC was committed to a policy of non-violence, even if it delayed the achievement of emancipation. One of his co-accused was so impressed by his demeanour in the witness box that as he stepped down to resume his seat in the dock, she wished to applaud, and wondered what the judges had made of what she called "this outstanding leader of the African people" (Helen Joseph, accused no. 2).

The Treason Trial eventually came to an end in 1961 when the three judges hearing the matter cut short argument by defence counsel and gave their verdict. They agreed unanimously that all the organisations charged in the indictment had worked together to replace the existing form of State with a radically different one based on the Freedom Charter. The prosecution had not proved, however, that such a State would be a communist one or that the accused had propagated the communist doctrine of violent revolution, and the court found it impossible to come to the conclusion that the ANC's policy was to overthrow the State by violence. The accused were accordingly found not guilty, and in great triumph they chaired their counsel to crowds of supporters waiting in the streets outside; they might have claimed that if their trial had borne any resemblance to the Reichstag Fire Trial, then it had been like that trial without even a Fire. The prosecution had been based on the assumption that campaigns for democracy in South Africa could only succeed by means of violence. The implications of such an approach were serious, but few of the accused seemed to have considered themselves in real jeopardy. If, however, the trial at times took on the aspect of farce, it can be argued that the legislative postscript was to rewrite the farce as tragedy.

The trial was concluded at a time of considerable political tension in the country. The ANC and a breakaway group led by Robert Sobukwe called the Pan-Africanist Congress (PAC) had both been banned after the shooting at Sharpeville in 1960, and later in that year the white electorate had decided by a narrow majority in a referendum that South Africa should become a republic. African leaders had protested about the fact that the African people had not been consulted about South Africa's new constitution, and they were now proposing to hold a conference to state their attitude. Fortuitously the banning orders on Mandela expired at this time, and Mandela emerged as the main speaker at the conference, voicing its demand for a national convention to be held representative of all groups in South Africa, at which a new non-racial, democratic constitution could be worked out. Later he wrote to the Prime Minister in the same terms, but the letter was handed over to the police, and Mandela then called for a general stoppage of work to coincide with the formal declaration of a Republic. To avoid capture by the police, Mandela went underground, the first prominent African leader to do so in modern times. The strike was only partially successful, but Mandela stayed underground, flitting from one part of the country to the next and earning for himself the name of the Black Pimpernel. The panache he had once exhibited as a lawyer he now displayed as an outlaw, but eventually after eluding the police for seventeen months, during which time he managed to go abroad and meet leading states-men in Africa and Europe, he was càptured and put on trial for inciting Africans to strike and for leaving the country illegally.

The defence which Mandela put up at this trial involved the most comprehensive and widely reported critique of the administration of justice ever made in South Africa. Mandela was not the first black man to challenge the right of racially constituted courts to sit in judgement over him. Individuals had done so before, and leaders of the PAC had boldly challenged the jurisdiction of the courts at the time of Sharpe-ville in 1960. Thus Robert Sobukwe had refused to plead to the charge on the basis that he felt no moral obligation to obey laws made by a white minority, and he had stressed that in his view unjust laws could not be justly applied. Yet Mandela's experience as a lawyer enabled him to examine the whole question of the administration of justice in South Africa with particular thoroughness, and his words, which were of special relevance to the theme of this study, will be quoted from extensively.

For sixty years lawyers defending rebels in South African courts had accepted the right and duty of the State to prosecute alleged law-breakers. Most defences had turned on questions of fact, with the accused either denying participation or else trying to minimise their role in activities that were admittedly illegal. Occasionally speeches in mitigation of sentence had alluded to political conditions in the country, and delicate suggestions had been made that autocratic behaviour on the part of certain officials had contributed towards rebellion. Some Afrikaner rebels in the Cape and Natal during the Anglo-Boer War had claimed that they were citizens of the Boer Republics and therefore entitled to be treated as prisoners of war, but the reports of trials during this period do not suggest that any attempt was made to challenge the overall legitimacy of the laws and the courts in the British Colonies. There had been over the years many unsuccessful challenges to martial law courts, but the authority of the ordinary courts had not been put in question. The defence, the prosecution and the judges had been at one in acknowledging the legitimacy of the ordinary legal system and the laws which it enforced. In juristic terms, the courts had held that they could not enquire into the legality of the authority which had constituted them. In political terms, conquered Afrikaners, defeated Africans and suppressed strikers had submitted to the jurisdiction of their victors.

Mandela began his defence by calling upon the magistrate to recuse himself on the grounds that he would not be able to ensure that Mandela had a fair trial. By means of this procedural device, Mandela threw into question the whole basis of law enforcement in South Africa. He stressed that from a personal point of view he held the magistrate in the highest regard, and apologised in advance for having to refer frequently to 'the white man' and 'the white people', because he detested racialism from any quarter, but was compelled to use this terminology because of the nature of the application. In essence he claimed that he feared he would not consider himself either legally or morally bound to obey laws made by a Parliament in which he had no representation.

From a technical point of view he based his application in the well-known principle that not only must justice be done, it must be seen to be done, and that any fact which gave rise to a reasonable apprehension in the mind of the accused that a judicial officer was lacking in impartiality rendered it necessary for such judicial officer to withdraw from the trial. Mandela went well beyond the usual limits of such application by alleging a bias arising out of a general social situation rather than from anything particular to the magistrate. In jurisprudential terms, his argument used natural law propositions to challenge the whole positivist foundations of the South African legal system. It attacked the concept of legal autonomy whose supporters claimed that it was possible for unjust laws to be justly administered. From a political point of view the application documented as clearly as any contemporary statement the transition of African nationalists from the politics of protest to the politics of revolution, since his challenge was directed not only at the political system in South Africa, but at the whole legal and administrative apparatus whereby it was maintained. Paradoxically, as an accused person in court, Mandela had a greater opportunity to articulate and get publicity for radical African demands than he had ever had whilst still unapprehended; this was the price the authorities had to pay for using the courts as an integral part of their system of social control.

His first proposition was that in a political trial involving a clash of the aspirations of the African people and those of the whites, it was wrong for whites to act as judges in their own cause, that is, for the aggrieved to sit in judgement over those against whom they had laid a charge. He conceded that an African in court enjoyed, on the surface, the same rights and privileges as a white person in that his trial would be governed by the same rules of procedure and evidence. Yet there was no real equality before the law. Africans had no right to participate in the making of the laws whereby they were governed, nor the right to get relief from the courts on the grounds that constitutional guarantees had been violated, nor the right to take part in the administration of justice. "The white man makes all the laws, he drags us before his courts and accuses us, and he sits in judgement over us. . . . I feel oppressed by the atmosphere of white domination that lurks all around in this court-room. . . . I have grave fears that this system of justice may enable the guilty to drag the innocent before the courts. It enables the unjust to prosecute and demand vengeance against the just." It was understandable, he said, that citizens who had the vote as well as direct representation in the country's leading bodies should be morally and legally bound by the laws governing the country; it should be equally understandable that Africans should adopt the attitude that they were neither morally nor legally bound to obey laws which they had not made, nor could they be expected to have confidence in courts which enforced such laws. He was aware that South African courts had often upheld the right of the African people to work for democratic change, and some judicial officers had openly criticised the policy which refused to recognise that all men were free and equal. He welcomed the existence of democratic values amongst some of the country's judges, but such honest and upright men were few and they had failed to convince the rest of the white population that white supremacy led to disaster. He added:

Even though now I happen to be tried by one whose opinion I hold in high esteem, I detest most violently the set-up that surrounds me here. It makes me feel that I am a black man in a white man's court. This should not be. I should feel perfectly at ease and at home with the assurance that I am being tried by a fellow South African who does not regard me as an inferior, entitled to a special kind of justice.

The court might say that he would be tried fairly and without fear or favour

> ... but broadly speaking Africans and whites in this country have no common standard of fairness. . . . Whatever the white man may say in his defence, his moral standards in this country must be judged by the extent to which he has condemned the vast majority of its inhabitants to serfdom and inferiority. We, on the other hand, regard the struggle against colour discrimination and for the pursuit of freedom and happiness as the highest aspiration of all men.

In conclusion, he declared that he made no threat when he said that unless these wrongs were remedied without delay "we might well find that even plain talk before the country's courts is too timid a method to draw the attention of the country to our political demands".

The magistrate interrupted Mandela a number of times, but did not prevent him from completing his statement. Not surprisingly, the magistrate rejected the recusal application and ordered that the trial proceed. (Mandela later brought another recusal application, alleging that the magistrate had been seen in a motor car in the company of two members of the Security Branch, who were assisting the prosecution, one of whom had given evidence. This application was also refused.) After evidence had been led for the prosecution, and Mandela had declined to go into the witness box, which would have been inconsistent with his challenge to the legitimacy of the proceedings, he was found guilty of both charges and asked if he had anything to say before sentence was passed on him.

Mandela was now presented with a second opportunity to address general remarks to the court. Unlike some American accused and their lawyers who recently (1969) deliberately broke established rules of etiquette in order to demonstrate their objections to the way justice was being administered, Mandela used recognised procedures to make his points and maintained normal court decorum throughout. Traditionally in South African practice a speech in mitigation of sentence related to the moral rather than the strictly legal aspects of the accused's conduct. Whereas at the beginning of the trial Mandela had concentrated on giving his views on the role of the courts in a racially stratified society, now he dealt primarily with the history of African submission to and resistance against the dominant legal order.

He spoke first of how as a boy in a village in the Transkei he had listened to the elders of the tribe telling stories of the good old days before the arrival of the white man, when his people had lived peacefully under the democratic rule of the kings and their councillors. "We occupied the land, the forests, the rivers; we extracted the mineral wealth beneath the soil. . . . We set up and operated our own government, we controlled our own armies and we organised our own trade and commerce. The elders would tell tales of the wars fought by our ancestors in defence of the fatherland as well as the acts of valour performed by generals and soldiers during these epic days." Leaders of different tribes had been mentioned as the pride and glory of the entire African nation. The foundation of government in early African societies was that all men were free and equal, and there were no classes, no rich and poor, and no exploitation of man by man. The council which governed the affairs of the tribe was fully democratic; chief and subject, warrior and medicine man, all took part and endeavoured to influence its decisions, and no step of any importance could ever be taken by the tribe without reference to it. There was much in such a society that was primitive and insecure and that could never measure up to the demands of the present epoch, but it nevertheless contained the seeds of a revolutionary democracy in which no one would be held in servitude, and it provided inspiration to those who sought to create a new democratic South Africa.

Mandela next dealt with his legal and political career, and pointed out that although many officials had treated him and his partner courteously, others had been openly hostile and discriminatory. He and Tambo had also been aware that however well they pursued their careers, they could never become prosecutors, magistrates or judges, and would have to deal with officials whose attainments and competence were no higher than theirs but whose superior positions were maintained by white skins. He saw it as a duty not only to his people but to his profession and to justice to cry out against this discrimination. It was opposed to the basic attitude towards justice which formed part of legal training in South Africa.

The whole life of any thinking African, he claimed, drove him continuously to a conflict between his conscience on the one hand and the law on the other. The ANC had for fifty years done everything possible to bring its demands to the attention of successive South African Governments. It had at all times sought peaceful solutions for the country's ills and problems. On the question of South Africa's new constitutional status, its members were neither monarchists nor believers in a Voortrekker type of republic, but were inspired by the idea of bringing into being a democratic republic where all South Africans would enjoy human rights without the slightest discrimination, where African and non-African would be able to live together in peace, sharing a common nationality and a common loyalty to the country.

The intention behind the strike he had called had been that it should go off peacefully. Nevertheless around the campaign an atmosphere of civil war and revolution had been created by the Government which sought "not to treat with us, but rather to present us as wild and dangerous revolutionaries intent on disorder and riot, incapable of being dealt with in any way save by mustering an overwhelming force against us. . . ." The Government had mobilised its armed forces and arrested African leaders, setting "the scene for violence by relying exclusively on violence with which to answer our people and their demands". The African people had learnt from bitter experience how demands forcefully made were always met by terror and massacre. Government violence could only do one thing and that was to breed counter-violence. "Already there are indications in this country that people, my people, Africans, are turning to deliberate acts of violence and of force against the Government, in order to persuade the Government in the only language which it shows by its behaviour it understands." By its conduct the Government demonstrated that it despised the process of representation and negotiation, and by its administration of the law it brought the law into contempt.

> I do not believe, Your Worship, that this Court in inflicting penalties on me for the crimes for which I have been convicted, should be moved by the belief that penalties deter men from the course which they believe is right. . . . I am prepared to pay the penalty even though I know how bitter is the situation of an African in the prisons of this country. . . . To men, freedom in their own land is the pinnacle of their ambitions, from which nothing can turn men of conviction aside. . . . When my sentence has been completed I will still be moved, as men are always moved by their consciences . . . to take up again, as best I can, the struggle for the removal of those injustices until they are finally abolished once and for all. . . . I

have no doubt that posterity will pronounce that I was innocent and that the criminals who should have been brought before this Court are the members of the Verwoerd Government.

These defiant words expressed in a forensic setting the new determination of African nationalists to work outside of and in conflict with the established legal order to achieve their goals. They ushered in an era of sabotage, insurrectionary activity and guerilla warfare, on the one hand, met with progressive suspension of habeas corpus, large-scale imprisonment and allegations of torture and brutality on the other. Mandela was sentenced to the maximum penalty allowed by the magistrate's jurisdiction, namely a total of five years imprisonment, and he was removed to Pretoria Central prison, where he was held in segregation and given mailbags to sew in his cell.

Fifteen months later Mandela was back in the dock in Pretoria, this time on trial before the Supreme Court for his life. In July 1963 a police raid on a secluded house in an outlying suburb of Johannesburg called Rivonia had led to the capture of a number of ANC leaders and supporters as well as the discovery of a series of highly incriminating documents. Some of these documents had been in Mandela's handwriting, while others had referred to him by name, and they had indicated that before his seizure by the police Mandela had played a leading role in organising sabotage and planning guerilla warfare.

When Mandela emerged from the cells below court as accused number one in what became known as the Rivonia Trial, people who had known him before as a dapper lawyer were shocked by his appearance. The wife of one of his co-accused wrote that his splendid figure seemed to have shrivelled; once noted for his elegant clothing, he now wore a khaki shirt, shorts and sandals of an African prisoner, and she wondered if fifteen months of sewing mailbags alone in his cell had reduced him from a proud and sophisticated man to the status of a 'boy' (Bernstein). Another of his co-accused, an attorney who was eventually acquitted, observed that Mandela appeared to have lost at least three stones, and was so frail as to be barely recognisable.

The leader of the prosecution team, well-known for his aggressive technique, described the trial as one of the most sensational ever held in South Africa (Yutar). The evidence established that all the accused, save for two who were found not guilty, had worked together in a clandestine manner and organised well over a hundred sabotage attacks against electricity pylons and other Government property. They had also sent abroad scores of young Africans to be trained for possible guerilla warfare. It was proved that Mandela had been the leader of a special wing of the ANC established to spearhead armed struggle, and that during his visit abroad he had undergone a short course of military training in Algeria.

Less than three years after the collapse of the Treason Trial, the State was leading uncontroverted evidence about what it called an ANC plot to bring about a violent and hellish revolution in South Africa. Mandela who during the Treason Trial had vehemently denied any intention on the part of the ANC to use violence, was now describing the circumstances which had led him and others to change their policy and embark upon violent struggle. For most of the eleven men in the dock, the dominant issue at the trial was not whether they would be found guilty, but whether or not they would be sentenced to death. In other trials held during the period a number of ANC and PAC activists were sentenced to death and later hanged, usually for homicide committed in the course of insurrectionary engagements.

South African law enabled an accused person at the close of the prosecution case either to remain silent, or to give evidence under oath and subject to cross-examination, or else to make a statement from the dock. Mandela chose to make a statement from the dock, since, although it carried less weight in law than evidence given under oath, it permitted him to make a speech uninterrupted by questions and answers, and was consistent with his earlier refusal to acknowledge the jurisdiction of the court. He was the first witness called by the defence, and for five and a half hours he took advantage of the legal system which threatened to take away his life to address the world.

Most of what Mandela had to say was devoted to explaining the philosophy of the ANC and why after fifty years of strict adherence to non-violence it had now sponsored the formation of a body (The Spear of the Nation) dedicated to the violent overthrow of the regime.

Firstly, [he declared] we believed that as a result of Government policy, violence by the African people had become inevitable, and that unless responsible leadership was given to canalise and control the feelings of our people, there would be outbreaks of terrorism which would produce an intensity of bitterness between the races which is not produced even by war. Secondly, we felt that without violence there would be no way open to the African people to succeed in their struggle against the principle of white supremacy. All lawful modes of expressing opposition to this principle had been closed by legislation, and . . . we had either to accept a permanent state of inferiority, or to defy the Government. . . . Only when the Government resorted to a show of force to crush opposition to its policies . . . did we decide to answer violence with violence.

Four forms of violence were possible: sabotage, guerilla warfare, terrorism and open revolution. Sabotage was agreed upon as the action which would involve the least risk to life, but preparations were also made to fight guerilla warfare should the need arise. "If war were inevitable, we wanted the fight to be conducted on terms most favourable to our people. . . . I started to make a study of the art of war and revolution and, whilst abroad, underwent a course in military training. If there was to be guerilla warfare, I wanted to be able to stand and fight with my people and to share the hazards of war with them."

The last portion of Mandela's statement was devoted to an attempt to refute the allegation that the ANC was being duped by communists who played upon imaginary grievances of the African people.

Our fight is against real and not imaginary hardships, or, to use the language of the State Prosecutor, "so-called hardships". Basically we fight against two features which are the hall-marks of African life in South Africa and which are entrenched by legislation. . . . These features are poverty and lack of dignity, and we do not need communists or so-called agitators to teach us about these things.

Our complaint is not that we are poor by comparison with people in other countries, but that we are poor by comparison with the white people in our own country and that we are prevented by legislation from altering this imbalance. . . . White supremacy implies black inferiority. Legislation designed to preserve white supremacy entrenches this notion. Menial tasks in South Africa are invariably performed by Africans. When anything has to be carried or cleaned, the white man will look round for an African to do it for him, whether the African is employed by him or not. Because of this sort of attitude, whites tend to regard Africans as a separate breed. They do not look upon them as people with families of their own . . . or realise that they have emotions . . . , that they want to earn enough money to support their families properly, to feed and clothe them and send them to school.

Above all we want equal political rights, because without them our disabilities will be permanent. I know this sounds revolutionary to the whites in this country, because the majority of voters will be Africans. This makes the white man fear democracy. But this fear cannot be allowed to stand in the way of the only solution which will guarantee racial harmony and freedom for all. . . . Political division based on colour is entirely artificial and when it disappears so will domination of one group by another.

During my lifetime I have dedicated myself to the struggle of the African people . . . against racialism . . . I have cherished the ideal of a democratic and a free society. . . . It is an ideal which I hope to live for and achieve, but if needs be, it is an ideal for which I am prepared to die.

The trial lasted many months, and during lunch-breaks Mandela took long prison-style walks with one of his co-accused, who was an attorney, weighing up as one lawyer to another the pros and cons of whether or not the death sentence would be imposed.

The last day of the trial was noted with interest throughout the world, and the jury box in the court was crowded with diplomats from many lands. The trial had been debated in the United Nations, where there had been overwhelming support for the accused and criticism of the South African Government on the grounds that its policies constituted a denial of human rights and threat to peace in Africa. At least seven Governments, including that of the United Kingdom, were reported to have pressed the South African Government to exercise clemency. The South African authorities, on the other hand, insisted that the matter was entirely one of domestic jurisdiction and that the South African Judiciary was independent and would not be influenced by pressure either from foreign Governments or from its own. It claimed that the policy of separate development offered all groups in South Africa the opportunity for self-determination, and declared that the only threat to peace in southern Africa came from communists and others who interfered from outside and threatened the country with sabotage and terrorism.

The defence called only one witness in mitigation, the author Alan Paton. Although it was not usual for such a witness to be cross-examined, in this case the prosecutor, with the help of a police dossier, proceeded to 'unmask this gentleman', and a sharp exchange followed between the two men which raised the tension in court. In the final plea in mitigation, counsel for the defence stressed that South Africa had a tradition of treating treason and rebellion with relative leniency.

Supporters of the accused had gathered outside the court to hear the result, whilst police with guns and dogs waited in the vicinity to deal with possible demonstrators. The judge ordered the convicted accused to rise–six Africans, one Indian and one white–and briefly gave his reasons for sentence. He said that the function of the court, as in any other country, was to enforce law and order and to enforce the laws of the state within which it functioned. The main crime of which the accused had been convicted was in essence one of high treason, but the State had decided not to charge the crime in that form, and accordingly he had decided not to impose the supreme penalty. The sentence in the case of all the accused would be one of imprisonment for life.

The accused were immediately taken to prison, where all were still being held in 1971. Mandela and six others were flown to Robben Island, historically the home of lepers and political prisoners, where along with approximately a thousand other persons convicted of security offences, they were subjected to the strict regime of maximum security prisoners. In terms of a statute passed in 1962 Mandela's name was placed on a list of persons whose statements may not be published or repeated in South Africa. To that extent he has been silenced, and his name no longer appears except in illegally produced literature, nor are his words ever publicly quoted. Later in the decade two persons close to Mandela were involved in important trials with a political background. The first was Bram Fischer, Q.C., who had been the leading counsel for the accused at the Rivonia Trial. Declaring that he could serve justice best by going underground, he changed his appearance and lived the life of an outlaw for nine months before being caught by the police. A grandson of a leading Boer statesman, son of a Judge-President, and himself a former leader of the Johannesburg Bar, Fischer was now brought as an accused person into the court where he had so frequently appeared as counsel. Eventually he too was sentenced to life imprisonment, and in 1971 he was still being held along with a number of other white persons convicted of security offences, in Pretoria Local Prison. Then in 1969 Mandela's wife, Mrs Winnie Mandela, was the principal accused in a trial of twenty-two persons charged with carrying on the activities of the illegal ANC. Both before and after her trial she was held for several months in solitary confinement and subjected to prolonged interrogation; her trial collapsed, and before she could leave the court-room she was re-detained by the police. This further detention following on her acquittal evoked considerable criticism from groups which had not previously taken a public stand on questions connected with the administration of justice in South Africa; students in various parts of the country mounted protest demonstration, and academic lawyers from a large number of universities voiced their disquiet. Eventually Mrs Mandela and most of her co-accused were put on trial again, but the defence plea of *autrefois acquit*, that is, that they had already been acquitted on the charges, was successful, and they were freed.

Meanwhile outside South Africa, Mandela's former law partner Tambo was helping to build up a guerilla army on the lines which Mandela had contemplated before his capture. Tambo had once been described by Father Trevor Huddleston as a most devoted churchman whose life showed the Christian motive at its best; now he was devoting himself to the destruction of the State in which he had formerly worshipped, and attempting to overthrow by violent means the legal system through which he had once made his living. In 1967 he announced in a public statement that ANC guerillas had entered Rhodesia in alliance with guerillas from the Zimbabwe African People's Union, each marching south for the liberation of their respective countries. A short while afterwards the South African Government reported that special units of the South African police had been sent to Rhodesia to combat the guerillas there, and other reports indicated that South African aircraft and armoured cars had proceeded to the battle zone.

The frontier wars were beginning again, but this time the combatants were equipped with modern weapons and inspired by modern ideologies. What was being fought over was no longer possession of land or cattle or water supplies, but who should rule in southern Africa. The struggle now had extensive international implications, with alliances being established between the white regimes on the one hand and the African nationalist guerillas on the other; the United Nations Organisation tended to lend its moral support to the latter. As acting-president of the ANC, Tambo frequently held up to the guerillas Mandela's example of total commitment, and issued a warning to the world that a racial war had begun in southern Africa which could escalate into an international confrontation of measureless dimensions.

CHAPTER EIGHT

Race Conflict and the Legal System

If increasing industrialisation intensified rather than reduced compulsory segregation in South Africa, it also highlighted the degree to which race differentiation was being artificially maintained. The absorption of Africans into a common society was coupled with their exclusion from civic rights, while the integration of Africans into a market economy was accompanied by the denial to them of the job opportunities and wage rates available to the whites. The very fact that legal intervention was necessary to enforce segregation established that race differentiation was neither natural nor divinely ordained. The more the police, the Judiciary and the prisons demonstrated their physical superiority, the more they undermined their moral authority. Large-scale evasion of the law and growing participation in crime constituted one expression of African resistance to the dominant legal order; crowd revolts and clashes with the police were another. More directly, Africans campaigned through a number of organisations, some political, some industrial, for a relief of burdens and an extension of rights. Their enemy was an internal colonialism rather than an external imperialism; they struggled against local masters rather than foreign overseers; they sought political integration under the slogan of equal rights, rather than political secession under the banner of independence.

In general the white electorate was vigorously antipathetic to African claims. In few countries can the voters have been beset by such a polychrome of perils as in South Africa: a Yellow Peril at the turn of the century (Chinese labourers), a Red Peril after the end of the Second World War (communism), and a Black Peril virtually all the time (not to mention the Khaki Election during the Second World War). The Supreme Court, however, tended to be less easily alarmed than the electorate, and for many decades adopted a relatively tolerant attitude towards agitation for social change in South Africa. The judges likened themselves to the guardians of the black people, and delivered strong lectures to white farmers, policemen and others found guilty of violence to black persons. Thus in the so-called Bultfontein case, five policemen, including a station commander, were sentenced to up to seven years imprisonment for thrashing, kicking, battering and giving electric shocks to two African suspects, causing one to die.

This benevolent judicial paternalism became increasingly difficult to maintain as social conflict became more acute. By 1960 the law began to lose much of its more tolerant, liberal aspect. Large-scale African protests were met with large-scale repression by the authorities; African movements went underground and began to plan insurrection, whilst the authorities abandoned normal procedures and counter-attacked with specially trained corps of police. Neither the African revolutionaries nor the white counter-revolutionaries conducted their struggle within the formerly accepted framework of the law. Africans were accused by the whites of terrorism, while whites were accused by the Africans of torture. Although the combatants were not rigidly divided along racial lines–many of the police were black and some of the revolutionaries were white–the issue was whether or not white rule would survive in southern Africa.

This concluding chapter will examine some of the major changes brought about in the legal system as a result of this conflict. First, attention will be directed to the way the traditional rules of criminal procedure were modified, next consideration will be given to the changing role of the police force, and finally there will be a discussion of how the Judiciary reacted to extensions of executive and police powers.

CRIMINAL PROCEDURE

In the sixty years since Union the law relating to criminal procedure developed in a manner distinctly disadvantageous to the suspect or accused person and markedly beneficial to the police and prosecution. Emergency powers which formerly could be invoked only after the declaration of martial law, have now become embodied in permanent legislation, and the scales in criminal trials with political background are at present firmly tilted in favour of the authorities.

Shortly after Union a start was made on the consolidation of the vast body of Colonial statutes dealing with criminal procedure, and the consequent Criminal Procedure and Evidence Act, 1917, became the procedural code for the whole country. The Act incorporated in its provisions English concepts relating to arrest, trial, evidence and procedure, but gave an accused person perhaps rather more protection than a criminal defendant received in England. For forty years the basic sections of the Act remained unaltered, and when a new Act was passed in 1955 to consolidate all the various amendments made in the intervening years, it differed from the old Act more in enumeration than in content. The provisions of the old Act had been temporarily suspended during periods of war and rebellion, but once the emergency situations had disappeared, the superstructures of emergency law had vanished with them and basic procedural rights had been revived. From 1962 onwards, however, a series of statutes were enacted which granted the authorities extensive powers to be used on an indefinite basis for the investigation and prosecution of widely defined security offences.

A comparison of the legal position of a suspect or accused person at the time of Union with his position in 1970 reveals how greatly his legal rights have diminished, especially if he is suspected or accused of a crime with a political background.

Arrest: Under the old law a suspect could be taken into custody only if he had been duly arrested, either on a judicial warrant or because the person effecting the arrest had reasonable grounds for suspecting that he was guilty of an offence. A suspect had to be cautioned that he was not obliged to answer any questions, and was entitled at all reasonable times to receive counsel from his legal advisers. If he had been arrested without warrant, the police were required to bring him before court as soon as possible, and never more than forty-eight hours after his detention. Anyone unlawfully arrested was entitled to use force to regain his liberty; alternatively, his family could apply for a writ of habeas corpus, or he could wait until he was released and then institute a civil action for wrongful arrest and detention.

The position today is substantially the same with regard to persons suspected of having committed common law offences, but radically different in respect of persons held under security laws. Members of the latter group may be detained not merely on the grounds that they have committed an offence, but on the grounds that they have information about the commission by others of an offence. Suspects or potential informants may then be held indefinitely in solitary confinement without access to counsel or the courts, and may be detained incommunicado until they have answered all questions to the satisfaction of the Commissioner of Police. No court of law may pronounce on the validity of such detention or order the release of such detainee.

Bail: Any accused person remanded in custody was entitled to apply to court to be released on bail, which, if granted, was not to be excessive. The question of whether or not bail should be granted was one to be decided by the Judiciary and not the Executive, the primary consideration for the court being whether or not the accused person was likely to stand his trial.

The Attorney-General of each province is now empowered in political matters, and in cases of murder, arson, kidnapping, armed robbery and aggravated housebreaking, to order that the accused be not released on bail, and the courts then lose their jurisdiction to consider the question.

Preparatory examinations: No person could formerly be charged on indictment before a superior court unless he had first appeared at a preparatory examination before a magistrate, at which all the evidence to be used against him had been led.

Today it lies within the discretion of the Attorney-General to decide in any matter whether or not a preparatory examination should be held; the more serious the charges, the more likely is he to decide that it is in the public interest not to disclose his evidence or witnesses in advance.

Juries: Originally all criminal charges in the Supreme Court were brought before a judge and jury. The employment of juries, however, was gradually reduced, until in 1969 juries were abolished altogether. Today the judge may sit on his own, but usually he is assisted on issues of fact by two assessors, who are generally retired magistrates or members of the Bar.

The abolition of the jury system has not been regarded as a setback for civil liberties in South Africa, since juries had always been racially constituted, and only white persons could feel that they were being tried by their peers. Jurors were empanelled from lists restricted to male white voters, who on occasions were guilty of flagrant miscarriages of justice in favour of white accused. One observer noted that whereas in other countries the prejudices of jurors tended to cancel each other out, in South Africa they all ran in one direction (Pugh). The main reason for the eventual abolition of juries appears to have been the inconvenience rather than the injustice that they caused.

The trial: The basic elements of the English accusatorial system have remained unchanged in South Africa, namely, that the accused be presented with a precise charge, that all evidence against him be given viva voce and be subject to cross-examination by him or his counsel, and that he be entitled to call witnesses and give evidence if he so wishes. The two main innovations which are disadvantageous to the accused are that his trial may, if it relates to offences under the security laws, be held in a court in any part of the country and not necessarily in the court serving the area in which the crime was allegedly committed, and secondly, that he may be joined in one indictment with other accused even although their alleged offences did not relate to the same transaction. Thus on 27th June 1967, thirty-seven South West Africans (Namibians) were charged in Pretoria with having taken part in guerilla activities more than a thousand miles away.

Confessions: No admission made by an accused person outside of court may be tendered in evidence against him at his trial unless it is proved by the prosecution to have been made freely and voluntarily. Even if made freely and voluntarily a confession to a police officer may not be admitted in evidence unless repeated before a magistrate and reduced to writing. No one may be convicted on the basis of a confession alone unless there is evidence *aliunde* that the offence has been committed. These basic rules relating to admissions and confessions have remained unaltered since the 1917 Act was passed, but the prosecution has been authorised to lead evidence of facts discovered as a result of inadmissible statements and also to produce testimony that the accused pointed out goods and places, even though such pointing out was done in the course of making an inadmissible statement. Thus although a statement extracted under duress would not be admissible, evidence gathered as a result of or in the course of receiving that statement may be admitted. Conflicting decisions have been handed down by the courts as to whether confessions made during detention under the security laws are admissible, but even if such statements are not admissible, the fruits of such statements are.

Witnesses and the privileges against self-incrimination: The most drastic change in the character of criminal trials in South Africa has been in the status of prosecution witnesses and the pressures to which they may be subjected. Originally a recalcitrant witness could be detained on the order of the court for periods of eight days at a time. His right to refuse to answer self-incriminatory questions, however, was fully recognised. Thus an accomplice could refuse to submit to being sworn and accept instead the risk of himself being prosecuted. Should an accomplice give evidence to the satisfaction of the court, he would be entitled to an indemnity from prosecution.

The position today is that potential witnesses may now be detained indefinitely under the security laws for interrogation in solitary confinement without any right to legal advice. They may then be brought straight from the cells to the witness box, with the prospect of not being released from police detention unless the evidence they give is satisfactory to the police. Alternatively, and even in relation to the more serious non-political trials, potential witnesses may be detained for 180 days on the warrant of the Attorney-General, and they may then be held incommunicado in police custody subject to interrogation until called to give evidence. Accomplices brought to court to testify may no longer refuse to be sworn or plead self-incrimination as an excuse for not answering questions, and any recalcitrant witness, whether an accomplice or not, may now be sentenced to a year's imprisonment. An accomplice who gives evidence to the satisfaction of the court is still entitled to an indemnity from prosecution, but the court has no power to order his release from detention by the police.

Evidence: Generally speaking the English law of evidence continues to be applied in South Africa. The rules with regard to relevance, best evidence, hearsay, similar facts, character evidence, and previous convictions are substantially unaltered, but one significant change has been brought about in respect of trials under the security laws, namely, that certain documents relating to organisations may be produced as proof of their contents.

The definition of offences and onus of proof: Formerly persons charged with attempting to subvert the State were prosecuted for treason or sedition, and in order to obtain a conviction the prosecution had to prove all the essential ingredients of the crime charged beyond a reasonable doubt. Now a series of new broadly-defined security crimes have been created by statute. Once certain minimum facts have been established by the prosecution, the accused must then disprove the existence of other crucial facts, and do so beyond reasonable doubt.

Autrefois acquit: Persons charged and acquitted under the Terrorism Act, 1967, may no longer plead such acquittal if arraigned on the same facts in terms of another law.

Minimum sentences: Minimum sentences in times of peace were formerly unknown in South African law. Now three major security laws provide that persons convicted of widely defined offences must receive sentences of at least five years imprisonment, and that the operation of such sentences may not be suspended.

The right of appeal: This is one area where criminal procedure has been altered significantly for the benefit of the accused. Originally an accused person who was tried and convicted in the Supreme Court could appeal to the Appellate Division on grounds of law only. Since 1948, however, it has been possible for an accused to appeal on grounds of fact as well, if the trial judge or the Chief Justice grants him leave to do so. Appeals from the magistrates' courts to the Supreme Court have always been permissible as of right on grounds either of fact or of law.

Legal aid: The provision of legal aid has hardly changed in the sixty years since Union. Counsel continue to be appointed *pro deo* for un-defended accused in capital cases–in fact they usually commence their careers by handling such cases–but otherwise there is no functioning machinery which ensures that criminal defendants in even the most serious matters receive legal representation. Legal aid in civil cases is available only to Supreme Court litigants who satisfy a stringent means test and who establish reasonable prospects of success. Such assistance is said to be granted *in forma pauperis* and is liberally given in matrimonial matters but less freely in other causes.

The desirability of extending legal aid more generally, especially in criminal matters, has been under active consideration by successive Governments since 1935. Voluntary legal aid bureaux were set up after that date in the main urban centres, and received subsidies from the Government. These were so small, however, that one writer observed: "During 1958 the State paid £5,304 in subsidising legal aid in South Africa, just over one hundredth of what has recently been set aside for research in the wine industry" (Abramowitz). In fact, the authorities appeared to become increasingly hostile to the concept of legal aid. The annual report of the Secretary for Justice for 1958 stated that legal aid in criminal trials not carrying the death sentence was redundant since "our whole legal system is designed to prevent the conviction of an innocent man, whether defended or not, and that it is the duty of judicial officers and prosecutors . . . to ensure that no miscarriages of justice occur". The report for 1965 suggested that legal aid was positively harmful since it would "undermine the administration of justice and would moreover be completely inconsistent with the general judicial and social pattern in the country". By then subsidies to voluntary legal aid bureaux had ceased, and only one was still in existence.

In 1966 the South African Defence and Aid Fund, which had raised funds for the defence of persons charged with political offences, was declared an unlawful organisation, and it subsequently became illegal for anyone to collect money to defend such persons. The banning of this organisation highlighted the absence of legal aid for criminal defendants, and discussions took place between representatives of the

Government and members of the legal profession about the establishment of a legal aid fund for indigent accused. After protracted talks, statutory authority was given in 1969 for the formation of a Legal Aid Board, which, in its second year of operation, was voted a sum of approximately £85,000.

DISCUSSION

From the above review it will be seen that substantial inroads have been made into the procedural rights of citizens without any corresponding procedural benefits having been conferred. The major changes have related to trials with a political background, but even in regard to common law offences the prosecution has been granted extraordinary powers. Thus in 1971 a ,law was passed in relation to drugs which reproduced many of the main features of the Terrorism Act.

There are few jurists who would deny that in situations of emergency the authorities are entitled to suspend the ordinary legal rights of citizens. The doctrine of martial law was based on the principle that in situations of grave conflict, the Judiciary would recognise the right of the military to rule in autocratic fashion, and would suspend temporarily its own jurisdiction; the military would later receive retroactive legislative indemnity for 'illegal' actions taken by it during martial law. South Africa has a long history of proclamations of martial law, and a large amount of judicial authority on the subject. In recent decades, however, the tendency has been to use the police rather than the military to counteract actual or threatened rebellion. Legislative arrangements have been made for the police to have extraordinary and permanent powers of detention and interrogation, and for trials under the security laws to be heavily weighted in favour of the prosecution. The ordinary Judiciary is still used for all trials, but its power to ensure the maintenance of what was formerly regarded as due legal process has been greatly limited.

The manner in which the South African courts have reacted to this situation will be dealt with later. At this stage it is appropriate to mention the justification which has been advanced for the abrogation of procedural rights. In a recent publication entitled *South Africa and the Rule of Law*, the South African Government stated that it subscribed to the rule of law, but was not prepared "to expose the peoples committed to its care to terrorist aggression because of a dogmatic insistence on the immutability of certain selective legal rules and procedures". The booklet dealt at length with the policy of separate development, which, it claimed, was not oppressive but was on the contrary designed to permit all groups to achieve prosperity and freedom. It emphatically rejected the allegation that Government policies were so inhuman and oppressive that they drove opponents to subversion, to which the Government then reacted by enacting legislation which violated individual rights in an attempt to stamp out opposition to its policies. When intimidation and other terrorist methods were used to bring about such a reign of fear that people dared not help the authorities maintain law and order, it was necessary to "supplement the traditional rules and procedures to meet these extraordinary situations. . . . *A Government does not then depart from the rule of law; it strengthens the rule of law.*"

The contrary viewpoint was elegantly expressed in a public lecture to students at the University of Cape Town by a former Chief Justice of the Federation of the Rhodesias and Nyasaland, who had resigned his post in protest against security legislation being considered by the Rhodesian Parliament. He said that repressive measures at variance with tradition were introduced with distaste and a more or less instinctive feeling that they were unworthy. Always there was an assurance that they were of a temporary nature, or simply to meet an emergency. They appeared inadequate and were strengthened. Government and people became conditioned to them, and an assumption gained currency that these measures were achieving results. No one thought to ask whether other and less objectionable measures would not have been effective without prejudicing the future, for, in the long run, injustice reaped a bitter harvest. Citizens were fortunate if in a relatively short time they were not living under a totalitarian system that had been the excuse and the justification for the descent to Avernus (Tredgold).

In a sense, all modern communities are confronted with danger and the threat of annihilation, and if the courts are to play an active and enduring role in public life some limitations must be placed on the concept of emergency. Thus it can be argued that to qualify as a genuine emergency warranting the suspension of normal legality the danger apprehended should be a clear and present one; disproportionate means of counteraction should not be used, heinous methods of repression should at all times be avoided, and the emergency should be brought to an end as soon as possible. Furthermore, extraordinary powers should be recognised as such and not become ordinary by long usage, and, finally, the emergency must not have been created by the actions of the authorities themselves.

This last is perhaps the most difficult of all the criteria to apply since it involves the kind of judgements which many lawyers are reluctant to make. On the one hand the courts and the legal profession must recognise the duty of members of all communities to maintain peace and order, on the other they must also acknowledge the right of the persons to pursue justice and overcome tyranny. An oppressive regime should not be able to justify suspension of basic rights on the grounds that it is threatened with being replaced by a more just society. Nor if such a regime violates the rights of large sections of the community and provokes them to resistance, should it be able to claim that suspension of legality is a legitimate means of self-defence. In relation to South Africa, lawyers arguing within the narrow positivist tradition can point out that legislation which grants permanent powers of unrestricted control by the police is inconsistent with the concept of a special emergency; they can claim that not even an emergency situation would justify the use of torture of the kind that has been alleged against the security police; they can argue that bringing witnesses from solitary confinement to court and placing the onus of proving innocence on the accused are both at variance with the notion of a fair trial; but they cannot deal with the fundamental question of when the stage is reached that rebellion against autocratic rule may be justified.

POLICE

In common with many other countries, South Africa has during this century witnessed striking changes in the power and public role of the police. These developments were accomplished not so much by an increase in the size of the police force, as by an alteration in its structure, its powers and its relationship with the Government. Shortly after Union the various police forces throughout the country were unified into a single body with headquarters in Pretoria. The new South Africa Police Force (SAP) embodied two traditions, the English one of making the police force subject to the law and placing it under the ultimate control of the civil authorities, and the home-grown tradition of equipping a paramilitary force with special powers and special weapons to enforce colonial-type laws against the black population. The organisational model for the new body was in fact the strongly centralised and highly mobile Natal Police, who in addition to combating crime and enforcing master-servant relations, had fought in military battles against Africans and Boers. After the Transvaal and the Orange Free State were annexed by the British, centralised police forces were established in these territories as well, so that after Union it remained only for the various forces in the Cape to be consolidated for uniformity to be achieved. The setting up of a Union Defence Force, the first permanent indigenous army in southern Africa since the days of Shaka's Zulu regiments, both enabled the Imperial garrison to be withdrawn and allowed the South African Police to reduce its paramilitary operations. The head of the new unified force was a serving officer entitled Commissioner of Police, and he was made subject to the control of the Cabinet through the Minister of Justice.

The growth of the police force from 1912 to 1968 is given in Table 24.

TABLE 24

AUTHORISED ESTABLISHMENT OF SOUTH AFRICAN POLICE COMPARED TO TOTAL POPULATION FOR THE YEARS 1912, 1938 AND THE YEAR ENDED 30TH JUNE 1968

Year	Total Population	South African Police	Police per 1,000 of Population
1912	6,102,000	8,705	1·42
1938	9,978,000	11,080	1·11
1968	19,826,000	33,628	1·70

(Annual Report)

It appears from Table 24 that the personnel of the police force increased first at a slightly slower then at a greatly faster rate than did the total population. It should be remembered, though, that two other sets of organisation were established which greatly assisted the police and made a significant contribution to the total number of arrests each year, namely the provincial and municipal traffic forces, and the 'native affairs' police. The total number of persons exercising police powers therefore increased at a far greater rate than did the total population.

In its internal structure the South African Police has always reflected the stratification of the society at large. White and black policemen are issued with different uniforms and different equipment, receive different training at different Police Colleges and are remunerated at different rates. The one item all policemen have in common is a whistle. No black policeman may be placed in command of a white policeman, and all black policemen are under general instructions not to arrest white offenders. Generally speaking, all white policemen are armed, whereas no black policemen are armed. White policemen may rise to any rank, whereas the first black lieutenants were appointed only in 1971. The whole commanding elite of the force is therefore white, and the growth of this white officer class has been particularly pronounced: between 1922 and 1968 the number of white constables increased by only about a half, whereas the number of white officers of the rank of lieutenant or above increased ten times. The growth of the force has accordingly taken the form mainly of an increase in white officers and an increase in black constables: black policemen now account for nearly half the total personnel, a larger proportion than before.

One of the main by-products of technological advance in South Africa has been the modernisation of the police force. Its communications now include telephones, the telegraph, a telex system and an extensive network of radio links; constables who formerly patrolled on foot, on cycles, on horses or on camels, now ride around in a fleet of 5,000 vehicles, which include 2,000 patrol vans, 600 riot trucks, 80 armoured cars, and 30 hearses. The force is armed with a wide variety of pistols, rifles and sten-guns, and has the use of 3 aeroplanes, 2 helicopters and 10 motor boats. In addition the security police are equipped with sophisticated electronic devices. The growth of the security police has been one of the most striking phenomena in recent South African history. Whereas formerly internal security was maintained largely by punitive expeditions of the military, now it is secured mainly by preventive operations of the police. Within the police force itself, the security branch has grown from a small, auxiliary group of detectives into a large, semi-autonomous section of police, and in the country at large they have developed from a relatively insignificant group of data-collectors into a major centre of power.

In the years immediately after Union there was more scope for Africans to agitate for fundamental change than there is today. A Deputy-Commissioner of Police in the Orange Free State wrote in 1920 that "the Native and the Coloured people are becoming better educated and organising with a view to obtaining what they consider is due and equitable to them". Ten years later, however, the annual police report mentioned that a "special branch" of the SAP had been established at headquarters to deal with "Communist and other agitators, unscrupulous persons who issued propaganda to ignorant and peaceable natives". The special branch grew slowly until the Second World War, when it co-operated with military intelligence in keeping pro-German Afrikaner sabotage and insurrectionary movements under surveillance. Thousands of militant anti-British Afrikaners were detained during this period, including Mr B. J. Vorster, the present Prime Minister of South Africa, and Mr H. J. van den Bergh, head of all security operations in South Africa today. Amongst the many persons put on trial after special branch investigations into spying and sabotage was Dominee D. Vorster, the present Prime Minister's brother who was imprisoned for seeking to pass on to the Germans information about personnel and gun emplacements at Simonstown naval base. Both brothers were in fact Generals in the para-military Ossewabrandwag (Oxwagon Sentinel). It appears, too, that vigorous but unsuccessful attempts were made to trap Mr C. R. Swart, later Minister of Justice and then the first President of the Republic of South Africa. According to his biographer, advocate Swart's office and his person were searched, a fabricated document was planted on him and he and his contacts were continuously watched. After the war, the special branch once more directed its attention to 'Communists and other agitators', and in the 1950s it became particularly active in raiding the homes of members of the African National Congress and allied organisations, and in recommending prosecutions and banning orders against them. A central head office was created to correlate the information received from approximately a hundred members in groups scattered throughout the country, and the whole section was renamed the Security Branch (Rademeyer, *Cape Times*, 22nd May 1957). In 1960 the head of the Security Branch was named Director of Security and placed on a special committee, including the chief chaplain and the head of the Criminal Investigation Bureau, which maintained direct liaison with the Commissioner of Police (Annual Report).

In the 1960s the power of the security police increased greatly. Shortly after Mr Vorster was made Minister of Justice in 1961, he transferred his old friend and fellow-internee, Mr van den Bergh, from the Criminal Investigation Department to head of the Security Branch. During their internment together they had built up a close personal understanding which was to stand them in good stead during their collaboration in office. While Mr Vorster sponsored legislation to suspend habeas corpus and give the police special powers of detention and interrogation, Mr van den Bergh set about reorganising and expanding the security police. The police reports are relatively reticent about the size and activities of the security police, but one such report does mention that during the comparatively quiet year ended 30th June

1966, special courses in internal security were given to 135 members of the security police and 125 other policemen, and special addresses on security were given to 5,106 ordinary policemen.

When Dr Verwoerd was assassinated in 1966, Mr Vorster became Prime Minister and relinquished his office as Minister of Justice. Departing from tradition, however, he continued to maintain special links with the security police. Two years later it was announced that Mr van den Bergh was to become head of the whole SAP, but shortly thereafter the public were informed that instead he would be made Security Adviser to the Prime Minister with the rank of full General. General van den Bergh was then promoted to head of a newly created body called the Bureau of State Security, popularly referred to by its initials as BOSS, a secret organisation attached to the Prime Minister's office and responsible for co-ordinating internal and external security. Its functions were stated to be to investigate all matters affecting the security of the State and to perform such other functions and responsibilities as were determined for it from time to time. Unlike other Departments of State, it did not issue reports on its activities, nor were its finances subject to public scrutiny, nor was it answerable to the Cabinet as a whole but only to the Prime Minister.

Shortly after the Bureau of State Security was established, the scope of the Official Secrets Act, 1956, was extended to render it a criminal offence for any person to possess without authorisation any information relating to any military, police or security matter. 'Police matter' was defined as meaning any matter relating to internal security or to the maintenance of law and order by the police, and 'security matter' was defined so as to include 'any matter dealt with by or relating to the Bureau of State Security'. At the same time the law relating to State privilege was amended so as to give the Prime Minister or his nominee power to prohibit any person from giving any oral or documentary information in court, the disclosure of which in the Prime Minister's opinion would be prejudicial to the interests of the State or public security. The combined effect of these provisions was to authorise the prevention of publication in the press or mention in court of any activity of the security police or the Bureau of State Security; thus an ex-detainee could be prevented from giving evidence of alleged torture or other irregularities.

General van den Bergh's new position led to his being described in the press as the second most powerful man in State service in South Africa, second only to Mr Vorster himself. His past utterances on communism and liberalism had led many people to assume that his Bureau would step up surveillance of people and organisations to the left of the Government, and undoubtedly they did so both at home and abroad but in fact the first known objects of his attention appear to have been members of a right-wing group inside the governing party itself (the so-called *verkramptes*). In a prosecution against a leading member of this group, he testified that the security police got their information by infiltration, tapping conversations, questioning and tailing suspects, and intercepting mail.

In the meanwhile paramilitary security units of the SAP had become involved in fighting with African guerillas in Rhodesia (Zimbabwe) and South West Africa (Namibia). Security operations were now being conducted outside as well as inside South Africa's borders and the influence of the security police was being felt in many countries.

THE JUDICIARY AND THE EXECUTIVE

In formal terms no changes of note have taken place in the years since Union in the relationship between the Judiciary and the Executive. Superior court judges continue to have security of tenure and may be removed for misbehaviour or incapacity only on the resolution of both Houses of Parliament, a procedure which has yet to be invoked. Short of such impeachment, the only penalty which an awkward judge need fear is that his promotion to the Judge-Presidency of a Provincial Division or to membership of the Appellate Division of the Supreme Court might be held back. Similarly, just as the constitutional independence of the Judiciary in relation to the Executive remains unaltered, so its legal subservience to the Legislature is essentially the same. The judges have always acknowledged their responsibility to pronounce rather than to make the law. Their oath of office has required them to judge according to the law, and this has obliged them to give effect to the will of Parliament as expressed in legislation, however obnoxious a particular enactment may have seemed to them. Nevertheless despite their adherence to what has been called the phonographic theory of the judicial function, they have not in fact been either obliged to or capable of acting as mere automatons. In interpreting vague words in a statute they could lean in favour of the Executive or of the citizen; in controlling the conduct of trials, they could initiate or discourage enquiries into police irregularities; in commenting on the evidence and giving reasons for judgement they had considerable scope for expressing approval or disapproval of the conduct of witnesses, and in passing sentence they had the opportunity, almost invariably taken, of delivering homilies on the behaviour of the accused.

Generally the South African judges have had a reputation for tempering harsh legislation, moderating inequitable Executive action, and restraining irregular police conduct. In the recent period of racial stress, however, they have come under strong criticism for aligning themselves too closely with the Executive and failing to show appropriate vigilance in relation to police behaviour.

No simple yardstick exists for measuring the Executive-mindedness of a Judiciary. A mere totalling up of decisions given for and against the Executive at any period would not be very revealing, because often the outcome of a case has little relationship to the point of principle decided by it, and in any event one leading decision can have more significance than a host of minor ones. In the absence of any express statement by the judges indicating a conscious change in policy, the most that can usefully be attempted is to seek out predominant trends at particular periods, as indicated by the line of reasoning followed in cases dealing with relationships between the citizen and the Executive.

Shortly after his elevation to the Cape Supreme Court in 1876, Chief Justice Henry de Villiers ordered the release of two Griqua leaders who were being held as prisoners of war by the Cape authorities. Holding that if they were British subjects they should be charged in court with rebellion, and if they were not, they should be set free since war had not been declared against their people, the Chief Justice declared: "The disturbed state of the country ought not in my opinion to influence the court, for its first and most sacred duty is to administer justice to those who seek it and not to preserve the peace of the country." In the Transvaal, Chief Justice Kotze in a similar matter emphasised that the court was bound to do equal justice to every individual within its jurisdiction, without regard to colour or degree, except where in a particular instance the law provided to the contrary. The foundation of their arguments was the common law principle, recognised both in England and in Holland, that every person was entitled to his freedom except in so far as the law specifically provided to the contrary. Should an individual's liberty or rights of personality be interfered with by the Executive in a manner not clearly sanctioned by law, then no matter who the person was or what the allegations against him were, he was entitled to an appropriate remedy from the courts. In the case of a person wrongfully detained, the judges would order that he be brought to court and released unless the detaining authorities could establish some legal warrant for continuing to hold him. The court's power in this regard was limited by only two sets of circumstances: a declaration of martial law, or the enactment of a statute which in clear language restricted the court's jurisdiction.

These points were emphasised by Sir James Rose-Innes shortly before and shortly after he became Chief Justice of South Africa in 1914. In one judgement he drew attention to the tendency of legislation to give departmental officials final power to affect the rights of the public to the exclusion of the courts. "Such legislation, unless carefully safe-guarded, may endanger private rights, and become a serious menace to the liberty of the subject. These are considerations to which the courts do well to draw attention", he said. In a second case he stigma-tised as unlawful and injurious the actions of a prison governor who subjected an unconvicted strike leader and suspected dynamitard to a specially rigorous regime. He described the governor's conduct as a wrongful and intentional interference with those absolute rights relat-ing to personality to which every man is entitled. His colleague, Solomon, J.A., declared that it would be a most dangerous doctrine to lay down that the police authorities are entitled to infringe upon the personal rights of liberty of any individual, merely because in their opinion it is desirable to do so in the interests of public safety. In a third matter Innes stressed that one of the features of the English constitution reproduced in self-governing dominions was the absolute supremacy of the law. "Every subject, high or low", he observed, "is amenable to the law, but none can be punished save by a properly constituted legal tribunal. If any man's rights of personal liberty or property are threatened, the courts are open for his protection. And behind the courts is ranged the full power of the state to esure enforcement of their decrees." Although he never failed to give effect to a law merely because he found its terms to be objectionable, he did not hesitate to criticise legislation which he felt unduly restricted the rights of the citizen and fettered the jurisdiction of the courts. Furthermore, he insisted that statutes which interfered with the liberty of the subject should be strictly construed in favour of the individual rather than the Executive. It should be noted that these observations were not made in respect of social welfare legislation, but with regard to racially dis-criminatory legislation and Executive actions undertaken during times of political stress.

In the 1930s the Appeal Court appeared to emphasise its subservience to the Legislature rather than its independence of the Executive. One

Judge of Appeal who later became Chief Justice stated in as many words that Parliament could make any encroachment it liked upon the life, liberty or property of the individual and the courts were bound to give effect to it (Stratford). As a statement of constitutional doctrine there was nothing exceptional in this formulation, but it did indicate a willingness rather than a reluctance to give effect to restrictive measures. It was at this time that a prominent African leader expressed his disappointment at what he considered to be a decline in the quality of justice being administered to Africans. "Thirty years ago", he wrote, "we used to regard British justice in the Cape ... as something infallible and above suspicion. But of late we have had to revise our catechism with regard to South African or Afrikaner justice" (Jabavu). His main complaints were about the functioning of the inferior courts, but he also quoted from an Appeal Court judgement which decided a test case against an African litigant by reading something into an Act which Parliament had failed to put in itself. The 1930s were not, however, entirely devoid of liberal judicial decisions; in one notable judgement the Appeal Court upheld the right of freedom of speech when it allowed an appeal against conviction and imprisonment of two communists who had been charged with insulting the King. One of the judges wrote: "We have travelled a long way on the road of freedom of speech and of political criticism since the days when it was a crime *laesae majestatis* to enter a house of ill-fame or a latrine with money in one's possession or a ring on one's finger, bearing the image of the Princeps." He added that if the language used was unduly strong, it should be remembered that Africans had no voice in Parliament or the Government and could only protest against grievances.

During the 1940s the major public law cases related to the situation created by South Africa's entry into the war against Nazi Germany. Some of the reported judgements indicated a tendency on the part of the courts to lean in favour of the Executive during this period, and many Afrikaners subsequently complained that judgements had been influenced by wartime hysteria. Notable amongst these critics were Dr Verwoerd, who lost a libel action against a publication which had accused him of making the newspaper which he edited into a tool of the Nazis, and Mr B. J. Vorster, who was interned for two years and whose brother was imprisoned for collecting important military and naval intelligence about Simonstown naval base. An Afrikaner jurist writing at the time observed that the phrase 'martial law' evoked ominous thoughts in the minds of South Africans, who associated it with war or rebellion on the one hand, and military rule on the other; it led to drastic curtailment of personal liberties and an unwillingness on the part of the courts to take a stand against even the most blatantly unlawful actions of the Executive. Precedent from the time of the Anglo-Boer War and the 1914 Afrikaner rebellion, he wrote, established that once war was raging the courts had indeed hardly any jurisdiction to interfere with the actions of the military, but this did not justify a recent decision which held that an order of internment issued without statutory authority by the Minister of Justice be regarded as an act of the military (Conradie).

The extension in the 1950s of Ministerial powers coincided with the more rigid enforcement then of segregation and led to a great increase in the number of court actions instituted to restrain the Government. In the well-known Votes cases the Appeal Court emphasised the independence of the Judiciary, and invoked a limited testing right to invalidate legislation which purported by a simple majority to take coloured voters in the Cape off the common electoral roll. It expressly overruled a dictum delivered by the Court in 1937 to the effect that Parliament was able to ignore the entrenched clauses in the South Africa Act, which stipulated that voting rights in the Cape could be diminished on grounds of race only by a two-thirds majority of both Houses of Parliament in a joint sitting. One judge stated that the purpose of the entrenched clauses was to place a check on legislative power in favour of the individual, and likened the argument that once Britain abdicated from South Africa the entrenched clauses lost their validity to the proposition that as soon as the policeman was round the corner there was no law (Van den Heever).

During this period freedom of speech and of assembly were frequently asserted by the courts, and it was held by a narrow majority that the Crown prerogative did not entitle the Minister of the Interior to revoke a passport validly issued. Again and again Chief Justice Centlivres stressed the great care with which the courts scrutinised statutes granting the Executive power to invade the liberties of the subject, though he added that once it was clear that the Legislature intended to grant 'autocratic powers' to the Executive, the courts had to give effect to the will of the Legislature. The Appeal Court also in two major decisions reaffirmed the rule of natural justice that persons should not be deprived of rights or made subject to restrictions without first being granted an opportunity to be heard; Parliament could always exclude such right of audience, but unless it did so in clear language, statutes should be interpreted on the assumption that such right was meant to be operative.

Towards the end of the 1950s and in the early 1960s the courts were approached on a number of occasions to grant writs of habeas corpus against farmers, policemen and prison officials, and in almost every instance they acceded promptly to these requests. Thus Africans arrested on the Rand under the pass laws and sent without trial to work for farmers in the Eastern Transvaal, where they were held in bad conditions against their will, were released on court orders after their relatives had applied for writs of habeas corpus. In 1960 speedy action on the part of lawyers and judges secured the release of several persons detained under Emergency Regulations which had been adopted but not yet promulgated. In Johannesburg a judge granted a rule nisi against the police at 7 a.m. returnable at 10 a.m. on the same day, and later in the day granted a further fifteen similar orders; in Durban a judge granted an order at 2.45 p.m. returnable at 4.30 p.m. that afternoon; in all these matters time was of the essence, since the regulations which would have authorised the detention were in fact promulgated on the next day.

In the following year considerable international interest was aroused by a habeas corpus application brought in the eastern Cape. The proceedings were based on a note smuggled out of a Transkei lock-up stating that a young African political refugee in what was then the British Protectorate of Basutoland had been kidnapped and brought by members of the South African Police to South Africa. The judge of first instance surprised observers by delaying his decision for two months, after which, in a 72 page judgement subsequently referred to as a 'curiosity of legal literature', he rejected the application. The matter went on appeal to a full Bench of three judges, who with 'unprecedented celerity' overruled their colleague's decision and granted a rule calling upon the police to show cause why they should not produce the detainee in court and release him. Dealing with the fact that the court had only scanty hearsay evidence on which to entertain the application, the judgement concurred in by the full Bench stated: ". . . the Supreme Court is the protector of the rights of the individual citizen, and it will protect him against unlawful action by the executive in all its branches. . . . From a practical point of view . . . I do not think the Court should be astute to find objections at this stage to the relief claimed. The Court should rather be astute to find a means of exercising its function and jurisdiction in the protection of a citizen from a potential inroad on his liberty". The detainee was eventually released, and after suing for damages for wrongful detention was paid an undisclosed sum in an out of court settlement. A full report on the case published by the International Commission of Jurists in Geneva criticised the conduct of the South African authorities, but went out of its way to praise what it termed a vigilant and independent Bench and a courageous legal profession in South Africa.

These various decisions, together with the acquittal in 1961 of the accused in the long drawn out Treason Trial, earned for the South African Judiciary a high reputation amongst lawyers both inside and outside South Africa. From 1963 onwards, however, a trend of judicial decisions began which reversed the flow of praise, and led to criticism being levelled at the South African Judiciary by the very people who had been its most enthusiastic erstwhile supporters; conversely, the South African Government, which had formerly been openly critical of the Judiciary, and especially of the Appeal Court, now began actively to extol its virtues. The main complaint of the critics was that in interpreting statutes which suspended habeas corpus and drastically curtailed the rights of individuals, the courts leaned unduly in favour of the security police. Some of the criticism was broadened into a general charge that the Judiciary showed an attitude of heartlessness towards black South Africans incompatible with the due administration of justice.

The background to the apparent shift in stance of the Judiciary was the outbreak of sabotage and the enactment of special security laws giving the police powers to detain suspects incommunicado for interrogation. The crucial provision which had to be construed by the courts was the so-called 'ninety-day law', which empowered the police to detain for interrogation in solitary confinement persons suspected of having information about the commission of security offences. The law authorised the police to detain such suspects 'from time to time', with the proviso that 'no such person shall be detained for more than ninety days on any particular occasion'. The first question that arose for judicial determination related to the meaning of this ninety-day proviso, and whether it was an effective bar to detention for consecutive periods of ninety days. The Natal Court held that a re-detention after ninety days had elapsed could be justified only on the basis that new grounds for detention had arisen, otherwise the proviso would be illusory, but the Appeal Court overruled this decision and held that the police could re-detain a suspect merely on the basis that fresh information had come to light supporting the original grounds of detention.

The ninety-day limitation thereafter became an easily by-passed legal formality, and many of the thousand persons held under the law in the next two years were in fact re-detained after being released for a matter of moments.

The second question which the courts had to decide was whether a detainee was entitled as of right to have an ordinary supply of reading matter and writing materials with him while in confinement, or whether the police could grant or withhold such matter at their discretion. The law explicitly stated that detainees might be held by the police in isolation with no access to the courts or to counsel, but otherwise it was silent on the conditions of detention. The issue before the courts was whether a specific police power to withhold the normal amenities granted as of right to awaiting-trial prisoners should be inferred from the general power to hold suspects for interrogation; it was common cause that the detainee could not have any materials which might enable him to receive communication from persons outside. The matter first arose in the Cape court, which upheld a claim made on behalf of a detainee that he be allowed to receive as of right a reasonable supply of reading matter and writing materials. The court followed a 1912 precedent in which Sir James Rose-Innes laid down that individuals were at all times entitled to all the normal rights of personality save those which had been expressly taken away by statute; since the object of the ninety-day law was not to punish the detainee but merely to place him in custody for purposes of questioning, there was no need to read into it an implied provision that his conditions could be made more rigorous than those of an awaiting-trial prisoner. The court referred further to the famous dissenting judgement of Lord Atkin in *Liversidge* v. *Anderson* and added as a gloss of its own that it was precisely when public passions were running high that the courts should be most ready to protect the rights of individuals. This line of reasoning was rejected by the Appeal Court, which held unanimously that "it was not the intention of Parliament that detainees should as of right be permitted to relieve the tedium of their detention with reading matter or writing materials". On the question of construing the section, the court said it would adopt neither a strict interpretation in favour of the subject, nor a strained interpretation in favour of the Executive, but would attempt to find the intention of Parliament from all the provisions of the section in the light of the background against which it was enacted. In this regard the court went further than counsel for the police who in the course of argument disclaimed the contention that the purpose of holding the detainee in isolation was to break his resistance to interrogation; the court asked whether "in the furtherance of the object of inducing the detainee to speak, the continued detention should be as effective as possible, subject only to considerations of humanity as accepted in a civilised country?"; and by its conclusion answered the question in the affirmative. In rejecting the argument that the detainee should retain all personal rights save those expressly taken away by Parliament, the court asked hypothetically whether this meant that a person who in happier days habitually enjoyed champagne and cigars should as of right have champagne and cigars while in detention. Although no evidence was led on the subject at the time, the writer of this book, who was the detainee concerned, is now in a position to reveal that in happier days he had in fact rarely drunk champagne and had altogether given up smoking, but had continued habitually to read law reports.

This judgement of the Appeal Court was extensively criticised. Former Judge of Appeal O. D. Schreiner regretted the court's reliance on the majority judgement in *Liversidge* v. *Anderson* and observed that the maxim *salus populi suprema lex* had no doubt a proper role to play as a substantive defence in certain cases but was not a rule of interpretation. A professor of law who had referred to the judgement of the court of first instance in support of his contention that the South African Judiciary was vigilant in maintaining common law rights in the face of an encroaching Executive, was compelled to add a footnote that the judgement had been reversed on appeal "for reasons that are not entirely convincing" (Beinart). Other writers stated that they could not see how holding a detainee in prolonged detention without any means of keeping himself occupied could be regarded as consistent with considerations of humanity. Finally, a Judge of Appeal who had not sat in this particular matter, argued strongly in a third test case heard on the ambit of the ninety-day law that the whole basis of the Appeal Court's reasoning had been wrong.

The issue in the third case was whether a judge had the power to order the production in court of a detainee, to substantiate by means of viva voce evidence allegations he had made in a smuggled note that he had been subjected to ill-treatment by the security police. A single judge and then a full Bench of three judges in the Transvaal rejected an application by the detainee's wife, who sought an order protecting her husband from further irregular treatment, that the detainee be brought to court to give the necessary evidence. In the Appellate Division, the

Appeal Court divided three to two in favour of upholding the decisions *a quo* and rejecting the application. One of the dissenting judges argued that in construing the object of the ninety-day law, it was far more reasonable to suppose that Parliament intended the detainee to be kept in isolation merely to prevent him from communicating with other possible conspirators, than to infer that Parliament intended a species of pressure to be brought to bear upon him to induce him to speak; accordingly, it was his view that the decision in the earlier case on reading matter had been based on faulty reasoning. In the present case, neither he nor the second dissenting judge could see how the purpose of the section could be defeated by the detainee being brought before court, where proper safeguards could be maintained to protect the interests of the police. Both the dissenting judges emphasised that a case of this kind should not be considered in a narrow or legalistic fashion. The majority of the court held otherwise, however, and stated that the object of the section would be frustrated if the detainee were to be brought before court; if he had in fact been ill-treated in the way he alleged, then his remedy lay in a claim for damages after his release.

The judgements in these three cases formed the foundation of a strongly argued critique of the South African Judiciary which appeared in the *South African Law Journal* under the heading 'The Permanence of the Temporary' (Matthews and Albino, 1966). The joint authors were respectively a professor of law and a professor of psychology, and they considered the implications of these decisions against the background of studies conducted in various parts of the world into the effects on prisoners of solitary confinement and stimulus deprivation. Their charge was not that the South African judges lacked integrity but that they failed to grasp imaginatively the implications of solitary confinement and the Western ideals of individual freedom. "In recent years", they wrote, "the courts have interpreted laws which have cried out for one of those resounding defences of individual liberty in the dignified and majestic language in which judges sometimes speak, but the opportunity has been passed by." In carrying out a general programme of laws which many regarded as oppressive, the courts had not shown themselves to be reluctant or even faintly troubled. Security laws were justified as a temporary measure to deal with an emergency, but the situation which arose was that of a permanent emergency with signs not of respite but of vanishing liberty and permanent insecurity.

Some months later Chief Justice Steyn rose vigorously to the defence of the Judiciary. The occasion was an after-dinner speech delivered to law teachers and students, and he directed his attention to what he called attacks made on the courts of South Africa, more especially on the Appeal Court, both in print and out of print, in regard to their decisions on the so-called ninety-day provision. He objected to the disparaging tone of the critics and the intemperate, derogatory language used, and reminded his audience of the factual circumstances in relation to which the provision had been passed and in the light of which it had to be interpreted. These facts had been established in the course of a number of trials beyond any shadow of a doubt, and had become so notorious as not to need repeating. Whether or not the ninety-day law was the most effective method of dealing with this situation was for Parliament and not for the courts to decide. The matter has occasioned a political storm and had been widely canvassed in Parliament and elsewhere. "In effect we have now been blamed, on the ground *inter alia* of the alleged effects of such interrogation–incidentally not in evidence before us–for not entering the political arena and taking a strong stand on a particular side, after the law had been passed. . . . It is not our function to write an indignant codicil to the will of Parliament. If in the eyes of some there is any blame in avoiding such a course, I have no doubt that our judges, one and all of them, will not thereby be pressed into unwise participation before or after the event in a political conflict" (1967).

The Chief Justice's hopes that the judges would continue to enforce the will of Parliament without revealing any flickers of independent judicial conscience, were not to be realised. In fact judges in the past had frequently commented upon the inequitable consequences of laws they had been obliged to enforce, and on occasion their recommendations had been acted upon by Parliament. Judicial criticisms were aimed particularly at laws which directly affected the administration of justice, such as the provision that confessions to a policeman were not to be admissible in evidence unless subsequently reduced to writing before a magistrate, or the provision that whipping be compulsory for persons convicted of certain scheduled offences. Receiving stolen property was one of these offences, and Chief Justice Centlivres observed in 1956 that compulsory whipping for receivers was not necessarily in the best interests of the administration of justice, the dignity of which would be better maintained if the courts had their discretion restored. Nine years later Parliament in fact restored the judicial discretion. More generally, Centlivres declared in another matter that the mere fact that a judge held strong views on what he considered to be an evil in society did not disqualify him from sitting in a case in which some of those evils were brought to light; his duty was to administer the law as it existed, "but he may in administering it express his strong disapproval of it" (1951). Judges had also been openly critical of a recently passed censorship law. One judge had in a literary magazine condemned the law before it was finally enacted, while another, who had been compelled to apply it, stated in a judgement that its terms were so wide that much harm could be done to the cause of literature without any corresponding good being done to the cause of morals. When this judgement was eventually taken on appeal, the Appeal Court judges divided three to two in favour of upholding the ban. The majority of the court, which included Dr Steyn, found that a number of passages in the book in question were objectionable; one of the minority judges, however, made a point of quoting in full all the salacious passages which the Chief Justice had delicately paraphrased, and went on to declare himself as follows: "When a court of law is called upon to decide whether liberty should be repressed . . . it should be anxious to steer a course as close to the preservation of liberty as possible. . . . In its approach to the law it should assume that Parliament, itself a product of political liberty, in every case intends liberty to be repressed only to such extent as it in clear terms declares."

Yet by the time Dr Steyn made his after-dinner speech in defence of the Judiciary, none of the judges had expressed any dismay at the manner in which the administration of justice was being affected by the operation of security laws. The holding of accused persons and witnesses for months and even years in solitary confinement prior to their being brought to court led to no expressions of judicial concern, nor was there any vigorous judicial reaction to allegations by State witnesses that they had been subjected by the police to violence and sleep deprivation. There were some rulings against the police, but they were so cautiously expressed that they did little to protect detainees in general from irregular treatment. The security police, accustomed to losing most of their cases in the 1950s became used to winning nearly all their cases in the 1960s. Emboldened by the favourable climate they encountered in court, they went so far as to disobey a habeas corpus writ served upon them ordering them to produce in a court a detainee (Heymann) taken into custody before an empowering law had been fully promulgated. By moving the detainee from one lock-up to another, they were able to avoid receipt of the writ by his jailor until the law authorising the detention had been duly promulgated. The judge hearing the matter criticised the action of the police as possibly being in contempt of court, but beyond awarding costs against the police, took the matter no further, and the detainee was not brought before him or released. In another case the security police detained in court twenty-two Africans who had just been acquitted after a lengthy trial.

Eventually legislation was passed which made it possible for the security police to continue to use the courts for the punishment of offenders but to disregard the courts for all other purposes (the so-called 'Boss' law, 1969). The Prime Minister or his nominee was empowered to prevent the courts from considering any matter which in his opinion affected the interests of the State or public security. This provision for excluding the courts' jurisdiction was consistent with a general increase in the power of the police and a decline in the authority of the courts in relation to security matters, but was so sweeping in its effect that it prompted hitherto silent members of the Judiciary into outspoken criticism. One judge declared at a public gathering that he was worried about the dignity, independence, and esteem of the Judiciary in the existing South African scheme of things. He emphasised that the independence of the Judiciary was the cornerstone of the administration of justice, and said that the Government had neither consulted with the Judiciary on the proposed legislation nor informed it of its intentions (Marais). Other judges also made public statements expressing serious misgivings about the legislation. Eventually after the law was passed a Judge of Appeal was appointed to act as a one-man Commission of Enquiry to investigate the machinery for dealing with threats to the security of the State and to consider whether the new law should be amended. Although the Commission's report is apparently not going to be published, the Commissioner has stated in a newspaper interview that he took into account the opinion of members of the Judiciary and legal profession in recommending alterations to the new law (*Sunday Times*, 25th April 1971).

JUDGING THE JUDGES

A feature of the judges who, in conflict with the Chief Justice's advice, entered the political arena and took a stand in defence of the court's jurisdiction, was that all of them were Afrikaners who during the Second World War had been active in the legal defence of pro-German saboteurs and spies. The first of the judges to speak out had in fact himself been interned during the war (Marais), and although neither he nor his colleagues had come from liberal backgrounds, they presented an appearance of much greater independent-mindedness than did their English-speaking colleagues on the Bench. There was some parallel to this in the Appeal Court where some of the most important pro-Executive judgements were delivered by English-speaking judges (Ogilvie-Thompson, Holmes), whereas the strongest dissentient judgements in favour of liberty were handed down by an Afrikaner judge who during the war had defended pro-Nazi rebels (Rumpff). Thus the policy in the 1950s of promoting Afrikaners to the Bench, most of whom were known to be generally sympathetic to the Government, did change the character of the South African Judiciary, but not in as total a fashion as some people had anticipated.

The accession to power of an Afrikaner nationalist Government in 1948 led to a rapid increase in Afrikaner influence in the South African legal system. British styles and procedures continued to be observed, but important posts were filled largely by Afrikaans-speaking persons, and the use of the Afrikaans language becaame more widespread. At the time of Union, Afrikaners who entered the legal profession became anglicised in speech and manner. The first Afrikaans-medium law faculty was established in 1920, the first superior court judgement in Afrikaans was delivered in 1933, the first Afrikaans law journal was published in 1937 and the first Afrikaans legal textbook appeared only in 1946. In 1922 only a quarter of the judges had Afrikaans names, and many of these came from thoroughly anglicised families, whereas in 1969 nearly two-thirds of the judges had Afrikaans names. The promotion of Afrikaners to the Bench was defended as a means of achieving linguistic parity between English and Afrikaans-speakers, but one of the consequences was to hold back the advancement of men whose attitudes to race were relatively liberal and to increase the proportion of judges who were generally sympathetic to the policies of the Government. Leading members of the Bar, especially those known for their liberal or left-wing opinions, were passed over in favour of Afrikaners known to be nationalists. Thus Dr L. C. Steyn, a Government law adviser, was appointed to the Transvaal Bench in 1951; the Bar protested vigorously and even attempted to boycott his court, but in 1955 he was appointed to the Appeal Court, and in 1959 he was made Chief Justice. He retired in 1971, having been Chief Justice for longer than anyone except Innes. The leader of the Government team in the Voters' cases of the early 1950s was appointed to the Cape Bench in 1955, to the Appeal Court in 1958, and then made Judge-President of the Cape in 1959. Unlike the Chief Justice, however, he did not regard race segregation in court as reasonable, and with the support of his colleagues managed to keep the Cape Supreme Court free of apartheid notices (Beyers). Thus changes in the composition of the Judiciary tended to make it more Executive-minded and to bring judicial attitudes to race more in line with official attitudes to race, but the process was by no means a complete one. For a number of years very few English-speaking judges were appointed to the Bench, and most of those who were appointed, or whose judicial careers were advanced, tended to have reputations for being Executive-minded. One of this latter group is Judge Ogilvie-Thompson, who in 1971 replaced Dr Steyn as Chief Justice; both he and Dr Steyn were generally regarded by lawyers as extremely able jurists who presided over their courts with a courtesy and dignity marred in the eyes of their critics by a tendency to lean in favour of the Executive. Some of the more recent appointments, however, have gone to men known to have relatively liberal attitudes, so that it would be dangerous to predict in an unqualified manner that the trend away from the comparatively liberal judicial era of the 1950s will continue.

The above-mentioned changes in the composition of the Judiciary together with the tendency of most of the judges, especially in the Appeal Court, to lean more towards the Executive than their predecessors had done, lost for the South African judges some of the prestige they had formerly enjoyed. Whereas until the beginning of the 1960s the judges had achieved an international reputation through the quality and character of their judgements, now the Department of Information was called upon to expound their virtues. Thus one publication declared that the legal traditions of South Africa were among the highest in the world, that law-abiding South Africans of all races did not fear the law but accorded it deep respect, and that the country's judicial officers were universally held in high esteem (Panorama, February 1968). Another claimed that even if the laws in South Africa were criticised, the judicial system and officers of the court were held in the highest esteem throughout the world (*Rule of Law*). The Minister of Justice declared that Chief Justice Steyn was a legal colossus who ranked among the most distinguished legal men in the world. He would be remembered after his retirement for his contribution towards restoring, Roman-Dutch law to its rightful place and his magnificent contribution to the use of Afrikaans in the country's legal development. "During his term of office as Chief Justice, our country had its share of turbulence, and he too was made a target for criticism. However, he would not be deviated and succeeded amicably in keeping the courts and its judges out of the political arena" (Pelser, *Rand Daily Mail*, 4th December 1970).

Reference to contemporary legal publications, however, indicates that the esteem claimed for the South African Judiciary was not in fact being universally acknowledged. A contributor to the *International Comparative Law Quarterly* stated that the changed composition of the South African Judiciary disposed it to be more inward-looking, more impervious to outside influences and more in accord with current legislative policy (Millner, 1962). Similarly, the International Commission of Jurists which had formerly gone out of its way to exempt the judges in South Africa from strictures, now issued a booklet entitled *The Erosion of the Rule of Law in South Africa*, in which it stated that the overall impression gained from recently decided cases was of a Judiciary as 'Establishment-minded' as the Executive, and prepared to adopt an interpretation that would facilitate the Executive's task rather than defend the liberty of the subject and uphold the Rule of Law. U.S. Senator Robert Kennedy, in an address to the Johannesburg Bar, stated that no Bar anywhere in the world held a higher position, but he hinted that to maintain that position the Bench and Bar would have to remain alert and active even during periods of social emergency. Speaking of American experience, he said that "in times of stress and hysteria we have temporarily given in to the cries of those who have claimed that suppression can bring security. But each time the Bench and the Bar have recalled us to the Constitution" (1966 SALJ).

Finally, inside South Africa itself criticism of judgements was being extended and developed into criticism of the judges themselves. Whereas previously legal writers had on occasion alluded in discreet and at times Aesopian language to the fact that when appointments were made to the Bench, individuals had been preferred or passed over because they happened to be Englishmen or Afrikaners, liberals or segregationists, now a law professor for the first time raised as a matter for legal discussion the fact that all the judges in South Africa were white. In an extensively reported inaugural lecture, the professor observed that comment or criticism which was commonplace in other countries was often avant-garde, daring and even dangerous in South Africa, and this was particularly true of any discussion of the judicial process. Nevertheless, he continued, absence of criticism did not promote infallibility, it merely encouraged belief in infallibility, with all its attendant dangers. South African judges had been frank about their law-making function in relation to the common law, but still adhered to the myth of judicial sterility in relation to the interpretation of statutes. In practice the judges were continuously filling in gaps in legislation in a manner coloured by their unconscious assumptions. Being drawn from one small section of the population—the white group—they tended to share a whole range of inarticulate but influential premises with members of the Executive, who were drawn from the same small group. In his view, the positivist legal tradition in South Africa helped to conceal rather than reveal these premises, and the distinction which it drew between law and morality enabled the Judiciary to apply the harshest laws with an easy conscience. He claimed that academics contributed to this situation by their failure to deal with fundamental legal theory and their unwillingness to examine the social functions of law. In Germany after the First World War, he said, positivism was the only legal philosophy acceptable to the legal profession. This stance, with its servile obedience to the will of the sovereign and strict distinction between law and morals, was exploited by Hitler and resulted in the debasement of the German legal system (Dugard, 1971).

Many judges appear to have discussed this address; a number publicly rejected its main thesis, while others remained silent. A colleague of the professor's, however, gave strong support for what he called the need for drastic de-mystification of the law in South Africa. In all civilised countries, he maintained, the investigation of the subtle undercurrents which went into the thoughts and mental make-up of a judge had been a legitimate field of investigation and research, and only in South Africa had there been a tendency to envelop the Bench with a halo of mystery and untouchability (Van Niekerk).

How to judge the judges is never an easy matter. Their conduct can be evaluated in terms of standards set by their predecessors or of goals which they proclaim for themselves, or of norms almost universally accepted in principle, such as the United Nations Declaration of Human Rights. Judicial behaviour can also be looked at from a procedural point of view, in which case the question might be asked whether it conforms with generally acceptable notions of fair practice, or else it can be examined in terms of its actual effects, in which case the query might be whether or not it promotes manifest injustice. If the judges are viewed merely as products of their society, they will be no more entitled to praise or immune from blame than any other member of their community; on the other hand, should a special legal conscience be attributed to them, then higher standards of conduct might be demanded of them. A positivist might ask simply whether the judges acted in accordance with the law as set out at the time in the decrees of dominant political authority, whereas a supporter of natural law might ask further whether these enactments contained at least that minimum core of morality which in their view distinguishes rules of law from tyrannical edicts. Both might say that just as special heinousness nullifies the excuse of a soldier that he was merely obeying orders, so gross inhumanity might deprive a judicial officer of the plea that he was merely carrying out the law. Much, of course, would depend on the forum in which the evaluation was being carried out, since the criteria adopted in the pages of a law journal might differ radically from those applied by a post-revolutionary domestic court, or those relied upon by an international legal tribunal.

In any society where courts exist they tend to play a significant role in the system of domination. They normally claim a monopoly of the right to sanction the use of force, and they speak in the name of the sovereign, usually on behalf of the community. Yet just as no individual can be judged simply in terms of his own opinion of his conduct, so no legal system can be evaluated simply in terms of its own traditions and concepts. It may be useful as a starting-off point to consider whether or not the Judiciary is departing from its own well-established norms, and then to examine the norms themselves, both in relation to internal consistency and in respect of international standards. A test frequently adopted in this connection is whether or not a legal system operates according to the Rule of Law, a concept easier to extol than to define. Yet to stop there would carry the risk of excluding matters of substance because of preoccupation with matters of form. The often asked question of whether the end can justify the means should perhaps be turned around to ask whether the means can justify the end. The actual effects of the legal system and the interests promoted or suppressed by it should be as much a matter for enquiry as its formal elegance or procedural equity. The enhancement of techniques to serve ends which are unjust promotes rather than reduces injustice. In this connection it should be noted that the courts give a sense of orderliness and regularity to domination. The measured language of the law and the decorum of the court-room help to calm persons who face punishment, while forensic combat diverts and absorbs hostility. The hope of an acquittal or that the maximum sentence will not be imposed gives individual defendants an alternative to confrontation and encourages compliant behaviour. In general terms, by placing a limitation on the powers of the rulers, the courts facilitate the accommodation of the dominated to the dominators, and thereby make rule more secure. What might otherwise be seen as a large question of social relationships gets converted into a series of small questions about individual guilt according to narrowly defined criteria.

Bearing some of these considerations in mind, it is suggested that a survey of the role and functioning of the Judiciary in racially divided South Africa makes it easier to deny to the judges any claim to special virtue than it does to impute to them any liability for special fault. The main criticism which could perhaps be advanced in relation to the conduct of most of the judges is not so much that they help to enforce race discrimination because they are corrupt, cowed or consciously biased, but that they do so willingly; not that they lack courtesy or decorum, but that they use polite and elegant language to lend dignity to laws which impose segregation and harshly penalise radical opponents of a system of government almost universally condemned. Instead of investing their office with the prestige associated with the pursuit of justice, they allow the prestige associated with their office to be used for the pursuit of injustice.

During such time as the Judiciary played some role in tempering or delaying the impact of differential legislation, it was possible for observers to concentrate on those aspects of judicial activity that stood apart from the rest of governmental action, and possibly to underplay the extent to which the Judiciary operated as a central part of the State machine. Decisions against the Government, such as the judgements in the Cape Voters cases and the acquittals in some of the many trials held under the security laws, tended to emphasise the extent to which the Judiciary was independent of the Executive, and to divert attention from the degree to which the court system as a whole was used to maintain domination. To legal practitioners and individual litigants operating within the system it might have been all-important whether the higher courts leant in favour of the Executive or in favour of liberty (the two in the South African context usually being regarded as mutually exclusive). But to the million Africans prosecuted under race-statutes each year such trends were largely irrelevant. While the judges were wrestling with large constitutional issues about whether in the absence of clear legislation to the contrary certain prominent individuals had the right to travel abroad, hundreds of thousands of ordinary people were being punished by the courts for moving without passes inside their own country. During the period when the Appeal Court was emphasising that guilt in murder trials should be determined on a subjective rather than an objective basis–thus seeming to favour the accused person–the rate of executions rose more steeply than it had ever done before. For a long while the courts protected individuals who complained about social injustice, but as soon as these individuals began to take active steps to correct the injustice, the courts were used to penalise them. The failure of the courts to save black people from being dispossessed by the processes of law can be defended on the basis of the constitutional subordination of the Judiciary to the Legislature, just as the penalisation by the courts of black and white rebels can be justified in terms of the courts' duty to help maintain the public peace. Yet to emphasise the concept of judicial subordination is to undermine the notion of judicial independence.

To make these points is not to advocate the elimination of the Judiciary or to decry the efforts of those individual judicial officers who are concerned about the effects of their judgements; the thesis that more direct repression automatically leads to more powerful counter-action is hard to sustain, especially in the light of South African experience in the 1960s. It is simply to stress that the mere existence of a Judiciary confident in its learning and independence is no guarantee that justice will in fact be administered by the courts. One might here reverse the well-known maxim, and say that not only must justice be seen to be done, it must be done. Certainly the judges today would have more difficulty than their predecessors might have had in resisting the charge that if the symbol of the administration of justice in South Africa is a two-edged sword, the edge that menaces the black population has become increasingly sharp, while the edge that restrains white officials and police grows increasingly blunt.

SOURCES AND BIBLIOGRAPHY

1. NOTE ON SOURCES

This study was based largely on material found in the Institute of Advanced Legal Studies and the library of the Royal Commonwealth Society in London. The questions asked and the comments made were naturally influenced by the writer's experience of the law in South Africa. One of the most difficult problems of method was to integrate information gained from a variety of sources, all bearing on the same subject matter but not normally related to each other, such as law journals, law reports, legal memoirs, government bluebooks, and African autobiographical literature. All the sources mentioned in the Bibliography were referred to in the preparation of this work. Abbreviated references are given in the text to some of the main materials used, and a more complete list of sources for each chapter is given in the following pages. The full references to the works cited in abbreviated form can be found in the list of abbreviations and the Bibliography.

Because of their special subject matter Chapters Five and Six contain a number of full references in the text. Readers wishing to have more detailed references for these Chapters and the rest of the book may consult the doctoral thesis submitted by the writer to Sussex University in 1971: "The Administration of Justice in a Racially Stratified Society–South Africa 1652-1970".

2. ABBREVIATIONS

The following abbreviations have been used in the text and footnotes:

AD	Appellate Division (LR)
ANC	African National Congress
BPP	British Parliamentary Papers
CILSA	*Comparative and International Law Journal of Southern Africa*
CLJ	*Cape Law Journal*
Cmd	Command
CPD	Cape Provincial Division (LR)
D	Durban Local Division (LR)
EDC	Eastern Districts Court (LR)
EDL	Eastern Districts Local Division (LR)
GN	Government Notice
GWLD	Griqualand West Local Division (LR)
HCG	High Court of Griqualand (LR)
HMSO	His (Her) Majesty's Stationery Office
ICJ	International Commission of Jurists

ICLQ	*International Comparative Law Quarterly*
LR	Law Reports
MLR	Modern Law Review
NLR	Natal Law Reports
NPD	Natal Provincial Division (LR)
OPD	Orange Free State Provincial Division (LR)
ORC	Orange River Colony
PAC	Pan-Africanist Congress
R v	Rex (Regina) v –
RCI	Royal Colonial Institute
RP	Republican Publication
S v	The State versus
SA	South Africa
SAIRR	South African Institute of Race Relations
SALJ	*South African Law Journal*
SANAC	South African Native Affairs Commission
SAP	South African Police
SAR	South African Republic (LR)
SC	Supreme Court (Cape LR)
SCC	Special Criminal Court (LR)
Sp. Ct.	Special Criminal Court (LR)
SWA	South West Africa Provincial Division (LR)
TLAD	Transkei Legislative Assembly Debates
TPD	Transvaal Provincial Division (LR)
TS	Transvaal Supreme Court (LR)
UG	Union Government (Publications)
UN	United Nations
WLD	Witwatersrand Local Division (LR)

3. REFERENCES

Chapter One (p. 17)

Early Legal Institutions. Various articles in CLJ and SALJ by C. Graham Botha, J. de V. Roos, C. H. van Zyl; G. Visagie (Acta Juridica 1963); J. C. De Wet (Tydskrif 1958); Hahlo and Kahn (1968); Burchell and Hunt (1970).

Slavery. De Kock; Cambridge History; Sklavius (Mediationes Medii 1970); Van den Berghe; C. Graham Botha (SALJ); Macrone; Brion Davis.

Torture. Various articles in CLJ and SALJ by C. Graham Botha, J. de V. Roos and C. H. van Zyl; De Kock; Leibbrandt.

Khoi Khoi. De Wet (Tydskrif 1958); Oxford History; Macrone; Alberti; Venter.

Postscript. C. G. Botha (SALJ 1915); Barrow (1806); Kahn (Death Penalty).

General. Simons (African Women); Macrone; Van den Berghe; Oxford History; Walker (History); Venter.

Chapter Two (p. 32)

Transition. Cole; biographical sketches in SALJ by C. G. Botha and F. St. L. Searle; Mellor; Cambridge History; Macrone; Saxe-Bannister; Hoffmann; Burchell and Hunt (1970).

Liberty, Equality, Servility. Mellor; Duly; Simons (Class and Colour); McCracken.

Robes and Oxwagons. Schreiner; biographical sketches in SALJ by F. St. L. Searle; *Mackay* v. *Philip,* 1. Menzies 455; Macmillan; *Letterstedt* v. *Morgan,* 1849, 5. Searle 373; Walker (de Villiers); Corder; Porter; Innes; In re Kok and Balie, 1879, Buchanan, p. 64; In re Sigeau, 1895, CLJ, 193; Walker (de Villiers).

Barristers and Gentlemen. Walker (de Villiers); Innes; Ex parte Kriger, 1945 CPD 254; biographical sketches in SALJ; Gandhi (Autobiography).

Attorneys and Law Agents. Cowen (Acta Juridica 1959); biographical sketches in SALJ; C. H. van Zyl, SALJ 1912.

Magistrates, Justices of the Peace and the Law Department. Oxford History; Schreiner; Porter; Corder; Walker (Schreiner); Cape Register 1894; Hook; biographical sketches in SALJ.

The Land Register. Various articles in CLJ and SALJ; Duly.

Law Enforcers: Army and Police. Cambridge History; Tylden; Porter; Barrow (Memoir); Cape Register 1894; an Ex-C.M.R.; S.A. Yearbook No. 6; Porter; Cape Bluebook 1884.

Prisons and Punishment. Venter; Cape Register 1894; Porter; Cole; Prisons and Borstals (1960); S.A. Yearbook No. 6; Morice, CLJ 1892.

White Justice. BPP C 2482/443; Cole; *Upington* v. *Solomon and Dormer,* 1879, Buchanan, 240; Innes; Tamplin, RCI 1910; Dick, SANAC (2); Elliot, SANAC (3); Glanville, RCI 1874-1875; Simons (African Women); Robertson; Marais (ed. Schapera); Oxford History; Macmillan; *Q.* v. *Vuso and Others,* 1900 CLJ, 77; *Mbangeni* v. *Falcon,* HCG (9) 1899, p. 1; Walker (de Villiers); Sweeney, SANAC (2); *East London* v. *Two Shillings,* 1899 CLJ, 3; Cape Register 1894; Cape Bluebook 1884; Simons (Class and Colour); *R.* v. *Bilibili,* 1892 CLJ, 245; *R.* v. *de Wee,* 1901 SALJ, 297; *Moquebele* v. *Peri-Local Board,* 1893 CLJ, 150; *Zigli* v. *McLeod,* 1904 SALJ, 394; *Umvalo* v. *East London,* 1892 CLJ, 246; 1893 CLJ, 42.

General. Notes, book reviews, biographies and articles in the CLJ and SALJ.

Chapter Three (p. 68)

Introduction. Oxford History; Walker; Macrone; Bell; J. P. Verloren van Themaat; Tydskrif 1954; *Cassim and Solomon* v. *The State,* 1892 CLJ, 58; Fraser; SANAC (2), 378; Modisane; Gandhi (Autobiography); Myrdal.

The Courts and Race in the OFS. Biographical sketches in CLJ and SALJ; Pirow; M. de Villiers, SALJ 1920; Pirow; Venter; *The State* v. *Gibson,* 1898 CLJ, 1; *Cassim and Solomon* v. *The State,* 1892 CLJ 58; *Anna* v. *The Village Management Board,* Jagersfontein, 1892 CLJ, 269; *Preller* v. *Schultz,* 1893 CLJ, 83; *Meyer* v. *The State,* 1892 CLJ, 120; Simons (African Women); Trollope; Fraser; *Segelecho* v. *do.* 1887 CLJ, 298; In re Jacob Ngakantsi, 1889 CLJ, 110, 259.

Law and Race in the Transvaal. Kotze; Kahn (SAR); Nathan; Reitz; Oxford History; Simons (African Women); Rhoodie and Venter; Marais (ed. Schapera); In re Marechane, SAR (1), p. 31; Kotze; Gordon; *Ismail Suleiman* v. *Landdrost,* Middelburg, SAR (2); p. 244; *Tayob* v. *SAR,* 1898 CLJ, 291; Gandhi (Autobiography); Venter; Bell; Innes; Simons (African Women); Q. v. *Sepana Kotze,* 1880, p. 172; Nellmapius, 1887 CLJ, 45; *Brown* v. *Leyds N.O.,* 1897 CLJ, 94; Pirow; *R.* v. *Padsha,* 1923 AD 281; *Habib Motan* v. *Transvaal Govt.,* 1904 TS 404.

Law and Race in Natal. Oxford History; Nienabur, Codicillus 1965; Simons (African Women); The Colony of Natal; biographies in SALJ; Hahlo and Kahn (1968); Marks (Rebellion); Welsh (President); Thompson (Unification); Venter; Natal Directory 1894, 1895; Holt; BPP C 5892/199; Railway Guide; Gandhi (Autobiography); Natal Law Reports 1903; Meer; Morris; In re Tilonko, 1908 SALJ, 184; Re Cukijana and Tobela, 1909 SALJ, 167; Beaumont, SANAC (3); Saunders, SANAC (3); Finnemore, SANAC (3).

General. Notes, book reviews, biographies and articles in Tydskrif, Codicillus, CLJ, SALJ and Butterworths SA Law Review (1954-1956).

Chapter Four (p. 95)

Administration of Justice in Tribal Society: Pre-Conquest. Oxford History; Marks (Historians); Schapera (Law and Justice); Hunter; Weber (ed. Aubert); Seymour; Trollope; Alberti; Needham; Welsh (President); Gluckman (ed. Fortes and Evans-Pritchard); Krige; Ritter; Modisane; Auerbach; Wilks (ed. Fage); Hammond-Tooke (ed. Thompson); Molema.

Dispossession Nine Points of the Law: Colonial Relationships and Attitudes. Gluckman (ed. Aubert); Weber (ed. Aubert); Seymour; Dick, SANAC (2); Saxe-Bannister; Alberti; Barrow (Memoir); De Kiewiet; Porter; Marks (Rebellion); Walker (History); *Upington* v. *Solomon and Dormer,* 1879, Buchanan, 240; Shippart, RCI 1896-1897; Fraser; *Ncumata* v. *Matwa,* 1882 (3) EDC 272; In re Kok and Balie, 1879, Buchanan, 64; In re Sigcau, 1895 CLJ, 193; Tylden;

Innes; Loveday, SANAC (4); Holt; Gandhi (Autobiography); Churchill quoted in Marks; Macrone; Oxford History; Gordon; Shippard, RCI 1894-1895; Morgan, RCI 1902-1903; Simons (Class and Colour); Cape Register 1894; McCracken; Mbeki; Trollope; Creswell, RCI 1883-1884; Chalmers; Tamplin, RCI 1910; Jabavu (ed. Schapera); Collins, SANAC (4); Pirow; Whitworth, SANAC (4); Scott, SANAC (4); sketches by F. Brownlee in SALJ 1933-1939; Hahlo and Kahn (Background). Professor Hahlo later moved to Canada.

The Administration of Justice in a Tribal Area: Post-Conquest Position. Krige; Gluckman (ed. Fortes and Evans-Pritchard); Hammond-Tooke (Bhaca); Elliot, SANAC (3); Jeffreys, SALJ 1956; Henley, SANAC (2); Hunter; Innes; In re Sigcau, 1895 CLJ, 193; Welsh (President); Simons (African Women); Wiechers, Tydskrif 1967; In re *Yako* v. *Begi*, 1948 (1) SA 388 (AD); Seymour; Davis *et al.*, Luthuli; Hunter; Mbeki; Sprigg, SANAC (2); R. Verloren van Themaat (Education); Carter *et al.*; SAIRR 1961; TLAD 1965 (1), p. 62; SAIRR 1962; Act 48, 1963; SAIRR 1968; TLAD 1967, p. 87; TLAD 1968-1969, pp. 131, 133, 145; TLAD 1968, pp. 237, 238, 244; Suttner; R. Verloren van Themaat.

General. Notes, book reviews, anecdotes and articles in the CLJ and SALJ, and articles in Tydskrif 1968, 1969.

Chapter Five (p. 123)

The Unification of the Courts: The Supreme Court of S.A. Reitz, with introduction by Smuts; On Smuts and Hertzog, 1908 SALJ; 1910 SALJ, 1950 SALJ, Pirow; Cleaver; Nathan; Bell; Innes; Times History; Harrison; Reitz; Walker; Martin; Pace; Codicillus 1966; Trapido; Windham, SANAC (4); Gumede, SANAC (3); T. Schreiner, SANAC (4); Pirow; Gandhi; Broome, RCI 1901-1902; Fraser; Morris; Tsewu, SANAC (4).

Judicial Attitude to Race. Trapido; Simons (Class and Colour); biographies in SALJ; Kovalsky, 1936 SALJ; Avin, 1969 SALJ; Roome, 1969 SALJ; biographies in Tydskrif; Who's Who 1969; Diemont, Acta Juridica 1968; Hoffmann; Maister; Kahn (Death Penalty); Cape Argus, 24/8/1954; 24/11/1965; SAIRR 1969; U.G. 47 of 1947, p. 70; Van Niekerk (Hanged by the Neck); Kahn (Crime); Welsh (Capital Punishment). On White rebels—1900 CLJ, 15, 169; Bell, pp. 200-40; 1896 CLJ, 129; Cape Treason Trials, 1901 SALJ, 164; Times History, pp. 550, 554; Harrison, p. 136; Reitz, pp. 234, 258; Kruger, p. 93; Times History, pp. 550-69; Walker, pp. 554-65; Tylden, p. 231; Rosenthal, pp. 177-206; Kestell, p. 238; Maritz, p. 104; Herd; Simons (Class and Colour), p. 296; Kentridge, p. 115; Walker and Weinbren, pp. 139-40; Welsh (Capital Punishment), p. 422. On black rebels—SAIRR 1961 to 1969; Annual Reports of Commissioner of Prisons; SAIRR 1970. Further, see: Penal Statistics 1949-1962; Simons (The Law); Corder; Beinart; Devitt;

Roux (Bunting); Simons (Class and Colour); Ferreira, reviewed by Dugard, 1967 SALJ; Centlivres, Acta Juridica 1962.

General. Notes, book reviews, biographies and articles in CLJ, SALJ, Tydskrif and Codicillus.

Chapter Six (p. 161)

The Franchise. McCracken, Mbeki; Women's Enfranchisement Act, 1930; Native Representation Act, 1936; Le May, 1957 SALJ, 33; Promotion of Bantu Self-Government Act, 1959; Separate Representation of Voters Amendment Act, 1968; Bantu Authorities Act, 1951; Transkei Constitution Act, 1963; Bantu Homelands Citizenship Act, 1970; Coloured Persons Council Act, 1968; South African Indian Council Act, 1968. On constitutional crisis, see Cowen, 1952 Modern Law Review, 1953 Modern Law Review; 1953 SALJ; H. Verloren van Themaat, 1954 SALJ; Le May, 1957 SALJ; for the Votes cases, see Chapter Five.

Racial Legislation. Native Labour Regulation Act, 1911 (Bantu Labour Act, 1964); Native Land Act, 1913; Native Trust and Land Act, 1936; Native Urban Areas Act, 1923; Native Administration Act, 1927; Native Taxation and Development Act, 1925; Immorality Act, 1927; Section 10 of Act 25 of 1945 inserted by Act 54 of 1952; Natives Abolition of Passes and Coordination of Documents Act, 1952; Bantu Education Act, 1953; Prevention of Illegal Squatting Act, 1951; Native Resettlement Act, 1954; Native Labour Settlement of Disputes Act; Bantu Laws Amendment Acts, 1963, 1964; Unlawful Organisations Act, 1960; Liquor Amendment Act, 1961; Mines and Works Act, 1911, 1926; Reservation of Separate Amenities Act, 1953; Population Registration Act, 1951; Prohibition of Mixed Marriages Act, 1949; Immorality Act, 1950, 1957; Extension of University Education Act, 1959; Group Areas Act, 1950; Act 77 of 1957; Industrial Conciliation Act, 1956; Suppression of Communism Act, 1950; Unlawful Organisations Act, 1960; Prohibition of Political Interference Act, 1968. Davis *et al.*, Simons (African Women); Welsh (State President); Horrell (Legislation).

Law Enforcement and Race. Annual Police Reports; Annual Prison Reports; annual surveys of SAIRR; People in Prison, England and Wales; Rhoodie; Lansdown Commission U.G. 47/1947; Rhoodie; Venter; Freed; Murder in England and Wales; Penal Statistics 1949-1962; Welsh (Capital Punishment); Simons (The Law); Tanner, Read, Seidman and Abaka Eyison, and Milner, in (ed.) Milner; Kahn (Crime); Capital Punishment; Van Niekerk (Hanged by the Neck); Thompson, Codicillus May 1969; Kahn (Death Penalty).

General. Articles, notes and book reviews in CLJ and SALJ.

Chapter Seven (p. 200)

Attitudes Towards Lawyers. South African Native Affairs Commission, 1903-1905, referred to as SANAC. Radebe, SANAC 3; Makubalo, SANAC 2; Jabavu, SANAC 2; Umhalla, SANAC 2; Hunter; Roux (Bunting); Joseph.

Attitudes Towards Police. Wilson and Mafeje; Jabavu (ed. Schapera; Noni Jabavu; Mphahlele; Luthuli; Modisane.

Passive Resistance – Advocate M. K. Gandhi. Gandhi (Autobiography); Gandhi (Satyagraha); Hancock; Walker; Prison Returns, Transvaal Colony, 1907-1908; Doke; Brookes and Webb; Meer; Simons (Class and Colour); The (Indian) Leader 17/11/1967; Sampson, SAIRR 1966, 1967.

Active Resistance – Attorneys Mandela and Tambo. Simons (Class and Colour); Marks; Blackwell; 1911 SALJ, 349; *Mangena* v. *Law Society*, Transvaal 1910 TS; Benson; Kuper; Sampson; Special Report, Bureau of Statistics No. 266, in 1965 SALJ, 544; Nokwe in (ed.) Friedmann; Horter's Law List 1969; Carter *et al.*; TLAD 1965; intro. by Tambo to Mandela; autobiographical sketch by Mandela in Kantor; annual Police Report for 1953; *R.* v. *Sisulu*, 1953 (3) SA 276 (AD); *Incorporated Society of Transvaal* v. *Mandela*, 1954 (3) SA 102; *Mathews* v. *Cape Law Society*, 1956 (1) SA 807; Millner, 1957 SALJ; Mbeki; Joseph; Horrell (Action); Forman; Strydom; SAIRR 1961; *R.* v. *Adams*, 1959 (1) SA 646 (SCC); 1959 (3) SA 753 (AD); *R.* v. *Pitje*, 1960 (4) SA 709 (AD); SAIRR 1959-1960, 1961; Unlawful Organisations Act, 1960; Snyman Report into Disturbances in Paarl, November 1962, RP 51/1963; Sobukwe (UN Unit on Apartheid, 3/1972); Sobukwe sentenced in 1960 to three years, held for a further six years on Robben Island, SAIRR 1969; SAIRR 1960; *R.* v. *Swartz*, 1868, Buchanan, 13; *R.* v. *Cumela*, 1915 SALJ, 293; *R.* v. *Luyt*, 1927 AD 1; *R.* v. *Torch Publishing Co.*, 1956 (1) SA 815 (C); Mandela (ed.) Friedmann; *Mandela* v. *The State*; *R.* v. *Milne and Erleigh* (6), 1951 (1) SA 1|(AO); Centlivres, Acta Juridica 1962; section 11 g *bis* of Act 44 of 1950, as inserted in 1962 restricted right to quote 'banned' persons; On freedom of speech: *R.* v. *Bunting*, 1929 EDL 326; *R.* v. *Brown*, 1929 CPD 221; *R.* v. *Nkatlo*, 1950 (1) SA 26 (C); Kadalie; Roux (History). On Rivonia Trial, see Bernstein, Kantor, Strydom, De Villiers, Mtolo; *Pogrund* v. *Yutar*, 1967 (2) SA 564 (AD); *SA Associated Newspapers* v. *Yutar*, 1969 (2) SA 442 (AD); Security Council Resolutions 181, 182/1963; 190, 191/1964; General Assembly Resolutions 11/10/1963, 16/12/1963; Reports of Special Committee on Apartheid 13/9/1963, 24/3/1964, 25/5/1964; Cape Times 2/10/1964; Fischer; Ludi and Grobbelaar; On Winnie Mandela – see SAIRR 1969; Rand Daily Mail 10/12/1970; *R.* v. *Ndou*, 1971 (1) SA 668 (AD), Sechaba, 1967 vol. 10; SAIRR 1967.

Chapter Eight (p. 230)

Introduction. Simons (Class and Colour); Pain, Acta Juridica 1960; *S.* v. *Maree*, 1964 (4) SA 545 (O); Lewin (Politics and Law).

Criminal Procedure. Strauss (Procedure); cf. rebellions and conflict in 1913, 1914, 1922, 1939-1945, 1960; Public Safety Act, 1953; 'Sabotage Act' (General Laws Amendment Act), 1962; Terrorism Act, 1967; various amendments to Criminal Procedure Act, 1955, and Suppression of Communism Act, 1950; Arrest–Code IV; Judge's Rules, in Swift and Harcourt; Hiemstra, 1963, 1965 SALJ. Bail–Code VII; Criminal Procedure Amendment Act, 1965. Preparatory examination–Code VI; Act 37, 1963. Juries–Abolition of Juries Act, 1969; Code IX, VIII; various Articles in SALJ, 1916, 1920, 1931, 1956. The trial–Code XI, XIII, XVII; Act 44 of 1950, sec. 12 as inserted by Act 37 of 1963; Terrorism Act, 1967 secs. 4 and 5. Confessions–Hoffmann; Code secs. 244, 245, 258; *S. v. Ismail,* 1965 (1) SA 446 (N); *S. v. Hlekani,* 1964 (4) SA 429 (E). Witnesses and privilege–Code, secs. 212, 234, 254; Code, sec. 215 *bis* as inserted by Act 96 of 1965; Code, sec. 212 as substituted by Act 80 of 1964; Terrorism Act, 1967, sec. 6; *S. v. Weinberg,* 1966 (4) SA 660 (AD). Evidence–Act 44 of 1950, sec. 12 (as amended); Terrorism Act, 1967, sec. 2. Definition and onus–Act 44 of 1950, as amended, sec. 11 (b) *ter,* Terrorism Act, 1967, sec. 2. Minimum sentences–'Sabotage' Act, No. 76 of 1962, sec. 21; Act 44 of 1950, as amended, sec. 11 (i) *bis;* Terrorism Act, 1967, sec. 5. On legal aid–Abramowitz, 1960 SALJ; 1942 SALJ, 372; Dugard; Solomon; Codicillus, September 1967; *S. v. Van Rensburg,* 1963 (2) SA 343 (N); *South African Defence and Aid Fund* v. *Minister of Justice,* 1967 (1) SA 263 (AD); Erosion; Street, 1967 SALJ; Legal Aid Act, 1969; SAIRR 1969, 1970.

Discussion. Rule of Law; Tredgold; 1961 SALJ, 13.

Police. Holt; Tylden; S.A. Yearbook No. 6; annual Police Reports, Justitia, November 1963; Police Commission of Enquiry, U.G. 50, 1937; *R. v. Vorster,* 1941 AD 472; Kruger (Swart); Simons (Class and Colour); *R. v. Andrews,* 1948 (1) SA 18 (SCC); *R. v. Adams,* 1959 (1) SA 646 (SCC); 1959 (3) SA 404 (AD); Sunday Express, 8th May 1966; Sunday Times, 6th October 1968; Cape Times, 26th March 1968; SAIRR 1969; Government Notice No. 808 of 16th May 1969; Public Service Amendment Act, 1969; Security Services Special Account Act, 1969; General Laws Amendment Act, 1969, secs. 10 and 29; Hoffmann, preface and appendix; Sunday Times, 6th October 1968; *S. v. Marais,* 1971 (1) SA 844.

The Judiciary and the Executive. South African Act, 1909. Chap. IV; Supreme Court Act, 1959; Bamford, 1956 SALJ; In re Kok and Balie, 1879 SC 43; In re Marechane (1882), ISAR 27; *Shidiak* v. *Union Govt.,* 1912 AD 642; *Whitaker and Bateman* v. *Roos,* 1912 AD 92; *Krohn* v. *Min. of Defence,* 1915 AD 196; *Dadoo Ltd.* v. *Krugersdorp,* 1920 AD 530; Stratford, A.C.J. in *Sachs* v. *Min. of Justice,* 1934 AD 11; Jabavu (ed.) Schapera; Innes, 1931 SALJ; Curlewis, J.A. in *R. v. Roux,* 1936 AD 271; *S. v. Byleveldt,* 1964 (1) SA 269 (T); *Verwoerd* v. *Paver,* 1943 WLD 153; *R. v. Vorster,* 1941 AD 472; Hepple Cape Times, 15th July 1958; Trumplemann, 1940 TPD 242; *Schoeman* v. *Fourie,* 1941 AD 125; Conradie, 1941 Tydskrif, referring to Trumplemann;

Welsh, 1941 SALJ; *Min. of Interior* v. *Harris*, 1952 (4) SA 769 (AD); *Ndlwana* v. *Hofmeyr*, 1937 AD 229; On Freedom of speech–*R*. v. *Sutherland*, 1950 (4) SA 66 (T); *R*. v. *Nkatlo*, 1950 (1) SA 26 (C); *Du Plessis* v. *Min. of Justice*, 1950 (3) SA 579 (C). Assembly–*Arenstein* v. *Durban*, 1952 (1) SA 279 (AD). Passports–*Sachs* v. *Donges*, 1950 (2) SA 265 (AD); *Fellner* v. *Min. Interior*, 1954 (4) SA 523. Generally–*R*. v. *Sachs*, 1953 (1) SA 392; 1957 SALJ, 3. Audi alterem partem–*R*. v. *Ngwevela*, 1954 (1) SA 123 (AD); *Saliwa* v. *Min. Native Affairs*, 1956 (2) SA 310 (AD). Habeas corpus: Unreported cases, in Kentridge 1962 SALJ; Ex parte Hathorn, 1960 (2) SA 767 (D); Charles; *Ganyile* v. *Min. Justice*, 1962 (1) SA 647 (E); Cape Times, 24th August 1963; *Abrahams* v. *Min. Justice*, 1963 (4) SA 542; '90' day law, sec. 17, General Laws Amendment Act, 1963; *Mbele* v. *Min. Justice*, 1963 (4) SA 606 (N); *Loza* v. *Police*, 1964 (2) SA 545; *Whitaker* v. *Bateman*, 1912 AD 92; *Liversidge* v. *Anderson* (1942), AC 206; *Rossouw* v. *Sachs*, 1964 (2) SA 551 (AD); Schreiner; Beinart, Acta Juridica 1962; Mathews and Albino; Williamson, J.A. in *Schermbrucker* v. *Klindt*, 1965 (1) SA 353 (T); 1965 (4) SA 60 (AD). Dugard, 1970 SALJ, 289; Steyn, 1967 Tydskrif; On judicial advice to Legislature–*R*. v. *Hans Veren*, 1918 TPD 218; *R*. v. *Arbee*, 1956 (4) SA 438 (AD); *R*. v. *Shaiknagh*, 1946 WLD 71; *R*. v. *Milne and Erleigh* (6), 1951 (1) SA 1 (AD); *Pierce* v. *Hay Mon*, 1944 AD 175; *Wolpe* v. *SAP*, 1955 (2) SA 87; *S*. v. *Levy*, 1967 (1) SA 347 (W); *Hitzeroth* v. *Brooks*, 1965 (3) SA 444 (AD). Kahn (Censorship); *Publications Control Board* v. *Heinemann*, 1964 (4) SA 137 (AD); *S*. v. *Weinberg*, 1966 (4) SA 660 (AD); *S*. v. *Heymann*, 1966 (4) SA 598 (AD); *Gosschalk* v. *Rossouw*, 1966 (2) SA 476 (C); *Singh* v. *Att. General*, 1967 (2) SA 1 (T); Davids 1966, 1967 SALJ; *S*. v. *Ndou and 21 Others*, Transvaal, 16th February 1970; Sec. 29, General Law Amendment Act, 1969; Potgieter, J.A., G.N. 3296 of 17th September 1969; On Afrikaners and the Law–D. Point Acta Juridica 1961; 1960 Tydskrif, p. 1; Codicillus, June 1964; Die Uitleg van Wette by Dr L. C. Steyn; S.A. Yearbook No. 6; Horters Law List 1969; Welsh (Capital Punishment); CLJ, SALJ, Tydskrif variously; Blackwell (Judges); Rubin. On segregation in court, *R*. v. *Pitje*, 1960 (4) SA 709 (AD); Cape Argus, 7th December 1963; Rapport 7th March 1971. Rule of Law; Erosion; Dugard (Justice); Sunday Times, 28th March 1971; *S*. v. *van Niekerk*, 1970 (3) SA 655; Tydskrif 1970, p. 323.

4. BIBLIOGRAPHY

1. Official Publications

South African

(a) PRE-UNION:

Cape of Good Hope Bluebook, 1884.

Cape of Good Hope Register, 1894.

Natal Directory and Almanac and Yearly Register, 1894, 1895.

Natal: Official Illustrated Railway Guide and General Handbook, 1903.

South African Native Affairs Commission, 1903-1905, *Report and Evidence*, 5 vols., Cape Town, 1905.

(b) POST-UNION

Annual Reports of the Commissioner of the South African Police.

Annual Reports of the Department of Justice.

Annual Reports of the Director (now Commissioner) of Prisons.

Annual Reports of the Native Affairs Department (now Department of Bantu Administration and Development).

Official Yearbooks of the Union of Africa, nos. 1-27, covering period 1910 to 1953, and no. 30 of 1960.

Statistics of Offences and of Penal Institutes, 1949-1962, South African Bureau of Statistics, Special Report no. 272.

Police Commission of Enquiry, U.G. 50, 1937.

Penal Reform Commission of Enquiry, U.G. 47, 1947.

Commission of Enquiry into the Events on 20th and 22nd November, 1962, at Paarl, RP 51, 1963.

Transkei Legislative Assembly Debates, May 1964 to June 1969.

English

People in Prison, England and Wales, Cmnd. 4214, H.M.S.O. 1969.

Murder 1957-1968, a Home Office Statistical Division Report, H.M.S.O. 1969.

Criminal Statistics, England and Wales, H.M.S.O. 1969, 1970.

2. Law Journals

South African

Extensive use has been made of:

Cape Law Journal (1884-1900)–CLJ.

South African Law Journal (1900-1970)–SALJ.

Tydskrif vir Hedendaagse Romeins-Hollandse Reg (Journal of Contemporary Roman-Dutch Law)–1937-1970–Tydskrif.

Comparative and International Law Journal of South Africa (1969-1970)–CILSA.

Reference has also been made to the following University Law Department Journals:

Acta Juridica–Cape Town.

Annual Survey of South African Law–Witwatersrand.

Codicillus–South Africa.

Meditationes Medii–Orange Free State.

Responsa Meridiana–Law Students of Cape Town and Stellenbosch.

Speculum Juris–Fort Hare.

English

Modern Law Review–1953.

Comparative and International Law Quarterly–1962.

3. Law Reports

Digests:

Digest of law reports from the Cape, Transvaal and Orange Free State in the Cape Law Journal (CLJ), 1884–1900.

Digest of law reports from all parts of South Africa in the South African Law Journal (SALJ), 1900–1946.

Early Cape law reports, covering the period 1828–1910:

Menzies

Searle

Buchanan

Supreme Court (SC)

Eastern Districts Court (EDC)

High Court of Griqualand (HCG).

Early Transvaal law reports, covering the period 1881–1910:

Kotze

South African Republic (SAR)

Transvaal Supreme Court (TS).

Early Natal law reports:

Natal Law Reports (NLR).

Law reports after Union until 1947:

(A unified Supreme Court of South Africa was divided into several Provincial and Local Divisions, with an Appellate Division in Bloemfontein.)

Appellate Division (AD), also referred to as Appeal Court.

Cape Provincial Division (CPD)

Eastern Districts Local Division (EDL), now a full Division.

Griqualand West Local Division (GWLD), now part of the North Western Division.

Natal Provincial Division (NPD)

Orange Free State Provincial Division (OPD)

South West Africa Division (SWA)

Transvaal Provincial Division (TPD)

Witwatersrand Local Division (WLD)

Special Criminal Court (SCC), established *ad hoc* to try cases of treason and sedition.

Law reports from 1947 onwards:

South African Law Reports (SA), consolidated reports of all superior courts, in four annual volumes.

4. Statutes

Statutes of the Union Parliament, 1910-1961, and of the Republican Parliament, 1961-1969.

5. Newspapers, Journals and other Periodical Publications

Occasional reference has been made to the following:

Africa South–Political quarterly (1960)

Contrast–Literary quarterly (1969)

Justitia–Monthly organ of the South African Police (1963)

Sechaba–Monthly organ of the African National Congress (1967)

Cape Argus–(Cape Town)

Cape Times–(Cape Town)

(Indian) *Leader*–(Durban)

Rand Daily Mail–(Johannesburg)

Rapport–(Cape Town)

Star–(Johannesburg)

Sunday Express–(Johannesburg)

Sunday Times–(Johannesburg)

Times–(London)

Transvaler–(Johannesburg)

6. Other Major Sources

Proceedings of the Royal Colonial Institute (RCI), 1868-1909, later the Royal Empire Society, now the Royal Commonwealth Society.

Annual Surveys of Race Relations in South Africa, 1948-1970, published by the South African Institute of Race Relations (SAIRR), presently compiled by Muriel Horrell.

United Nations documents, including resolutions of the Security Council and the General Assembly, and reports of special commissions on apartheid.

Publications of the *International Commission of Jurists*, Geneva.

Hortor's Law List and Diary, Johannesburg, 1969.

7. Books and Articles

ALBERTI, *Alberti's Account of the Xhosa in 1807* (trans.), Cape Town, 1968.

AN EX-C.M.R., *The Cape Mounted Rifles*, London, 1881.

(Ed.) AUBERT, V., *Sociology of Law*, Penguin Readings, London, 1969.

AUERBACH, F. E., *The Power of Prejudice in South African Education*, Cape Town, 1965.

AVINS, A., *Race Separation and Public Accommodation:* Some Comparative Notes Between South African and American Law–1969 SALJ.

BARROW, SIR JOHN, F.R.S., *Autobiographical Memoir*, London, 1847.

BELL, W. H. S., *Bygone Days*, London, 1933.

BENDIX, R., *Max Weber, an Intellectual Portrait*, University Paperback, London, 1966.

BENSON, MARY, *The Struggle for a Birthright*, Penguin African Library London, 1966.

BERNSTEIN, HILDA, *The World That Was Ours*, London, 1967.

BLACKWELL, L., *African Occasions*, London, 1938.

—— *Are Judges Human*, London, 1962.

BRION DAVIS, D., *The Problem of Slavery in Western Culture*, London, 1970.

BROOKES, E., *Apartheid, A Documentary Study of Modern South Africa*, London, 1968.

BROOKES, E. and WEBB, C., *A History of Natal*, Pietermaritzburg, 1965.

BURCHELL, E. M. and HUNT, P., *South African Criminal Law and Procedure* (formerly Gardiner and Lansdown), Vol. I, Cape Town, 1970; Vol. IV in page proof.

CAMBRIDGE HISTORY, *Cambridge History of the British Empire*, Vol. VIII, 2nd edition, 1963.

Capital Punishment, Part I, Report 1960, Part II, Developments 1961 to 1965, United Nations Department of Economic and Social Affairs, New York, 1968.

Capital Punishment in the Republic of South Africa, UNESCO Commission on Human Rights working paper E/CN, 4/AC 22/20, 25th June 1969.

CARTER, GWENDOLEN, KARIS, T. and STULTZ, N., *South Africa's Transkei, the Politics of Domestic Colonialism*, London, 1967.

CHALMERS, J., *Tiyo Soga*, Edinburgh, 1877.

CHARLES, PETER, Q.C., *South African Incident–The Ganyile Case*, International Commission of Jurists, Geneva, 1962.

CLEAVER, *Mostyn Cleaver: A Young South African* (Second State Prosecutor, 1870–1900) by his mother, Johannesburg, 1913.

CODE, The Criminal Procedure Act, no. 56 of 1955.

COLE, HON. MR JUSTICE, *Reminiscences of My Life and of the Cape Bench and Bar*, Cape Town, 1896.

CORDER, H. L., *The Truth and Nothing But*, by the Late Civil Magistrate, Wynberg, Cape Town, 1964.

DAVIS, G., MELUNSKY, L. and DU RANDT, F., *Urban Native Law*, Port Elizabeth, 1959.

DE KIEWIET, C., *A Short History of South Africa: Social and Economic*, London, 1940.

DE KOCK, V., *Those in Bondage*, an account of life of the slaves at the Cape, London, 1950.

DE VILLIERS (see WALKER).

DE VILLIERS, DAWID, *The Case for South Africa*, London, 1970.

DE VILLIERS, HON. MR JUSTICE H., *Rivonia*, Johannesburg, 1964.

DEVITT, N., *More Memories of a Magistrate*, London, 1936.

DOKE, J., *M. K. Gandhi, an Indian Patriot in South Africa*, London, (n.d.) circa 1909.

DUGARD, J., *The Right to Counsel, South African and American Developments*, 1967 SALJ.

——— *Justice and Civil Liberty*, inaugural lecture, in *Rand Daily Mail*, 25th March 1971.

DULY, L., *Land Policy at the Cape 1795–1844*, Duke University, 1968.

ELKINS, S., *Slavery: A Problem of American Institutional and Intellectual Life*, Chicago, 1959.

Erosion–Erosion of the Rule of Law in South Africa (Staff Study, Legislation and the Courts, Prof. R. Falk, Observer's report on the *State v. Tuhadeleni and Others*). International Commission of Jurists, Geneva, 1968.

(Ed.) FAGE, J. D., *Africa Discovers Her Past*, London, 1970.

FALK, R. (see *Erosion*).

FERREIRA, J. C., *Strafproseswet in die Landdroshof* (Criminal procedure in the Magistrates' Court), Cape Town, 1967.

FISCHER, ABRAM, Q.C., *What I Did Was Right*, address from the dock, Mayibuye Publications, London, (n.d.) circa 1966.

FORMAN, L. and SACHS, E. S., *The South African Treason Trial*, London, 1957.

(Ed.) FORTES, M. and EVANS-PRITCHARD, E., *African Political Systems*, London, 1940.

FRASER, J. G., *Episodes in My Life*, Cape Town, 1922.

FREED, L., *Crime in South Africa: An Integralist Approach*, Cape Town, 1963.

(Ed.) FRIEDMANN, MARION, *I Will Still Be Moved: Reports from South Africa*, London, 1963.

GANDHI, *Satyagraha in South Africa*, Madras, 1928.

GANDHI, M. K., *Autobiography. The Story of My Experiments with Truth* (trans.), paperback, London, 1966.

GENOVESE, E., *The Political Economy of Slavery*, New York, Paperback, 1965.

GLUCKMAN, M., *The Kingdom of the Zulu in South Africa* in (ed.) Fortes and Evans-Pritchard; *Judicial Process Among the Barotse of Northern Rhodesia* in (ed.) Aubert, p. 161.

GORDON, C. I., *Aspects of Colour Attitudes and Public Policy in Kruger's Republic*, African Affairs No. 3, Oxford, 1969.

HAHLO, H. R. and KAHN, E., *The Union of South Africa: The Development of Its Laws and Constitution*, London, 1960.

—— *The South African Legal System and its Background*, Cape Town, 1968.

HAMMOND-TOOKE, W., *Bhaca Society*, London, 1962.

—— *The 'Other Side' of Frontier History: a model of Cape Nguni political process*, in (ed.) Thompson.

HANCOCK, W. K., *Smuts: The Sanguine Years*, London, 1962.

HARRISON, W., *Memoirs of a Socialist*, Cape Town, 1948.

(Ed.) HELLMANN, ELLEN, *Handbook of Race Relations in South Africa*, Cape Town, 1949.

HEPPLE, A., *Verwoerd*, London, 1967.

HERD, N., *1922: The Revolt on the Rand*, Johannesburg, 1966.

HOFFMANN, L., *South African Law of Evidence*, 2nd ed., Durban, 1970.

HOLT, H. P., *The Mounted Police of Natal*, London, 1913.

HOOK, MAJOR, *With Sword and Statute* (On the Cape of Good Hope Frontier), London, republished, 1908.

HORRELL, M., *Action, Reaction and Counteraction*, SAIRR, Johannesburg, 1963.

—— *Legislation and Race Relations*, Revised edition, SAIRR, Johannesburg, 1966.

Horter's Law List and Diary, Johannesburg, 1969.

HUNTER, M., *Reaction to Conquest*—Effects of contact with the Europeans on the Pondo of South Africa, 2nd edition, London, 1961.

INNES (SIR JAMES ROSE-INNES), *Autobiography*, ed. Tindall, Cape Town, 1949.

JABAVU, NONI, *Drawn in Colour*, London, 1960.

JABAVU, PROFESSOR D. D. T., *Native Grievances* in (ed.) Schapera.

JOSEPH, HELEN, *If This Be Treason*, London, 1962.

KADALIE, C., *My Life and the I.C.U.*, the Autobiography of a black trade unionist in South Africa, London, 1970.

KAHN, E., *The History of the Administration of Justice in the South African Republic*, in three parts, 1958 SALJ, 294; 1958 SALJ, 397 and 1959 SALJ, 46.

—— *Pass Laws* in (ed.) Hellmann.

—— *Crime and Punishment since 1910*, 1960 Acta Juridica.

—— '*When the Lion Feeds*', and the Censor Pounces, 1966 SALJ.

—— *The New Constitution*, 1961 SALJ.

—— *The Death Penalty*, address to Society of Teachers of Law, published in 1970 Tydskrif.

KANTOR, J., *A Healthy Grave*, paperback, Berlin, 1968.

KENNEDY, SENATOR ROBERT, *Address to the Johannesburg Bar*, 8th June 1966, published in 1966 SALJ.

KENTRIDGE, M., *I Recall*, Johannesburg, 1959.

KENTRIDGE, S., *Habeas Corpus Procedure in South Africa*, 1962 SALJ.

KESTELL, REV. J., *Christiaan de Wet*, Cape Town, 1920.

KOTZE, SIR JOHN, *Memoirs*, I, Cape Town, (n.d.) circa 1934.

KRIGE, E. J., *The Social System of the Zulus*, 4th edition, Pietermaritzburg, 1962.

KRUGER, D. W., *The Making of a Nation 1910–1961*, Johannesburg, 1969.

KRUGER, J. J., *President C. R. Swart*, Cape Town, 1961.

KUPER, L., *An African Bourgeoisie*—Race, class and politics in South Africa, Yale, 1965.

LEIBBRANDT, V., *Precis of the Archives of the Cape of Good Hope Journal 1699–1723*, Cape Town, 1896.

LEWIN, J., *African Native Law*, Cape Town, 1948.

—— *Politics and Law in South Africa*, London, 1963.

LUDI, G. and GROBBELAAR, B., *The Amazing Bram Fischer*, Cape Town, 1966.

LUTHULI, CHIEF A., *Let My People Go*, autobiography, paperback, London, 1963.

MACMILLAN, W. M., *Bantu, Boer and Briton*–The making of the South African native problem, London, 1929.

MACRONE, I. D., *Race Attitudes in South Africa*, Johannesburg, 1957.

MAISTER, RUTH, *Judicial Attitudes to Race*, Responsa Meridiana, 1969.

MANDELA, N., *No Easy Walk to Freedom*, speeches and documents, (ed.) Ruth First, London, 1965.

Mandela v. The State, pamphlet, London, (n.d.).

MARAIS, J., 'The Imposition and Nature of European Control', in (ed.) Schapera. *Bantu-Speaking Tribes of South Africa*, Cape Town, 1937.

MARITZ, M., *My Lewe en Strewe* (My Life and Struggles), Cape Town, (n.d.) circa 1939.

MARKS, SHULA, *Reluctant Rebellion*, London, 1970.

—— *Historians and South Africa*, in (ed.) Fage.

MARTIN, A. C., *The Concentration Camps*, Cape Town, 1958.

MATHEWS, A. and ALBINO, R., *The Permanence of the Temporary*, 1966 SALJ.

MBEKI, G., *South Africa, The Peasants' Revolt*, London, 1964.

MCCRACKEN, J. L., *The Cape Parliament, 1854-1910*, London, 1967.

MEER, FATIMA, *Portrait of Indian South Africans*, Durban, 1969.

MELLOR, G. R., *British Imperial Trusteeship 1783-1850*, London, 1951.

MILLNER, M., *Eclipse of a Judiciary*, 1962 ICLQ.

(Ed.) MILNER, A., *African Penal Systems*, London, 1969.

MODISANE, B., *Blame Me on History*, London, 1963.

MOLEMA, S. M., *Montshiwa*, Cape Town, 1966.

MORBASCH, H. and G., *Attitudes towards Capital Punishment in South Africa*, British Journal of Criminology, 1967.

MORRIS, H. H., *The First Forty Years*, Cape Town, 1948.

MPHLAHLELE, E., *Down Second Avenue*, paperback, Berlin, 1962.

MTOLO, B., *Umkhonto We Sizwe, Road to the Left*, Durban, 1966.

MYRDAL, G., *An American Dilemma*, 20th Anniversary Edition, New York, 1962.

NATAL LAND AND COLONISATION COMPANY, *The Colony of Natal*, London, 1861.

NATHAN, M., *Not Heaven Itself*, Durban, 1944.

NOKWE, D., *An African Barrister*, in (ed.) Friedmann.

OMER-COOPER, J., *Aspects of Political Change in the Nineteenth Century Mfecane*, in (ed.) Thompson.

Oxford History of South Africa, Vol. I, 1969.

PIROW, O., *J. B. M. Hertzog*, Cape Town, n.d.

POLLAK, W., Review Article on *Hahlo and Kahn*, 1961 SALJ.

PORTER, W., *The Porter Speeches* (1839-1845), Cape Town, 1886.

REITZ, D., *On Commando*, paperback ed., London, 1968.

REITZ, H., *The Conversion of South African Nationalist*, Cape Town, 1964.

RHOODIE, E. M., *Penal Systems in the Commonwealth*, Pretoria, 1966.

RHOODIE, N. and VENTER, H., *A Socio-Historical Exposition of the Apartheid Idea*, Cape Town, 1960.

ROBERTSON, H., *South Africa, Economic and Political Aspects*, Cambridge, 1957.

ROSENTHAL, E., *General de Wet*, Cape Town, 1946.

ROUX, E., *S. P. Bunting*, Cape Town, 1944.

—— *Time Longer Than Rope*.

RUBIN, L., *Nationalist Contempt of Court*, Africa South, 1960.

Rule of Law–Department of Foreign Affairs–*South Africa and the Rule of Law*, Pretoria, 1968.

SAXE-BANNISTER, *Humane Policy of Justice to the Aborigines, etc.*, London, 1830, reprinted 1968.

SCHAPERA, I., 'Law and Justice', in (ed.) Schapera, *The Bantu-Speaking Tribes of South Africa*, Cape Town, 1937.

—— (ed.) *Western Civilisation and the Natives of South Africa*, London, 1934.

SCHREINER, HON. MR JUSTICE O., *The Contribution of English Law to South African Law; and the Rule of Law in South Africa*, London, 1967.

SEARLE, F. ST. L., Biographies of various nineteenth century Cape judges, in SALJ.

SEYMOUR, S. M., *Native Law in South Africa*, 2nd edition, Cape Town, 1960.

SIMONS, H. J., *African Women: Their Legal Status in South Africa*, London, 1968.

—— *The Law and its Administration*, in (ed.) Hellmann.

SIMONS, H. J. and R. E., *Class and Colour in South Africa, 1850-1950*, London, 1969.

SOLOMON, BERTHA, *Time Remembered*, Cape Town, 1968.

STRAUSS, S. A., *Criminal Procedure in South Africa*, 1910-1960, Acta Juridica, 1960.

STRYDOM, L., *Rivonia Unmasked*, Johannesburg, 1965.

SUTTNER, R., *Legal Pluralism in South Africa*, 1970 ICLQ, 134.

SUZMAN, A., *Race Classification in Legislation 1910-1960*, Acta Juridica, 1960.

SWART (see J. J. KRUGER).

SWIFT, I. L. and HARCOURT, A. B., *The South African Law of Criminal Procedure*, Durban, 1957.

(Ed.) THOMPSON, L. M., *African Societies in Southern Africa*, London, 1969, (incl.) *The Forgotten Factor in Southern African History*.

Times History of the South African War, Vol. VI, London, 1909.

TRAPIDO, S., *The Origin and Development of the African Political Organisation*, unpublished seminar paper, presented at Institute of Commonwealth Studies, London, 1970.

TREDGOLD, SIR ROBERT, J. B. Davie Memorial Lecture, University of Cape Town, 4th September 1963.

TROLLOPE, ANTHONY, *South Africa,* Vol. II, London, 1868, reprinted 1968.

TYLDEN, G., *The Armed Forces of South Africa*, Johannesburg, 1954.

VAN DEN BERGHE, P., *South Africa: A Study in Conflict*, paperback, Los Angeles, 1967.

VAN NIEKERK, B. D., *Hanged by the Neck Until You Are Dead*, two articles, 1969 SALJ, 1970 SALJ.

VENTER, H. J., *Die Geskiedenis van die Suid-Afrikaanse Gevangenisstelsel 1652-1958* (The History of South African Penal Policy), Pretoria, 1959.

VERLOREN VAN THEMAAT, R., *Legal Education of the Bantu in South Africa*, 1969, CILSA.

WALKER, E., *A History of Southern Africa*, 3rd edition, London, 1957.

—— *Lord de Villiers and His Times*, London, 1925.

—— *W. P. Schreiner, A South African*, London, 1937.

WALKER, I. and WEINBREN, B., *2,000 Casualties*, Pietermaritzburg, 1961.

WEBER, M., *Rational and Irrational Administration of Justice*, (ed.) Aubert, p. 153.

WELSH, D., *Capital Punishment in South Africa*, in (ed.) Milner.

—— *The State President's Powers under the Bantu Administration Act*, Acta Juridica, 1968.

WESSELS, J. J., *History of Roman-Dutch Law*, Grahamstown, 1908.

WILSON, M. and MAFEJE, A., *Langa: A Study of Social Groups in an African Township*, Cape Town, 1963.

Index